Globalization and the Nation State

Also by Robert J. Holton

Cosmopolitanisms
Global Networks
Making Globalization

Globalization and the Nation State

Robert J. Holton

Emeritus Professor and Fellow, Trinity College, Dublin, Ireland

SECOND EDITION

First edition 1998
Second edition 2011
Published by PALGRAVE MACMILLAN

Palgrave Macmillan in the UK is an imprint of Macmillan Publishers Limited, registered in England, company number 785998, of Houndmills, Basingstoke, Hampshire RG21 6XS.

Palgrave Macmillan in the US is a division of St Martin's Press LLC, 175 Fifth Avenue, New York, NY 10010.

Palgrave Macmillan is the global academic imprint of the above companies and has companies and representatives throughout the world.

Palgrave® and Macmillan® are registered trademarks in the United States, the United Kingdom, Europe and other countries.

ISBN 978–0–230–27455–6   hardback
ISBN 978–0–230–27456–3   paperback

This book is printed on paper suitable for recycling and made from fully managed and sustained forest sources. Logging, pulping and manufacturing processes are expected to conform to the environmental regulations of the country of origin.

A catalogue record for this book is available from the British Library.

Library of Congress Cataloging-in-Publication Data
Holton, R. J.
Globalization and the nation state / Robert J. Holton. – 2nd ed.
p. cm.
Includes index.
ISBN 978–0–230–27456–3 (pbk.)
1. International economic relations.   2. International trade.   3. Nation-state.
4. International economic relations—Social aspects.   5. Cultural relations.   I. Title.
HF1359.H648 2011
306—dc22   2011008062

10   9   8   7   6   5   4   3   2   1
20   19   18   17   16   15   14   13   12   11

Printed in China

Contents

List of Tables and Figures

Tables

Figures

Acknowledgements

Globalization is a topic that still generates intense passions several decades after the term was first used to refer to rapidly multiplying cross-border connections and dependencies. The issues and challenges involved defy easy analysis and policy prescription, partly because globalization is a very complex set of processes, and partly because global activities, problems, and crises seem to emerge and evolve so rapidly. This second edition of a book first published in 1998, tries to make sense of global complexities, taking into account new trends and events like the rise of China, 9/11 and the intensified challenge of global terrorism, and the global financial crisis of 2008–9. While general themes in the study of globalization remain very much the same as in 1998, this volume updates the arguments and range of evidence used in the first edition. It also gives greater emphasis than before to global futures.

My thinking in these endeavours has been influenced by many individuals and by a global odyssey that led me from Australia to Ireland in 2001, and then back to Australia in 2009. Working at Trinity College, Dublin, I was fortunate to have been involved in the establishment of the Institute for International Integration Studies, and to have worked with Kevin O'Rourke, Rosemary Byrne, Ronit Lentin, Barbara Bradby, Hilary Tovey, and Adam Drazin.

The longer term influence of Roland Robertson on my approach to globalization has also continued and intensified since 1998, while I have also learnt from many other colleagues and collaborators including Sandra Holton, Chris Rumford, John Braithwaite, Constance Lever-Tracy, Tony McGrew, Graeme Thompson, Zlatko Skrbis, and Tim Phillips. I am also grateful to Anthony Elliott and Flinders University of South Australia for intellectual and academic support in the writing of this volume.

I should also like to thank my old friend Steve Edwards for his continuing interest in my work, and for being such a mainstay of civil society.

Such errors and confusions as remain in this work are nonetheless entirely my own.

Much of the impetus for this second edition came from the excellent editors at Palgrave Macmillan, firstly Emily Salz and more latterly Anna Marie Reeve.

The global family networks of which I am part, remains multi-centred on Australia and the UK, and I am, as ever, profoundly grateful to Sandra, George, and Flora, for their encouragement and forbearance in relation to the vicissitudes involved in my conduct of global research and publishing.

The author and publishers wish to thank Sage Publications for granting permission to reproduce Figure 8.1, reproduced by permission of Sage Publications, London, Los Angeles, New Delhi and Singapore from Roland Robertson, *Globalization: Social Theory and Global Culture*, copyright © Roland Robertson, 1992.

ROBERT J. HOLTON

1
Introduction to the Second Edition

Globalization has come to be regarded, over the past two decades, as a major feature of contemporary life. From global environmental sustainability to the global financial crisis, the internet to global celebrities, global epidemics to global cultural events like the World Cup, and from global terrorism to questions of human rights, headlines and conversations are full of globe-talk. In the period since the first edition of this book appeared in 1998, global issues, institutions and events have continued to dominate discussion on the direction of social change, the prospects for economic development, human welfare and social justice, the fate of the planet, and the values on which social life should be based. The purpose of this new edition is not simply to recognize these continuities, but also to identify what has changed since 1998, and to explain why understandings of globalization remain so controversial and contested.

In this first chapter a range of questions about globalization are raised and some major responses and arguments scrutinized. Attention is given first to questions about the meaning, scope, dynamics and limits of globalization, an exercise which reveals many confusions and some myths, right at the centre of public debate. Such questions are impossible to pursue very far without giving simultaneous consideration to the place of the nation state in a globalizing world. Does globalization mean the end of the territorially bounded nation state or are nation states able to respond to globalization, reshaping themselves and globalization at the same time? Put another way, can globalization and nations co-exist and if so what kinds of connections, conflicts and forms of cross-fertilization link global and national processes, institutions and cultures? This book is entitled *Globalization and the Nation State* because its subject-matter is the complex and multiple interactions that link globalization with nation states.

1

Such issues are at the heart of this book. They are pursued across time and space, introducing important questions of history and geography, as well as insights from sociology, political science and economics. At the end of the chapter, a summary is given of the way this study approaches definitions, concepts, and representations of globalization. This is followed by a condensed plan of the structure of the remainder of the book to help readers with a variety of interests navigate through it.

Debate and Controversy

Controversies over globalization and global challenges abound. Yet what exactly do terms like 'global' and 'globalization' mean? Are they best defined as any kind of cross-border connection, including relationships between states as well as those between businesses, cultural communities and individuals? Or do they signify only those transnational processes that somehow stand above nation states? If so does globalization really mean the end of the nation state and nationalism? Or are national and regional institutions and loyalties ultimately stronger and more enduring? In which case does globalization really exist? Or is there a third possibility that global and national processes often interact and adapt to each other, creating processes that reflect both global and national or local elements? Complicating these debates still further is the question of whether globalization has one distinct and unitary character, built, for example, around free trade and multinational corporations, or whether there are multiple globalizations, political and cultural as much as economic?

Beyond all this are normative and ethical questions that relate to basic human values, and feed into political debate and social action. Put simply the question here is whether globalization is a good thing or a bad one.

For some, globalization is seen negatively, and at times almost demonically, as the dominance of Western economic and cultural interests over the rest of the world. This dominance, according to those who hold this view, means the perpetuation of inequality between rich and poor countries and regions. It also, for many, means the degradation of the natural environment. Globalization, from this perspective is described variously as the operation of the capitalist world-system or, more polemically, as the 'New World Disorder'. The problem here is not only the perpetuation of gross inequalities, but also what has been referred to as the 'Coca-Colonization' of the world, whereby Third World populations are incorporated into the global economy as cheap labour or passive consumers of standardized products and nothing more. In this view, globalization rests on foundations of cultural imperialism based on the cultural mores of the West, at the expense of non-Western traditions interests and traditions.

For others, globalization is evaluated more positively. Some see it in a triumphalist light, as the penetration of capitalism into every corner of the world, bringing with it the possibility for all of the world's population to participate in the fruits of the international division of labour and market economy. The arrival of McDonald's hamburgers in Moscow nearly two decades ago symbolized a characteristic moment in this type of thinking. McDonald's, a symbol of global consumer capitalism, had now triumphed, so it was supposed, in what had previously been seen as a hostile political and cultural environment. And in wider debates about global welfare as measured by income levels, many economists point to evidence of gradual, if uneven material improvement across the globe, even in the midst of poverty and inequality.

In a somewhat different vein, political aspects of globalization have been associated with the advent of institutions like the United Nations (UN) and World Council of Churches, or social movements such as Amnesty International and Greenpeace International. This apparently disparate set of bodies have for many become new vehicles for political and religious desires for the creation of a single world community governed by peace and justice. Such a world, many hope, might be free from conflict, while planet Earth might at the same time be liberated from exploitation and environmental degradation. Alternatively, globalization is simply something to be enjoyed, as seen in the worldwide audience for global sporting contests – like the soccer World Cup and Olympic Games – or global music and film – from U2 and the Buena Vista Social Club to Hollywood, Bollywood and Hong Kong martial arts – developments fostered by new communications technologies and cultural entrepreneurs.

A range of values have been used as a basis for the evaluation of globalization. These include human welfare, as measured by economic growth and real incomes, social justice and freedom of choice, environmental sustainability, democratic accountability, personal and national security, and the sovereign rights of nations to determine their destiny. The simplest moral response is to be 'for' or 'against' globalization. Often, however, people like some parts of globalization and not others. Some see human rights or freedom of movement, for example, as good, while *laissez-faire* capitalism or world government are regarded more critically. Others like markets but not global political regulation. Such conflicts between different globalizations are especially evident where deep conflicts of principle are perceived between social justice and economic freedom or between environmental sustainability and the rights of acquisitive individuals to do what they like with their own property and resources.

Moral and policy choices may proceed with varying degrees of concern for supporting or rebutting evidence-based analysis, which is sometimes missing altogether, and at others confused and misleading. The aim of this study is then to provide an analytical underpinning to moral and political debates over globalization, providing analytical insights well grounded in logic and evidence from the clamour of rhetoric, outrage and the resulting closing of minds. One key element of this perspective is to clarify which contemporary trends and problems may justifiably be seen as a product of globalization, and how far other causes are involved.

Globalization and Inequality

An obvious starting point is to ask how far globalization is responsible for world poverty, the abuse of cheap labour and periodic economic crises? Or do these 'bads' have many causes – local and national as much as global? On the face of it, global inequality between countries has increased significantly over the long term. In 1820 the richest nation was roughly three times better off than the poorest, yet by the early 1990s the ratio of the wealthiest to the poorest was in excess of 70 (Milanovic, 2005: 46). Today the richest and poorest seem worlds apart in terms of income, health and literacy. And the group of countries that have incomes per head that are one-third or less than the wealthiest have actually increased in recent years to over 70, mainly in Africa and Asia.

Economists, however, disagree about whether things have worsened in the recent decades of globalization. There is considerable evidence that globalization in the form of trade liberalization and cross-border capital and labour mobility has actually contributed to rising real incomes for many, even amid patterns of gross inequality (Dinopoulos *et al.*, 2008). O'Rourke (2001) argues that evidence of per capita income over the last 150 years reveals that between-country inequality is now decreasing after many decades of increase, while within-country inequality has started to increase. Much of this is, however, a 'China effect'. Here recent economic development has prompted upward shifts from a very low income of $1 per day to a slightly higher level of $2 per day, making a vast difference to inequality figures for the world as a whole, because China is the world most populous country. East Asia has been the fastest-growing region in the last decade, despite near stagnation in Japan, and greater affluence is evident in many parts of Asia outside China, including South Korea, much of South East Asia, and certain parts of India. In this sense globalization may be working to a degree in spite of continuing inequalities.

Is the problem for many of the world's poorest nations, such as much of sub-Saharan Africa, then too little globalization, including too little access to rich-country markets for primary products, rather than too much? And even if this more optimistic view is taken, could it not also be that globalization might be more economically beneficial if its fruits were better distributed?

Such fundamental questions are tackled in more depth in Chapter 3. For the moment, attention remains with critics of economic globalization, for whom inequality and poverty, in some shape of form, are unacceptable. For a number of commentators, global market freedom has simply gone too far (Rodrik, 1997). This point connects with the recent global financial crisis, where excessive market freedom took the form of lax lending practices by financial institutions, combined with new financial instruments, such as credit default swaps, that were totally unregulated and a mystery even to many bank directors. These created unsustainable risks and corporate failures which citizens have been mobilized to pay for rather than market institutions themselves.

Yet how far would more regulated markets help by themselves to alleviate rather than worsen inequality and injustice by avoiding crisis and creating a greater sense of fairness? There are, after all, many causes of inequality and injustice, including political and cultural authoritarianism, ethnic conflict and corruption. In this sense, more effective economic globalization may be impossible without more effective political globalization built around some kind of enhanced global democracy. This leads us back to questions about the relationship between globalization and political institutions, and the changing and rather unclear place of nation states in a global world.

Globalization and the Environment

Another fundamental criticism of free markets is that economic growth is an inadequate response to environmental sustainability. Increased economic growth, even if its fruits are more fairly distributed, does not secure the future of the planet. From the new awareness of environmental issues that came to the fore in the 1960s to the attempts at institutional regulation begun in the 1980s, a sense of increased momentum has been evident in the global politics of environmentalism (Lechner, 2009: 250ff). By the 1990s, as pointed out in the first edition of this book, the relatively successful response to the depletion of the ozone layer suggested that reform was possible.

This momentum may have been checked in 2009, though perhaps not irrevocably, by the failure of Copenhagen negotiations over greenhouse gas emissions and climate change. In spite of the Kyoto Protocols of 1997, the reduction of emissions – or at least the rate of growth of emissions – has been poorly implemented even where agreed, and the refusal of the USA and others to comply, simply compounds the problem. Lechner believes climate change has become the global problem (ibid.: 258). The protracted character of climate change debates and initiatives is not primarily about the scientific evidence, upon which there remains a large measure of agreement, nor the lack of effective activist political pressure. The difficulties lay rather in the conflict of interests between those economic groups – whether connected with fossil fuels exploitation or with economic growth in the poorer underdeveloped countries – who gain materially from processes that produce greenhouse gas emissions, and those concerned with environmental sustainability who assert an overriding interest in the future of the planet. Conflicts over climate change in this respect show the limits as well as scope of 'one world' thinking, adding a further level of insecurity to popular anxieties already heightened by global financial crisis and global terrorism.

Limits to Globalization

In addition to all of this, there are major questions about the limits to globalization (Scott, 1997; Rieger and Leibfried, 2003), and the extent to which globalization can be reversed, or at least reshaped? Since there is so much hype involved in discussions of globalization, maybe globalization is on the way out? All questions of this kind rely on the presumption that the 'global' can clearly and neatly be distinguished from the 'non-global' or 'anti-global'.

At first sight, this seems quite reasonable. Economic globalization, associated with free trade and deregulated movements of capital and labour are quite distinct from 'non-global' or 'anti-global' trade protection and barriers to capital and labour inflows. Similarly, globalization in politics is usually associated trans-national political organizations and ideas of human rights and cosmopolitanism, all apparently distinct from decision-making by sovereign states and non-global or anti-global ideas of nationalism and the ethnic distinctiveness of particular peoples.

While there is some obvious logical merit in these contrasts between what is and what is not part of globalization, the idea of a sharp conceptual distinction between the two is inadequate. Where, for example, does this sharp contrast stand if globalizing trends are enacted by nation states, or where some varieties of nationalism find ways of expressing wider loyalties to those in other nations, in the name of humanity, democracy or peace. For Sassen (2006: 2), some though not all globalizing trends are 'structures inside the national', and do not necessarily become visible solely in trans-national organizations that stand above nation states and their citizens. Rather we may think of them as becoming embedded in national legislatures and judiciaries, the operations of corporations and NGOs, or in particular households. Examples of these embedded global trends and practices include the usage of trans-national norms like human rights in national politics and law (Berman, 2004–5), world's best practice in particular corporations (Sklair, 2001), the sending home of remittances by migrants in new countries to families in the homeland, or long-distance caring for relatives in the homeland by migrants overseas (Maimbo and Ratha, 2005). According to Sassen's argument, these are 'global' in logic, even though they emerge out of or become embedded in particular national and local contexts.

Problems inherent in drawing sharp contrasts between global and national processes mean some care is needed in thinking through what is and is not a limit to globalization. Limits, here, are not simply represented by unambiguous forces that expressly oppose globalization in the name of nation or local community. There are also other more subtle limits. These may apply where ostensibly 'trans-national' institutions are mistakenly placed in the 'global' category when in reality they function in a more nation-centred way. This criticism is levelled by Hirst and Thompson (1996) against much research on the global economy, which, they claim conflates trans-national processes with what are often international connections between intact nations. Whichever view is taken here, there is clearly a high degree of ambiguity in deciding whether ostensibly global arrangements are really transnational, as well as in determining whether national-level activities are anti- or non-global.

Another kind of limit is set wherever non-global institutions, such as national political and legal systems, are unable to underwrite the kinds of social and political order that most strands of economic globalization rely on. Rieger and Leibfried (2003), for example, argue that the legitimacy and stability of economic globalization depends, in large measure, on the capacity of welfare states and social policy to underwrite social citizenship and engender social cohesion and compliance. Since social citizenship rights have become fundamental to the institutional structure of many liberal-democratic societies, the provocative implication of this argument is that such rights, and the expectations and institutions based upon them, can limit the scope for globalization – at least in its economic form. Rather than welfare states being undermined and destroyed by an unlimited globalization, as many early theorists of globalization errone-ously believed (see the criticisms of this belief reviewed in Holton, 2005), it may be that the argument works better the other way round, namely that economic globalization is more vulnerable than national welfare capitalism. One acid test here is whether national trade policies become more rather than less mercantilist, sacrificing, as it were, aspects of global economic integration for domestic political cohesion and stability?

Commentators such as Benjamin Barber (1991, 1995) have placed great emphasis on the limits set to globalization by what he sees as quite contrary trends towards tribalism and divisive cultural fundamentalism. This involves a dichotomy between what he calls McWorld and Jihad. Whereas the former stands for the global networks of capitalism and electronic communication, an amalgam so to speak of McDonald's and Apple MacIntosh, the latter stands for a retribalization process or 'Lebanonization' of nation states, in which cultures stand opposed to each other, 'driven by parochial hatreds'.

Where Barber sets limits to globalization by emphasizing polariza-tion and tribalization, others challenge theories of globalization by referring to a proliferation or explosion of difference in modern life. Instead of the integration of all parts of the globe to a common pattern, what we find instead is the emergence of a complex plurality of different and often divergent economic, political and cultural trends. These may be expressed at a national level, within the revival of ethnicity, and through major politico-cultural movements such as the resurgence of Islam. However, they may equally be found in the proliferation of lifestyles and identities built around individual, local, or small group modes of social action. Examples include the gender politics of difference based on the assertion of individual rights of sexual preference and women's rights of self-determination, or, alternatively, the proliferation of local forms of community involvement and politics.

This leads us on to questions of the reversibility or reshaping of globalization. Will powerful nation states turn out after all to be the best counterweight to the insecurities of a borderless world? Or are bounded nation states too small and/or too self-interested to deal with challenges of global proportions? If so, does this mean that environmental sustain-ability and a world free from disease and injustice are inconceivable without globally applicable principles delivered by global institutions? And if so, are international institutions like the UN and World Bank, driven by alliances of powerful nation states, such as the G7, G8, and G20, likely to produce consensus-based global responses. Or are regional institutions such as the European Union (EU) more likely to provide a more effective though spatially limited basis for economic and social coherence? There is, meanwhile, a further set of issues to do with the weaknesses of essentially top-down governance. Have such top-down institutions really only become effective when pushed to extend and radicalize their thinking on questions like environmental sustainability or the Third World debt programme by social movements and advocacy networks? And to the extent that this is the case, do such movements and networks themselves form part of a new global civil society of non-state actors (Keane, 2003)?

Understanding Globalization: Old Themes and New Challenges

Many of the questions listed above were tackled in the first edition of *Globalization and the Nation State*. They remain of central concern. But added to them are additional themes and emphases that are not necessarily new, but which have recently expanded in importance. The most obvious of these stem from the events of 9/11 and the growing concern for geopolitical security. This event signified the globalization of terrorism and the permeability of borders to political violence as much as commodities, information and ideas from outside. The destruction of the Twin Towers and subsequent retaliatory military action by Western powers and their allies in the Middle East have long-term as much as short-term causes. Nonetheless these events have intensified the realization that the global order is not simply dominated by economic power or the dynamics of capitalism, and that territorial security matters, even in a globalized world of permeable borders and mobility of capital, technology and people. Most of those concerned with the future are now far less confident than they were of the imminent creation of a borderless world. Rather 9/11 and the intractable Middle Eastern conflict lend some credibility to the idea of a present and future dominated by global cultural wars (Huntington, 1996), such as that between the 'West' and 'radical Islam'.

However, 9/11 and the reaction to it also dramatize the vulnerability of states centred on political and military institutions to the capacity of trans-nationally networked organizations like Al-Qaeda to surmount and transcend the defences of even the most powerful quasi-Imperial nation state (Kellner, 2007; Holton, 2008). This in turn raises challenges not simply for national and global security, but also for the prospects for democracy in a global epoch. If the political boundaries that separate individual national polities are so permeable to terrorism, this somehow renders outmoded the way that representative democracy is currently organized, on the basis of national jurisdictions.

A second set of events around the recent 'Global Financial Crisis', also have long-term causes, but nonetheless require changes in the way we think about the global order and the place of markets, global economic institutions and democratic politics within it. The global economy expanded at a very rapid rate over the last few decades, with cross-border trade, investment and economic migration all showing overall growth. There were, to be sure, moments of serious crisis prior to this, such as the oil price shocks of the 1970s, the collapse of the Mexican currency in 1982 and the Asian economic crisis in the late 1990s. These generally affected individual nations or regions rather than the stability of the global system itself. And the main concerns about the global economy as a whole were less to do with its economic buoyancy, than with its environmental sustainability, its capacity to lift poorer populations and nations out of economic misery and social distress, and its accountability to democratic process. This has turned out to be very short-sighted.

What the global economic crisis now adds to this picture is a sense that liberal capitalism based on lightly regulated markets and powerful global corporations may not provide a sufficient basis for the onward and upward development of the global economy (Crotty, 2009). The problem here is not simply one of excessively risky lending practices by global banks or the hugely controversial bonus payments to traders and executives. Behind this lay structural problems of financial imbalances between national economies, and a savings glut, which, together with low real interest rates, drove up asset prices in increasingly risky assets like sub-prime mortgages in the USA (Wolf, 2010). At some point the bubble had to burst, and burst it did in 2008. A major symptom of the crisis that ensued was the catastrophic business failure of major corporations – including banks, insurance companies and automobile makers – leading either to complete collapse, as with Lehman Brothers, or to major injections of public funding to remain afloat. The costs of this crisis, will reverberate for generations not only in terms of losses in the value of assets measured in the trillions of dollars (IMF, 2009), or in terms of public debt burdens (Wolf, 2010), but also in relation to the legitimacy of capitalism itself (Soros, 2010).

The financial crisis challenges the assumption that markets are best left to their own devices free from strong forms of regulation. Free trade, free movement of capital and flexible labour markets would, so it was thought, provide an ongoing framework for economic growth, and a buoyant tax base to fund public expenditures by nation states. Yet this is precisely what is now thrown into doubt with the overhang of massive public funding to support collapsing corporations challenging the future capacity of public expenditure to meet needs for social welfare and social cohesion. Alan Greenspan, once the confident head of the US Federal Reserve charged with steering the US economy to continuing growth with financial stability, in his testimony to Congress, made the admission that, 'to exist you need an ideology. The question is whether it is accurate or not. And what I am saying is, yes I found a flaw' (cited in Blankenburg and Palma, 2009: 531). The flaw here lies with unregulated *laissez-faire* capitalism as a secure and effective basis for economic globalization.

Global Complexities

The combined effects of 9/11 and the global financial crisis and the trends associated with them, further complicate the original task of making sense of globalization, undertaken in the first edition of this study. One of the main arguments I made back in 1998 was that, while a powerful reality, globalization was not an all-powerful economic process that was necessarily undermining nation states. This was partly because most forms of economic globalization need nation states to provide some kind of infrastructural and cohesive framework for economic activity. But it was also because economic globalization is not the only global process at work in the contemporary world. Two other general kinds of development are evident, in no way separate from economic globalization, but operating very often according to a different logic.

The first involves other types of globalization centred on politics and culture (Robertson, 1992; Held, 1995; Beck, 2002; Holton, 2005). There are, in other words, multiple globalizations, not simply one single unitary economic globalization. These include emerging forms of global governance in areas such as human rights and environmental regulation, expressed within norms such as crimes against humanity or global environmental sustainability. Empire is another form that political globalization may take, both historically and in the contemporary arena. Some analysts see the imperial process at work in the operation of US foreign policy, and in the hegemonic presence of powerful economic interests and states within the global military and geopolitical arena, as much as bodies like the International Monetary Fund and World Bank.

Governance processes of the two different kinds sketched here are very far from world government, but they do, in certain respects go beyond a world of sovereign states, making unilateral decisions according to narrow national interests. Multi-level governance, based on multilateralism binds parties together in multi-actor systems that seek out common norms, agreements and standards. Governance of this kind may channel inevitable conflicts between national interests into dispute resolution processes, such as that provided for trading disputes by the World Trade Organization. This has largely replaced the tariff wars and economic nationalism of the 1930s, although echoes of this earlier epoch still appear in much governmental rhetoric. Technical-standard setting to harmonize potentially divergent national or corporate standards, through bodies such as the International Standards Organization (ISO) or the International Telecommunications Union (ITU), also represents a practical shift away from unilateralism.

In the case of Empire, meanwhile, patterns of domination reflect a highly unequal world, focused on institutions and processes that represent far more than the functioning of markets. Empires in the past were typically centred on a particular homeland, developing extensions beyond into regions of political domination and often settlement by the ruling power – whether ancient Rome, early modern Spain, nineteenth-century Britain, or the twentieth-century Soviet Union. Alternatively, in the work of Hardt and Negri (2000), a new kind of post-national systemic Empire is enveloping the global arena of nation states and international organizations. This represents a universal global form of domination, rather than domination working outwards from a particular territory and, as such, adds to the range of theories dealing with politics and globalization.

Both these forms of political globalization are clearly linked with economic globalization. This is true in the sense that economic development has drawn upon political resources, such as the Navy that sustained the British Empire, to secure its domination and stability. More generally, economic development creates many of the challenges that politics engages with. These extend from trading relations between nations, and movements of economic migrants across borders entering new communities in search of employment, to environmental degradation and global economic crises. It is also true that the quest for geopolitical security, reflected in international military alliances against terrorism in places like the Middle East, links the political search for a stable world with the economics of resource extraction and capital investment opportunities. In this way it is just as much a mistake to argue that the Gulf Wars have nothing to do with command over the world's oil resources, as to argue that they are only about oil. Security is a bigger question than the security of capitalism alone.

There are also connections between a third kind of global politics and broader processes of globalization, namely global democracy. This may rightly be seen as less developed than multi-level governance or Empire. As Held points out, those who are affected by many global processes and decisions are not located neatly within individual national polities. Rather, those affected by terrorism and other global 'bads' are located within overlapping communities of fate that bear no straightforward relationship to national political arrangements or constituencies (Held, cited in Albrow and Glasius, 2008: 2). The same argument applies to issues of environmental sustainability or human rights, which know no political boundaries. At a formal institutional level there is really no clear-cut representative or deliberative forum. Yet an emerging sense of a global public sphere is to be found beyond the level of states in a complex range of civil society organizations and networks such as the World Social Forum (Albrow and Glasius, 2008).

Further globalization processes may be located within cultural spheres, some of which, like global consumerism, are closely related to economic globalization. Others, like religious globalization, are not. The range of cultural globalization processes includes world religions, Islam as well as Christianity, as well as more secular outward-looking cultural processes linked with sport and the arts. Whether in football, cricket, or athletics, theatre, literature, or the visual arts, styles, influences, meanings and identities cross political boundaries. Globalization takes multiple forms, which, though inter-related cannot simply be reduced to economic processes and challenges.

The Robustness of the Nation State

In this expanded sense of multiple globalizations it remains the case that the nation state has survived politically and culturally as well as economically, a proposition explored in more depth in Chapters 4, 5 and 6. It still makes sense to speak of national economies, while individual nations remain significant players in economic policy-making. National polities seek the autonomy to promote and regulate markets and economic interests, expressed through national political structures located within territorial borders. For most practical purposes, democracy is also imagined by most of its supporters in terms of nations and localities, rather than in more remote global and regional terms. Nations also still function as sources of identity – real and imagined – generating solidarity and loyalty.

Yet in none of these senses do we see nation states and identities survive unchanged. They have rather been re-configured within processes that involve interaction between the global and the national. Put this way, global and national institutions and movements often seek to harmonize multilateral relations with each rather than being locked necessarily into conflict and opposition. One important example is that of the UN, created by nation states to mediate international conflict and promote peace and stability in relations between nations. Another somewhat different example is that of the modern Olympic Games, created as a global contest, reflected in the Olympic symbol of five interlocking circles representing the five continents, but coordinated through the sporting associations and governments of nation states under whose banners individual athletes compete. The point here is not simply that nations have remained resilient in the face of globalization, but also that the 'national' and the 'global' are in many ways complementary rather than necessarily conflicting social forces.

Theories of 'glocalization', developed by Robertson (1992, 1995) and Swyngedeouw (1992, 1997), are one sociological contribution to understanding the harmonization or interpenetration of global and national/local processes. With origins in Japanese business discourse in the 1980s (Ohmae, 1990; Robertson, 1995), glocalization began as a reference to the ways in which global corporations tailored products and marketing to particular local circumstances to meet variations in consumer demand. Such debates sought, in part, to identify what remained particular to Japanese national traditions even during the process of increasing integration into the global economy (Miyoshi and Harootunian, 1989). Robertson goes even further in seeing glocalization, or the interpenetration of the global and the local, as a defining feature of global society, evident not merely in business, but also in many other aspects of social life. For example, the nineteenth-century extension of nationalism was very much an international process, in the sense that particular nationalisms drew on other nationalist movements for support and inspiration, such that a transnational sense of what nation-building entailed developed. The point is not that each nationalist movement or nation looked the same but that highly particularistic national movements depended on a broader stock of global ideas and models as well on a distinctive sense of identity bound up with a particular history.

Others have spoken of 'glocal' states (Brenner, 1998), in which nation states do not disappear under the dominance of global scales of economic life. What happens instead, is that nation states are rearticulated and re-territorialized in relation to global challenges and opportunities. One major state focus has become the promotion of the global competitive advantage of nations centred on regions of economic innovation and global cities. The political geography of globalization is no longer entirely or perhaps predominantly nation state-centric. Insofar as states are relevant, they now might better be thought of in terms of glocal-state-centrism.

Even so, harmonization of this kind is far from universal, since there are many other circumstances of global/national conflict. This is expressed in many forms, from popular support for protection and industrial subsidies to industries undercut by foreign low-wage labour, to calls for tighter immigration controls, to resistance to global and regional integration, around issues like acceptance of the jurisdiction of the International Criminal Court, or compliance with EU directives. Democratic politics, after all, is organized largely through nationally bounded territory, in which politicians and parties must address national concerns.

Nationalism and Ethnicity

Issues of conflict and harmonization in global/national relations cannot then simply be deduced from a general theory of global expansion and national decline. Rather they require sustained analysis of a second related set of trends at work in the contemporary world. This involves a variety of movements associated with nationalism, ethnicity and tribalism, discussed in Chapter 6. The contemporary world has seen renewed episodes of genocide and 'ethnic cleansing', in defiance of ideals of human rights.

Yet ethnicity takes a multiplicity of forms, by no means all of which are inward-looking or xenophobic (Pieterse, 2007). This has been obscured by the myth that ethnicity always means trouble and conflict. Pieterse, by contrast, identifies four main types namely (a) domination, (b) enclosure, (c) competition and (d) optional. Of these only the first is typically monocultural, hot-blooded and xenophobic where associated with a majority group feeling under threat. Enclosure ethnicity, by contrast, when adopted by minorities, often seeks to bury itself in larger societies. Competition ethnicity has more affinity with conflict, yet competition can take many forms, including competition for resources from governments by participating in ethnic politics. Lastly, optional ethnicity is typically more private and cooler in its orientations.

Given this proliferation of ethnicities, there is no singular relationship between ethnicity and globalization. In the case of domination ethnicity, globalization is often the target, as in expressions of racial exclusion and ethnic superiority to other ethnic groups, entering the society through processes of global migration. With the other types of ethnicity, a more ambivalent and complex relationship may exist. Cross-border labour migration or refugee movement, for example, creates diaspora populations created through globalization processes, yet maintaining an ethnic distinctiveness. On the other hand, where global migrants employed as cheap labour for multinational enterprises or low-status service work in global cities within the country of settlement, they come into conflict with the raw edges of economic globalization.

Nationalism also takes many forms. Civil nationalisms, for example, are based less on particular 'historic' 'blood' ties and more upon ideas of citizenship rights for those within a given territory, and may often be more able to harmonize with cross-border norms and institutions such as democracy and human rights, shared across boundaries. This is broadly because citizenship rights in different nations take similar forms and may generate international solidarity, such as developed historically during and after the French Revolution of 1789 or the European uprisings of 1848.

The foregoing discussion indicates why this book links together the theme of globalization with those of the nation state and ethnicity. The justification for this is that globalization is not a limitless and all-encompassing social trend, but one that is both multidimensional and mediated through developments affecting the nation state and ethnicity. Equally, however, the development of globalization, in its political and cultural as well as economic forms, sets limits to the sovereignty of nations and the capacity of those groups who would seek to retribalize the world. Such issues are discussed throughout Chapters 4–7 of this book.

Understanding Globalization: Questions of Time and Space

The burgeoning commentary upon and analysis of globalization challenges many of the ways in which we think about human society, especially the practice of defining society in terms of the activities that go on within individual nation states. This approach has been termed 'methodological nationalism' (Beck, 2000; Wimmer and Glick Schiller, 2002). It was the typical procedure of nineteenth- and twentieth-century social science, in which the objects of analysis typically have been entities such as 'British society' or 'German society', considered as largely autonomous and self-constituting. The emergence of discourses about globalization, in contrast, represents a shift towards thinking of those aspects of social life that permeate national borders and connect the functioning of nation states and localities with each other. While territory and borders still matter, they no longer function in a self-contained manner as proposed in the Westphalian model of self-standing nation states emerging from the Thirty Years War fought in the seventeenth century. New ways of understanding globalization might then be regarded as 'methodological globalism', starting out from the idea of global interconnection rather than national separation.

To understand globalization means giving a renewed attention to issues in both history and geography. Is globalization a very modern development that post-dates the nation state, accelerated by new information technology which simultaneously stretches across space as well as permitting virtually instantaneous transactions. This sense of time–space compression (Harvey, 1989) is clearly central to globalization, but has this developed suddenly or through a longer-term phasing? Does globalization then have a longer history, both before and during the rise of nation states over the last 200 years? And if so, what spatial patterns are evident if we take this longer temporal view? What kinds of connectivity foster and create global linkages, and what are the spatial relationships between the component parts?

Further questions abound. Is globalization synonymous with the history and contemporary power of the West? Or does it derive from a range of regions and civilizations, remaining accessible to the non-Western world? If so, is it necessary to displace the West from the central dominant role within all processes and phases of globalization, in favour of a more multi-centred geography of global connectivity and power? And if this is done, would this necessarily mean the demise of ideas that treat globalization as homogenization and, more especially, Americanization? Does globalization encourage diversity, rather than or as much as, homogenization? And finally, is globalization invariably a constraint on human action and choice, a source of opportunity and resource for creative deployment, or a complex mixture of all these things?

The History and Geography of Globalization

This identification of globalization with quite recent developments has some merit. Two hundred years ago the world was far more fragmented, economically, culturally and in terms of communications, than it is today. Notwithstanding the expansion of the international economy and Western power since the sixteenth century, significant areas of the globe remained embedded in hunter-gathering and subsistence agriculture as late as the nineteenth century. In 1800 no standardized world time existed, while the reliance on sail and animal power for both long-distance transport and communication created what the Australian historian Geoffrey Blainey (1966) calls a 'tyranny of distance' separating many regions from each other. Geographical separation encouraged cultural parochialism and separatism.

Contrast this with the current organization of time and space. World-time based on the dominant Western calendar is ubiquitous, leaving Chinese, Orthodox and Islamic calendars to perform limited cultural and religious functions. Meanwhile, the 'tyranny of distance' has been obliterated by a communications revolution commencing with the telegraph, telephone, radio and television, and continuing electronically via the computer and satellite broadcasting systems, the digitalization of information transfer by means of the fax machine and the advent of the internet. These, together with air transport, have clearly shrunk the world, such that information can be transmitted instantaneously and people can move from one side of the world to the other in no more than 24 hours.

These recent changes are clearly of fundamental importance. Yet processes of change leading towards globalization (what Robertson (1992) calls 'mini-globalizations') are evident much further back in time. Cross-regional trade, imperial conquest leading to cross-regional transfers of resources, technology and culture, the surging movement of religious conviction and enthusiasm across existing political and cultural boundaries, and, last but not least, population movement, whether through enslavement or the search for new land, have all been long-term features of world history for several millennia (McNeill, 1986). Such developments were very far from being purely Western developments, for they involved China and the Islamic world as well as the classical civilizations of the Mediterranean and early modern Europe (Hopkins, 2002a).

These examples are drawn mostly from the world prior to Western colonization. Added to this are global processes during the colonial and more recent post-colonial periods, in which non-Western populations co-produced global processes and institutions. Involving, as it does, migrants, preachers, anti-colonial activists, writers, or sportsmen and women, the early twenty-first-century world is criss-crossed by networks of influence, commerce, family and religious influence that are not simple refractions of Western initiative and innovation (Werbner, 1999; Holton, 2005, 2008). These have been forged in part as responses to a global economy and political world in which Western power is undeniable, but it is not one in which this power is total or unambiguous in character. On any measure of cultural influence, as the case of Islam shows, the West is very far from having hegemonic control. And behind all this lies the larger theoretical point that the global co-production of the modern world has undermined any sense of the West being a separate entity, given the extent of cross-cutting economic and cultural influences. In this sense it is better to speak of a post-Western world.

While this understanding of pathways from the past to the present is well known to historians (Bayly, 2004), it is not fully appreciated either in popular globe-talk or in social science. This neglect has political as much as cognitive roots. Politically, the problem lies, as post-colonial theorists have pointed out (Said, 1978, 1993; Chakrabaty, 2000; Boatca and Costa, 2010), with Euro-centric assumptions that assert a dichotomy between the progressive West and static East, enshrouded in tradition, poverty and victimhood. This was allied in the nineteenth century to racial stereotypes, and in the twentieth century recast within modernization theory. In their different ways, neither was alert to the capacities and traditions which might reflect a more active capacity among non-Western populations to remake the world.

The neglect of the world beyond Europe and North America may also be linked with the 'failure' of many early episodes of mini-globalization to generate the self-sustainable expansion required to create one single interdependent world. Both the far-flung Roman Empire and the subsequent Islamic expansion of the Middle Ages eventually faltered. Similarly, the economic and technological dynamism of Sung China between the tenth and fourteenth centuries, which gave the world advances in movable-type printing and the use of gunpowder as an explosive, proved unable to sustain itself over the longer term (Elvin, 1973).

Such episodes may be seen as 'failures', but they clearly indicate that the world before the Industrial Revolution of the eighteenth and nineteenth centuries was very far from static and far from being dominated by self-contained rural communities and horizons of localism. Accordingly, the mini-globalizations of the world before industrialization may be said to have 'succeeded' in influencing the present via the transmission of technology, models of imperial and trading organization, cross-cultural practices and ideals of a single harmonious world linked with the great religious systems, such as Christianity and Islam.

Another important historical question is whether globalization is the necessary product of human evolution. Is there some kind of expansive logic in history involving a steady and inevitable accumulation of ever-widening inter-relationships between different segments of human society? The major problem with this argument is that there is no historical necessity embedded in social change, whether this is seen in terms of progress, globalization or the perfectibility of humankind (Holton, 2005). Such arguments are typically philosophical speculations. They exclude 'awkward' facts, such as historical discontinuities, major reversals and the sheer contingencies that generate alternative pathways of development, including alternative futures. Globalization is not the end-point of history since reversibility is always possible.

This study rejects the social evolutionist presumption that recent globalization is the culmination of previous mini-globalizations. Rather it draws attention to alternative interpretations of history, suggested in part by Barber's symbol of Jihad standing for tribalization and the primordial claims of ethnicity. Ethnicity, in its various forms, and the fusion of ethnicity, either with nation states or within patterns of global cultural dispersion, also have histories and futures that must he taken into account. They may act both as potential limits to globalization, but also sometimes in a more complex way as constituent parts of global processes.

Globalization clearly emerges as a set of processes that can be located in both time and space. However, it is easy to misconceive exactly what this means. It might simply mean that globalization can be identified temporally and spatially, along the lines of 'here it is back in cross-regional trade in 2000BCE' or 'over there in the Straits of Malacca in South East Asia, as much as the Mediterranean'. Yet there is a stronger sense in which we can locate globalization in time and space. In this alternative view, globalization constitutes notions of time and forms of space, whether these take the form of periods or cycles detectable in world history, or the cross-border spatial forms and connections that link social actors within networks of interdependence.

Rather than seeing time and space as absolutes that exist independent of human society, as in Newtonian physics, they may equally be seen, as Harvey (2006), points out, in relational terms. 'Processes', in his view, 'do not occur in space but define their own spatial form' (ibid.: 123). But to put it this way also implies that space cannot be divorced from time, which is clearly an intrinsic property of any process. In this sense we may speak of space–time. And as we have noted above, the idea of space–time compression developed by Harvey (1989), captures processes at the heart of globalization, namely the development of virtually instantaneous time made possible by new information technology, which simultaneously obliterates previous limits imposed by geographical distance.

Alongside time–space compression, there nonetheless remains a sense of multiple worlds and spaces. For Immanuel Wallerstein (1974, 1979, 1984), globalization represents the triumph of a capitalist world economy tied together by a global division of labour, driven by the logic of capital accumulation. Nations and regions, from the sixteenth century onwards, occupy specific places in a hierarchical organization of power and space, subdivided between the core economies of the Western world, the poorest exploited peripheral sections of the developing world and a semi-periphery in between. This is one way of imagining global space and time–space configurations.

One World or Many?

Another version of the idea of multiple worlds, is the vocabulary of First, Second and Third Worlds, and the more recent addition of a Fourth World. The idea of Three Worlds was elaborated by Alfred Sauvy in 1952 (Worsley, 1990: 83). This drew attention to the superpowers' drive to dominate the entire globe, that is, to the conflict between the First or Western and Second or Communist World, but also reflected the existence of a Third World beyond the first two. With the post-war expansion of colonial revolution, decolonization, post-colonial nationalism and the establishment of the Non-Aligned Movement in 1955, the term gained wider currency. It also shifted from a description of the non-Western world by Westerners into a form of self-ascribed identification for many post-colonial nations as well. Later still the pan-nationalist élan of these years became tarnished with the centralization of much post-colonial power in oppressive regimes, together with new wars between ex-colonial states. Attention turned away from issues of decolonization towards those of economic underdevelopment. From the 1970s onwards the concept of the Third World became synonymous with economic underdevelopment and deprivation.

The continuing use of the term 'Third World' is nonetheless problematic for two general reasons. First, there is the tendency to place all underdeveloped or non-Western nations in the same category, thereby minimizing important differences between them. Economically, for example, the Brazil, Russia, India and China (BRIC) group of developing countries are clearly constituent nations in the so-called Third World, yet are in a far more advantageous position than are countries such as Bangladesh or most of sub-Saharan Africa, whose economic resources and market power are far less marked. Similar contrasts are evident between industrializing nations such as Taiwan, Singapore, or Malaysia, and the primary product dependency of large parts of Africa and Latin America. In addition, the success of parts of the Third World rebounds on the assumption that all parts of the Third World are somehow less developed than any part of the First World. This is no longer tenable as 'Third World' successes overtake the developmental backwaters of Europe and North America, including areas of traditional industry decline in mining, steel making and automobile manufacture with its associated urban decay.

A second problem in the practice of identifying the Third World with all nations outside the first two worlds is more directly related to the issue of globalization. This involves the identification of various worlds with sets of nation states. This national focus fails to consider the possibility that integration into and position within global economic arrangements may occur at a subnational level rather than for nation states as a whole. A major example of this involves world or global cities (Friedmann, 1986; Sassen, 1991, 2009; Marcuse and van Kempen, 1999). For Sassen, the recent shift in global economic activities to services and finance brings about a renewed importance for key cities as strategic centres for global economic power, leaving surrounding areas to become increasingly peripheral. This applies not only to global cities such as Paris and Frankfurt within the First World nations of France and Germany, but also to global cities such as São Paulo and Mexico City within the supposedly Third World nations of Brazil and Mexico (Sassen, 1994), and more recently Shanghai in China (Chen, 2009).

A second problem with the nation state focus is that it fails to address issues concerning political and cultural diversity within nation states. Two groups are of particular importance here. The first is indigenous or aboriginal peoples marginalized in places such as the USA or Australia by colonial conquest and the processes of nation state-building. The second is those peoples or nations who are politically and culturally distinct but who do not possess a state apparatus with sovereign control of a given territory. Examples here include the Palestinians, Kurds and Catalans. It is to groups of these kinds that the designation Fourth World has often been applied.

To speak of four worlds is symptomatic of the divergent location of different parts of the world within structures of economic and political power, and is equally evidence of the divergent life chances and different types of cultural identity that emerge within this context. Beyond this, none of the four differentiated worlds is unitary in character or necessarily stable in terms of its internal composition. Inequalities and conflicts within each of the worlds are significant, as is the possibility of movement from one category to another, seen spectacularly in the economic rise of China and India.

What the preceding analysis has established is the unhelpful nature of any fixed notion of separate worlds. Space–time configurations are dynamic rather than static. This argument applies with particular effect to the confusions arising from the continuing use both of the vocabulary of First World–Third World difference and the idea of an East/West divide. Global spatial distinctions need to be more carefully drawn.

Definitions, Concepts and Representations

This chapter began with some sense of the normative and moral as much as intellectual debates and controversies that surround globalization. Attention then moved through questions about the scope and limits of globalization, its history and spatial characteristics. This approach deliberately avoided starting with a precise definition of globalization, preferring to identify and examine the breadth of usages for this controversial term. This has the advantage of broad coverage, but the potential difficulty that it has not really distilled out a clear sense of what globalization is, and what it is not. It is now time then to turn to questions of definition in a way that is better informed by the debates, controversies and evidence introduced in the first part of this chapter.

Within the babble of globe-talk, words such as 'global', 'international', 'transnational' and 'multinational', or simply 'worldwide', often appear as synonymous and interchangeable, but in other cases they may be used to make fine-grained distinctions. For example, the term 'international' is sometimes used to refer to relationships between nation states, whereas terms such as 'trans-national' are, in contrast, often meant to suggest processes that somehow stand above or beyond national determination and control. Corporations operating on a worldwide scale are referred to as 'trans-national' in UN circles, in part to draw attention to their presumed power over nations. In much academic literature, the term 'multinational' is used instead, implying perhaps that such enterprises operate in many countries and can switch activities between them. Such variations in terminology abound, yet, in the absence of any widely agreed conceptualization, it is dangerous to read too much into them in any particular case.

While there is a certain semantic arbitrariness in the way in which concepts are constructed, it is clear that concepts gain meaning only in terms of that with which they are contrasted. The 'global', for example, is usually contrasted with the 'national', more precisely with the assumption that social life is organized and structured within the boundaries of nation states. The rather minimal working definition of 'globalization', provided by Holm and Sorensen (1995: 1) reflects this, seeing globalization as 'the intensification of economic, political, social and cultural relations across borders'. This definition invites historical exploration of the dynamics of social change, by which the permeability of the political borders of the nation state has become intensified. This definition is also useful in stressing that globalization is not simply an economic phenomenon.

What needs to be added to this is a greater sense of global complexity and an awareness of the existence of different social worlds. One of the difficulties here is how simultaneously to draw attention to the development of the world as a single society, while doing justice to evidence of differentiation in the conditions of existence and forms of identity that the world's inhabitants express. Is globalization simply to do with the former, or is it intrinsically bound up with both processes?

Albrow (1990) takes up the former option, defining globalization as 'all those processes by which the peoples of the world are incorporated into a single world society', a society in which 'humanity' becomes for the first time a 'collective actor'. This latter role is closely connected with 'globalism', defined as 'those values which take the real world of five billion people [at the time of writing] as the object of concern, the whole earth as the physical environment, everyone living as world citizens, consumers, and producers, with a common interest in collective action to solve global problems' (ibid., 8).

Another approach to globalization, which starts out from a position quite similar to that of Albrow, is suggested by Robertson (1992 *passim*). He uses 'globalization' to refer 'both to the compression of the world', and the intensification of 'consciousness of the world as a whole'. This offers a useful working definition for a number of reasons. First, it is somewhat broader than Albrow's definition, including both the economic institutions and communications technologies that have helped to create a single interdependent world as well as understandings of the world as a single place. Such understandings are not, however, restricted to the idea of humanity as a collective actor, seeking collective solutions to common problems. Robertson, like Albrow, wants to draw attention to political and cultural ideas such as human rights, global environmental responsibility and cosmopolitanism, which, in their various ways, project a sense of a single humanity.

Coming to the study of globalization from the sociology of religion, Robertson emphasizes the meaningful and interpretative aspects of social life, including the world images within which globalization is represented. Globalization involves our understandings, experience and actions within the world and not simply the large trans-national structures that form the subject matter of political economy or international relations. This approach means that globalization is an inescapable part of the 'human condition'. The inescapability of globalization is reflected by its salience as a reference point for those who reject it as much as for those who celebrate it.

This leads Robertson beyond the idea of globalization as a large-scale, world-centred process that is distinct from and antagonistic to smaller-scale processes that occur among individuals within the nation or locality, or moving across borders. Globalization occurs, in his view within a larger 'field'. Put in the simplest terms, the global 'field' is the singular social world within which social interaction and social change of various kinds take place. Globalization is the process by which a single global field has come into being, but it is not the only component part of the global field. Other components include states and individuals. Alongside globalization may be found glocalization, wherever the global and local interpenetrate.

This way of thinking about globalization offers a number of advantages. One is that it allows us to avoid the presumption that globalization is an all-encompassing and unstoppable trend, without limits. Another is that we can leave open questions of the extent to which globalization operates as a system and the nature of the limits to globalization as one trend among several within the global field. Meanwhile, the associated concept of glocalization offers ways of connecting large-scale (macro) and small-scale (micro) aspects of the social world, connections that have often been obscured by the association of globalization solely with macro-processes, such as the world market, the multinational enterprise, or UN Declarations and Conventions, in contrast to the particular micro-worlds in which individuals house-holds and communities are assumed to live. Glocalization, in short, offers ways out of the global/local, macro/micro dichotomies that plague many analyses of globalization.

We have rehearsed issues arising in the definition of globalization in order to foreshadow questions to be pursued later in this book. Issues of definition and conceptualization cannot be fully addressed, however, without confronting the problem of representation.

When trying to interpret and decode any linguistic discourse, two inter-related problems arise. First, there is the issue of how far distinctions between concepts refer to distinctions between different kinds of observable social events, processes and phenomena, distinctions that can be subjected to empirical analysis. Second, there is the problem of how far distinctions arise from variations in the purposes of observers. To ignore the second issue is to ignore the ways in which terms such as 'global' and 'globalization' are used not merely for intellectual analysis, but also for moral evaluation and exhortation as well as for corporate public relations and the selling of commodities.

Two contemporary examples may be used to demonstrate the way in which particular interests represent the 'global' and the way in which notions of the 'global' are given meaning in relation to contrasts with the 'local'. Both cases also shed more light on the importance of glocalization.

The first example is that of corporations that describe themselves as 'global' in order to draw attention to the cross-national scope and commercial strength of their operations. Localism, here, implies commercial weakness and vulnerability. The problem in selling this message, however, is that potential customers or investors are generally located in particular localities with their own specific market conditions. This requires some way of depicting global corporations in a manner that is responsive to individuals based in particular localities. Financial service providers have, for example, placed great emphasis on their capacity to link together the 'global' and the 'local'. Citibank claims a history of 'breaking down barriers' and 'building cross-border relationships', representing itself as 'a partner with global outreach and local expertise' (1995 advertisement). In a similar vein, the Zurich Insurance Group trades under the slogan 'Global Strength: Local Knowledge'. In these examples, the 'global' has a strong positive resonance connected with the extensive power of multinational companies. Global power by itself is, however, represented as insufficient, requiring further augmentation by 'local' relationships or sources of knowledge to be effective in the market. Whether this kind of rhetoric means a genuine blending of trans-national and local interests of mutual benefit to each is implied but remains a matter of some contention (see Chapter 3).

Another contrasting representation of global–local relations may be found in the exhortation to 'Think Globally: Act Locally'. The origins of this slogan are not entirely certain, although its popularity among non-governmental movements, including Oxfam, environmental and women's movements, is clear. Whereas the corporate representation of global–local linkages has a significant top-down element, this second 'social movement' focus is projected in a grass-roots, 'bottom-up' manner. Instead of relying on trans-national organization for strength, it is the myriad of local actors who are enjoined to think about the global consequences of their actions before acting locally. Such consequences include the impact made by local actions on the environmental sustainability of planet earth as well as the political solidarities that emerge from widespread local actions in support of a global goal, as in women's rights campaigns.

These two examples of the language of global–local linkage indicate a vocabulary embedded in commercial and political or moral rhetoric as much as social analysis. Such representations should not be neglected because they tell us much about how social actors understand and evaluate globalization. To ignore the issue of the empirical reliability of representations is, however, to say that the 'global' is simply whatever people say it is. To leave the matter there reduces analysis to the deconstruction of rhetoric, foreclosing on the opportunity to ask how far understandings of globalization are sustained by research findings established through the critical scrutiny of data. This study is thus not simply about accounts of globalization, their logical rigour and conceptual coherence; it is also about their plausibility when judged against evidence.

Globalization and the Need for a Multidisciplinary Research Base

The research upon which this book relies is drawn from a wide-ranging set of intellectual sources and disciplines. While it is true that much academic work remains focused on the nation state as the core unit of social analysis, the study of aspects of globalization is now well established. This is evident in the following disciplines:

- **Sociology** (Featherstone, 1990; Robertson, 1992; Featherstone *et al.*, 1995; Giddens, 1999; Urry, 2000; Beck, 2002; Holton, 2005; Martell, 2010);
- **International Relations** and political science (Rosenau, 1980, 1990; Keohane, 1984; Held, 1991, 1995; Holm and Sorensen, 1995; Held *et al.*, 1999; Scholte, 2005);
- **History** (Abu-Lughod, 1989; McNeill, 1986; Hopkins, 2002a; Bayly, 2004);
- **Political Economy** (Carnoy *et al.*, 1993; Lever-Tracy *et al.*, 1996; Hirst and Thompson, 1996; Burawoy *et al.*, 2000);
- **Management and Business** (Dunning, 1993; Bartlett and Goshal, 2000; Dunning and Lundan, 2008);
- **Anthropology** (Hannerz, 1992, 1996; Friedman, 1994; Werbner, 2008).

This is also evident in more explicitly interdisciplinary activities such as world-system theory (Wallerstein, 1974, 1979, 1984, 1991; Chase-Dunn, 1989; Frank, 1990; Chase-Dunn and Barbones, 2006), world society theory (Meyer *et al.*, 1997; Meyer, 2009), policy-relevant debates on issues of development, global regulatory institutions and cosmopolitan democracy (Stiglitz, 2002; Held, 1995, 2004; Rodrik, 2007), migration and diaspora studies (Gilroy, 1993; Cohen, 2006), work on regulation (Braithwaite and Drahos, 2000; Braithwaite, 2008), religion (Beyer, 1994, 2006; Banchoff, 2008) and urban studies (Friedmann, 1986; Sassen, 1991, 1994; Marcuse and van Kempen, 1999). These major contributions are backed up by a proliferation of new journals dealing with global themes, such as *Transnational Corporations, The International Journal of Global Legal Studies, Diaspora* and *Global Networks*.

The Author's Social Location

The analyses developed in this study are therefore profoundly interdisciplinary in scope and are designed for a broad, cross-disciplinary audience. However, they also necessarily derive from the personal experience and particular viewpoints of the author.

Social science must rest upon some kind of trans-contextual appeal to truth and analytical rigour in order to have any credibility as scientific knowledge rather than opinion. Yet the numerous critiques of positivism over the past 100 or so years caution us to the realization that social knowledge can never be approached or understood in isolation from the social context, presuppositions and interests of the author. I have thus written this book in the English language, as a white, middle-class, trans-continental academic migrant, albeit from one English-speaking liberal-capitalist nation, namely Britain, to another, namely Australia. The decision to write about globalization, and the interpretations offered in this study, has been very much influenced by the process of migration, which often acts as a solvent of pre-existing views and an eye-opener to new experiences. In my own case, migration has done something to unsettle a Eurocentric northern hemispheric vision of global order.

Migration is, of course, profoundly mediated by class, gender and ethnicity, and my own experience is therefore neither more nor less typical or significant than that of others caught up in this quintessentially global process. Even though I have remained within the orbit of the liberal-capitalist English-speaking world, migration has given me a greater awareness of the Asia-Pacific as an emergent region than would otherwise have been the case. The experience of dual nationality and citizenship within the context of Australian multiculturalism is also significant, in that it has led me to consider more directly the desirability of inter-culturalism as a way of life and the political challenges to the cultural integrity of nation states that are entailed.

This personal background does not render the analytical propositions advanced here any more or less true, or give then greater or lesser persuasiveness, but it may help to explain a good deal of what is present and what is absent in the analysis. Yet the scope and limitations of what has been said here are equally rooted in a body of scholarship and the way in which I have interpreted that scholarship according to norms of logical rigour and empirical plausibility. This book is thus written on the presumption that the search for truth matters, while realizing that my interests and discursive reference points are – like anyone else's – partial, selective and culture-bound.

Book Plan: Linking Globalization with the Nation State

The plan of the book is thematic. Each chapter centres on particular aspects of globalization, with particular emphasis given to relationships between global processes and nation states. Chapter 2 provides an emphatic argument as to why any understanding of globalization should take a long-run historical approach, and where the nation state fits within the phases of global development. Chapter 3 deals with processes of economic globalization, focusing on markets, corporations and on market regulation by states and trans-national bodies. It also includes very recent developments such as the rise of China as a global economic power. Connections between economy and polity, markets and states, introduced here are expanded on in more depth in Chapter 4, with particular attention given to the senses, if any, in which national sovereignty may be said to still exist. Chapter 5, meanwhile, goes on to ask whether and how far a global political order is under construction, together with the place of nation states and regional bodies as well as global institutions within it. In Chapter 6, the relationship between nationalism, ethnicity and globalization is explored, with consideration of the significance of multiculturalism as a form of state policy within a globalizing world. Attention then moves, in Chapter 7 to global culture, around an analysis of the complex variety of trends within it, including cultural standardization, polarization and hybridization. This identifies ways in which national and global cultural processes interact and sometimes fuse, as well as forms of trans-national culture with which nation states either identify or come into conflict. In the concluding Chapter 8, the overall arguments of the book are restated. Globalization and nation states are seen not as fundamentally warring parties where global economic power necessarily always conflicts with national democracy, but in more complex terms. Power and inequality are major themes here, but so are issues of human rights, environmental protection and cosmopolitan cooperation. Attention then moves on to the question 'Is globalization reversible?', and if so, whether this means a strengthening of nation states. This serves as a way of projecting analysis into the future.

2

The Long History of Globalization

When did globalization begin? Is it a very recent development centred on cross-border flows of capital, labour and commodities, and on new communications technology like the internet? Or is the history of globalization far longer and, if so, how far back do its origins lie and what does study of its past tell us about the present and likely futures? Is this history one of an ever onward and upward progression, and is it marked by distinct phases? Or does history indicate reversals and disabling weaknesses in global institutions and relationships?

And where does the nation state fit into this picture? Does globalization pre-date the nation state and, if so, what part do globalizing processes play in the emergence of nations? And what are the current trajectories of globalization and nation states? Even if globalization has a very long-run history, is it now on the wane, as some have recently argued, pointing both to the robustness of nation states and a shift of commentators' preoccupations away from the language of globalization and a renewed concern for national security and national policy-making (James, 2001)?

The aim of this chapter is to explore this battery of questions. The argument is that globalization, in its various forms, does have a long history, and that this can be understood in terms of a variety of phases of globalization. Yet at the same time reversals and limits are also evident, suggesting that there is no underlying, necessary, or unstoppable logic to globalization.

This argument about the long-run nature of globalization challenges the idea that peoples and nations are and remain the fundamental building blocks of history. This does not mean that the history of globalization is consistently more significant than the history of nations. It is rather that the history of globalization, in the sense of cross-border interconnections, is as long-term as the history of particular peoples, and far longer than the institution of the nation state. This has been obscured over the last 250 years as the nation state and nationalism consolidated themselves and created versions of history in which peoples and nations are represented as the main players, and the global arena seen exclusively in terms of *international* relations, rather than any kind of trans-nationality.

Preliminary Issues

Terms like 'globalization' and the 'global village', and their equivalents in languages other than English, have come to prominence from the 1960s onwards. This does not mean that globalization itself is a very recent development. Nor does it mean that attempts to understand matters that we now label 'global' have only emerged in the past few decades. So where should a survey of understandings of globalization begin?

A conventional way of looking at this question is to identify earlier commentators who somehow anticipated the significance of processes now seen as central to what is today called globalization. Attention within sociology, for example, focuses on nineteenth- and early twentieth-century forebears. A classic example is that of Karl Marx and Friedrich Engels, whose familiar conception of the expansiveness of the capitalist mode of production throughout the globe and through all sectors of society is worth recalling:

> The need of a constantly expanding market for its products chases the bourgeoisie over the surface of the globe. It must nestle everywhere, settle everywhere, establish connections everywhere.
>
> The bourgeoisie has through its exploitation of the world-market given a cosmopolitan character to production and consumption in every country ... In place of the old local and national seclusion and self-sufficiency, we have intercourse in every direction, universal inter-dependence of nations. And as in material, so also in intellectual production ... National one-sidedness and narrow-mindedness become more and more impossible, and from the numerous national and local literatures, there arises a world literature. (Marx and Engels, 1962 [1848]: 37–8)

This remarkably prescient text, with its emphasis on global economic interdependence and the erosion of national and local autonomy in culture as in the economy foreshadows many themes in the contemporary literature on globalization.

Marx and Engels were not the only nineteenth-century social observers to perceive and anticipate the importance of global themes.

They were, like many others, children of the eighteenth-century Enlightenment. This movement of thought had, in a general sense, set much of the intellectual agenda for the nineteenth century by elevating the claims of reason as a universally valid foundation for knowledge. This in turn offered the promise of constructing universally valid social institutions that many believed capable of emancipating all corners of the world from ignorance and exploitation. The late eighteenth-century philosopher Immanuel Kant had articulated one element in this ideal by exploring the conditions for the emergence of cosmopolitan law and citizenship grounded in universal reason, which could take precedence and superseded the particularistic claims of national identity.

As Robertson (1992: 15–21) points out, Marx's immediate nineteenth-century forebears, Saint-Simon and Comte, had both advanced views of social science as an element in the unification of humanity. For Saint-Simon, science and industrialization reflected the same logic of advancing internationalism and interconnection between nations. The legacy of Saint-Simonian and Comtist internationalism of this kind is symbolized on the Brazilian flag, which depicts the globe as a single place united by the twin ideals of Order and Progress.

Nonetheless, as the nineteenth century proceeded, these early ventures in the social scientific understanding of what we have called globalization became eclipsed by the rise of nationalism, the nation state and primarily nation-centred ways of thought. The presumption was that human society was subdivided into bounded sets of peoples, be these nations or races. Assumptions of a racial hierarchy between peoples qualified any universal sense that all peoples had the potential to become a nation. Nonetheless, for those perceived as nations, each was seen as possessing a discrete national character. This was formed from a complex variety of political, military, demographic, religious and linguistic elements. The idealized representations of national history and character that emerged drew extensively on Romantic conceptions of the essence of a people in ways that generally stressed boundaries rather than bridges between nations.

Undoubtedly, the emerging world of nations was by no means obsessed with national particularism, being implicated in the growth of world markets, improved communications and intensified processes of imperial conquest by the leading European nations. Nationalism, in some variants, may embrace forms of internationalism or cosmopolitanism (Appiah, 1996; Kleingeld, 1999; Malachuk, 2007). One example is the liberal-democratic presumption that democracy, free trade and peace require and enhance international cooperation between nations. Some types of socialism also lent themselves to ideals of international solidarity between the working-class movements of different nations. Having said this, it remains the case that more parochial and self-interested variants of nationalism prevailed. This applied both in the world of political action and in understandings of how human society operated. This state of affairs is symbolized by the failure of Socialist Internationalism to combat nationalist political mobilization and thus prevent the outbreak of the First World War in 1914.

A national focus has thus been built into the analytical framework of social enquiry, social science and historiography over the past 150 years (Wallerstein, 1976). The nineteenth- and early twentieth-century legacy of thinking of society in terms of individual national societies is still very much with us. It is only very recently that alternatives to methodological nationalism have emerged, building first on Wallerstein and world-system theory and then moving beyond in many directions. One important strand here is the development of a richer and more sophisticated appreciation of global connections within historical scholarship by writers such as Hopkins (2002a), Bayly, (2004), Euben (2006), McNeely and Wolverton (2008).

History of Global Structures and Networks

If we associate globalization with developments such as the emergence of world markets for commodities and technological improvements to communication, then the search for origins attention shifts back five centuries. Wallerstein (1974), for example, cites the sixteenth century as a crucial watershed in the development of a capitalist world-economy. This is symbolized by the arrival of Christopher Columbus in the Americas in AD1492. In the next three centuries, Western Europe developed not only the Industrial Revolution based on wage-labour, but also the plantation economies of the Caribbean and southern states of America using slavery, the West African region from which slaves were obtained and the serf-based landed estates of Eastern Europe. All these are connected through the international exchange of commodities, be they Barbadian sugar, Polish grain, West African slaves, or Manchester textiles.

In contrast with Marx, it is not the presence of 'free' wage-labour relations that is crucial for capitalism but rather the integration of production within an international division of labour geared to capital accumulation. In this sense, Wallerstein regards slavery or serfdom as perfectly compatible with the operation of the capitalist world-system. This conceptual revision of orthodox Marxism enables him to draw attention to many facets of the global expansiveness of capitalism over a 400-year period that have been played down by analysts who focus mainly on indigenous change within the core region of Western Europe.

Wallerstein's emphasis on the sixteenth-century origins of the capitalist world-system is not by any means conclusive. Even if we define globalization in narrow terms as economic globalization, alternative analyses identify earlier world economic systems or interconnections. These are not literally global in a geographical sense, that is, covering virtually every corner of the Earth, but 'global' or 'world' phenomena in a more restricted sense, namely that they apply to long-distance intercontinental and cross-cultural networks and linkages. Janet Abu-Lughod (1989), for example, discerns the existence of a world-economy based on long-distance trade between Europe and Asia, organized through a chain of trading cities from Bruges and Venice, via Cairo and Baghdad, to Samarkand and Canton, as early as the thirteenth century. At this time, Chinese fleets of a size much larger than anything seen again before the eighteenth century sailed regularly to South East Asia, India, East Africa and the Middle East.

Philip Curtin (1984) also picks up the theme of cross-regional and cross-cultural long-distance trade. He argues that this process may he traced back several thousand years to the period 2500–1500BCE. In breaking with the emphasis on AD1500 as the turning point in global economic history, this longer-run focus includes types of economic activity generally excluded by Wallerstein, notably the long-distance trade in luxuries. The reasons for this exclusion are, as Frank (1990: 188) points out, rather arbitrary and seem to depend on a fixation with establishing a clear-cut divide between 'modern' systems and those which went before, a divide that serves, in turn, to dramatize the supposed historical novelty of the post-AD1500 modern capitalist world-system. Others have criticised Wallerstein for failing to appreciate how luxuries were not simply consumption goods for elites, but played a wider function in patronage and symbolic displays of social ties within households and cities (Schneider, 1977).

Many analyses, as we have seen, reject Wallerstein's periodization by projecting the understanding of globalization as a primarily economic phenomenon further and further back in time. Yet this longer-run approach to the expansion of the world-economy is not presented as a smooth cumulative process of development. Rather, the pattern is one of expansion, crisis and sometimes contraction and collapse. Abu-Lughod's thirteenth-century world-system, for example, stretching from North West Europe to China, subsequently collapsed under the impact of factors such as the Black Death – arguably the first global epidemic – and the Mongol invasions of China and India. Abu-Lughod goes on to develop the argument that the 'fall of the East' preceded the 'rise of the West' (Abu-Lughod, 1989). This did not mean the end of any kind of Eastern dynamic within world-systems. However, the axis of central Asia, Anatolia, northern India and the Levant–Egypt was never again to play a central world role. Over subsequent centuries, the arena of change moved outward from the Mediterranean and points East to the Atlantic and North West Europe, while the Western invasion and colonization of much of Asia established new mechanisms of global interconnection. The underlying mechanisms of change are thus discontinuity as well as persistence in the loci and forms of world-system development. In this sense, there is no evolutionary necessity for a fully fledged global economy to emerge directly from earlier historical episodes of global economic interconnection. Put another way, the 'rise of the West' was not predicated in any necessary way upon the previous 'rise of the East'.

So far we have focussed mainly on economic forms of globalization. Yet in the long-run processes of historical development under scrutiny economic relations were largely embedded within broader political, military and cultural processes. Trade routes, for example, were established to support the material needs of expanding political empires, whether in ancient Rome (Finley, 1999) or Ming China (Van der Ven, 2002). Similarly the expansion of the world-religions of Christianity (Mignolo, 2000) and Islam (Bennison, 2002) often followed military conquest, also further encouraging trading diaspora, located in cosmopolitan cities, whether around the Mediterranean, or along the Silk Road to China (Wood, 2002). Scholars, priests and migrants circulated along cross-border transport links alongside traders, as Wood's account of central Asian cities on the Silk Road makes clear (ibid.: 90).

If we widen the historical focus further to consider political and cultural connections with no particular connection with trade and trade routes, there are further plausible arguments for projecting the origins of globalization even further back in time. Andre Gundar Frank (1990) and his associates (Frank and Gills, 1993), for example, speak of 5,000 years of 'world system history', taking the analysis back to 2500BCE and before. This argument, synthesized from many specialist texts, emphasizes the significance of systematic interconnections between the European and Asian worlds. These include trade but also involve cross-cultural contact through conquest, such as Alexander the Great's forays into the Middle East and India. Other supporting evidence includes the diffusion of cultural ideas and practices, including religion and forms of knowledge. The argument is that increasing cross-border interconnections between the Hellenized Mediterranean, India, Africa, China and the later Islamic world were developed over the long-run generating a legacy of experience and innovation that serves as a backdrop to more familiar and more recent episodes in global history in the last 500 years (Bayly, 2002).

Yet if Wallerstein's time-frame for the history of globalization, is arbitrarily short, Frank's '5,000 Years argument' may be indiscriminately long, elevating rather limited and episodic cross-border connections into a temporal extension of globalization resting on rather thin evidence (Hopkins, 2002c: 22–3). The suspicion is that for the first 3,000 years of this 5,000-year time period, it is dubious to speak of a 'system' of major trans-regional significance.

One attempt to produce a more plausible evidence-based approach to global history is through the idea of distinct phases of globalization, developed by Hopkins (2002b) and Bayly (2002). Although the analysis is based on concepts that are suggestive, heuristic, provisional and thus in no way final, four possible phases are identified (see Table 2.1). These are labelled *archaic*, *proto-modern*, *modern* and *post-colonial*.

Unlike Frank's very long-run perspective, the tentative phasing in this account commences not 5,000 years ago, but is mostly confined to the last two millennia. Archaic globalization, the first phase, is identified with political and military developments including warrior dynasts from Alexander the Great and Attila onwards as well as pre-modern

Table 2.1 Globalization: four broad phases

1. Archaic	Associated with pre-modern empires, expansive world-religions and cross-regional trade. Increasingly evident in the millennium leading up to the seventeenth century, thereafter in decline.
2. Proto-modern	Associated with the emergence of stronger states with somewhat greater fiscal and military control over territory, and with growth in financial services, pre-industrial manufacturing and plantation agriculture. Evident between 1600 and 1800.
3. Modern	Associated with industrialization and the rise of the nation state. Global expansion linked with political empire, and also free trade. Heyday in the nineteenth and first half of the twentieth century.
4. Post-colonial	Associated with a set of changes evident from the 1950s onward including not simply colonial independence, but also the growth of new supra-territorial and regional organizations, together with spatial e-alignment of global economy to greater linkages with East Asia.

Sources: Adapted from Hopkins (2002b, 2002c) and Bayly (2002).

empires from ancient Rome and Byzantium to Mughal India. It also incorporates cross-regional trade and the world religions, emphasized by most other scholars. While not extending to the Americas or Australasia, it links Europe, Asia and much of Africa, and is seen as reaching its apogee around 1650. Thereafter the components of archaic globalization either fell into decline or were incorporated into the next two phases.

Proto-globalization is posited as a specific phase of globalization, prior to the more familiar modern phase, in order to draw attention to dynamic features of global significance in Europe, Asia and parts of Africa. These included the strengthening of states in terms of sovereignty and fiscal stability in Western Europe headed by Britain, as well as India and China (Bayly, 2002: 63–4) and further expansive economic processes connected with the British Empire and the *dar-al-Islam* (the world of Islam). In the Islamic world, as Bennison (2002.: 80–6) points out, the Ottomans, Moroccans and Safavids (based in Persia) were actively consolidating their rule, while merchants in these regions were involved in trading networks across the Muslim–Christian divide. The world beyond the West was coming under challenge, but was by no means lacking in dynamism. Bayly (2002: 27), believes that it is probable that 'revitalized and competing state systems in Asia', together with the continuing spread of 'universal religions' such as Islam and Buddhism, both contributed to the evolving shape of the global order, and hence 'should not be edited out of the text or treated as passive recipients of European forces'.

It is clear, nonetheless, that Euro-American capitalism assumed a major transformational role in the *modern* phase of globalization after 1750. This succeeded in drawing together commercialization and industrialization, under the aegis of the nation state (ibid.: 68). It moved beyond the remnants of both archaic globalization, and the limits of proto-global plantation capitalism and mercantilism. This involved a growth in free trade, far-reaching changes in industrial and military technology, and increasing cross-border mobility of capital. Political imperialism, meanwhile, helped to tie the globe together, whether by diplomacy in the case of Japan, or by force in India, South East Asia and much of Africa.

Even so, Bayly (2004) speaks of the co-production of the modern world by Western and non-Western populations over the period 1850–1950, rather than its unilateral reshaping by the West alone. Support for this argument may draw on socio-economic, political and cultural evidence in areas, such as the resilience and dynamism of diasporic trading networks in South East Asia (Harper, 2002) and by the significance of indigenous institutions in Japan, which launched a kind of regional globalization in the second half of the nineteenth century (Hopkins, 2002b: 7). Movements such as pan-Islamism and pan-Africanism, meanwhile, emerged as cross-border alternatives to Western Imperialism, looking forward to a post-colonial global world. And underlying all this is the important point that empires were 'too big' and 'too hard to control', as well as being 'ambiguous in their moral constitution' (Cooper, 2001: 38). Rather than total Western domination, they may better be seen as mosaics including 'islands of productive exploitation' within 'seas, where imperial control was shallow'. Susan Bayly (1999: 447–8) adds to this the idea of an 'invisible Empire' of inter-cultural engagement within realms such as law, religion, science and education, and greatest in Asian colonial cities, where new commercial or professional callings were being called into being; all this in spite of racism and racial residential segregation (Holton, 2008, 89)

The final phase in this tentative history of globalization, premised on post-war colonial independence, is better thought of as *post-colonial*, than post-imperial. This is because the end of political empire did not necessarily bring with it an end to economic and cultural Imperialism. Nonetheless the end of political empire, as we shall see in later chapters, did usher in a new set of supra-national organizations of global and regional governance. These include the World Bank or the European Union, as well as the multinational enterprises that emerged in the modern period, as successors to proto-modern trading ventures, such as the East India Company. Whether or not this array of organizations means the end of the nation state is highly unlikely, as will be seen in Chapters 4–6. It is nonetheless clear that the so-called post-colonial phase is one in which the international system of states, inherited from the nineteenth century, is being further reshaped in a more complex set of global, regional and local directions (Holton, 2009)

And, beyond all this, the cultural dimensions of the post-colonial phase, are themselves significant indicators of further change beyond the modern period. Continuing mass migration, new information technology and the growth of radical Islam are all responsible for profound mobilities of persons, cultural repertoires and visions of alternative worlds. This brings opportunities, but also risks, as indicated in the 9/11 attack on the USA and the continuing versatility of terrorist networks, so far able to outflank the formal military strategies of even the most powerful nation states.

Cultural conflicts within the post-colonial phase of globalization, bring in a further important concept, namely that of civilization. In Chapter 7, we explore how far global culture is polarized by wars between civilizations, as suggested by Huntington (1996). This later discussion may usefully be set within a broader discussion of the relationships between globalization and civilization. A key question here is how far globalization involves inter-civilizational engagements, and how far globalization constitutes a single central civilization.

Globalization and Civilization

The term 'civilization' first arose during the eighteenth-century Enlightenment as a description of the progressive application of reason in human affairs. 'Civilization' applied both to social and political life as well as to individual 'civilized' behaviour. By the nineteenth century, as Delanty (1995: 93–4) points out, 'civilization' began to be used in the plural, whereby individual nations, regions, or races were classified as civilized or uncivilized, according to whether they possessed (or were perceived to possess) specific institutions, such as stable states, the rule of law and private property. Further, the civilized could be divided into different civilizations. This classification had a moral and political as well as a descriptive function in that it became a device for assertions of white European superiority over Asian or Oriental and African society. Europe was part of the process of civilization, whereas other societies lying beyond merely possessed culture.

This approach to civilization led to the construction of a view of history in which the rise of the European or Western history proceeded through a series of phases quite independently of the non-Western world. Eric Wolf has described this view of Western history in genealogical terms as one in which:

> Greece begat Rome, Rome begat Christian Europe, Christian Europe begat the Renaissance, the Renaissance the Enlightenment, the Enlightenment political democracy and the Industrial Revolution. Industry, crossed with democracy, in turn yielded the United States, embodying the rights to life, liberty, and the pursuit of happiness. (Wolf, 1982: 5)

The exclusively Eurocentric constructions of world history, of the kind Wolf describes, have repelled many scholars from having anything to do with notions of civilization. Many critics of the term see it simply as an ideological celebration of Western culture; that is, as a focus that excludes the greater part of humankind from the making of history. Norbert Elias put the objection well, as noted by Stephen Mennell, namely that 'the notion of civilisation represents the self-satisfaction of Europeans in a colonialist age' (Mennell, 1990: 369). Notwithstanding this major problem, there are ways of rescuing the idea of civilization from Eurocentric bias, as a way of shedding light on the history of globalization.

The case for retaining the idea of civilization across the broad sweep of history is that it provides a way of characterizing distinct cross-border assemblages of institutions, and ways of life that endure across multiple generations. This enables an assessment of whether there exist common connections between different peoples spread across different territories, rather than fragmenting the picture of global history to particular groups. Civilizational analysis, in this sense, involves lumping together rather than splitting apart. In a fragmented world with few interconnections between groups, civilization might not exist; in an interconnected world, by contrast, one of more civilizations are possible, depending on the evaluation of comparison and contrasts

Where might the analysis of civilizations intersect with the study of globalization? The answer to this question involves us returning first to the issue of whether there is a unifying connecting thread in human history and, second, to whether such a thread links together the history of different regions or civilizations into a single interconnected global history. Such a global history, it must be emphasized, need *not* take the form of a single unitary process (or meta-narrative), such as the triumph of reason or Western civilization. Nor should it be taken to imply an inexorable process of homogenization to a single pattern. Nor, finally, need it entail any sense of evolutionary or teleological purpose, whether globalization is seen as a force for progress/good or domination/evil. In contradistinction to all of these, the minimum that is required for us to be able to speak of a single global connecting thread is that tangible interconnections exist between distinct regions, leading to interchange and interdependency.

Within this broader civilizational framework, exemplified in the work of Toynbee (1934–61), the development of human history is conventionally linked with a set of dynamic centres such as ancient Sumer (Mesopotamia), the Indus valley, ancient Egypt, the ancient Mediterranean worlds of Greece and Rome, and, moving forward in time, the Chinese empires between AD500 and 1500 and medieval Islam. Each is considered as possessing a significant innovative capacity and a sufficient degree of autonomy to warrant description as a civilization. At the same time, these criteria do not necessarily rule out some elements of diffusion of influence from one to another. However, where the extent of diffusion becomes highly significant across all previous civilizations another possibility arises, namely the creation of one single civilization – a global civilization.

Behind this argument lies an analytical point that has often been obscured. As Curtin puts it, 'no human group could invent by itself more than a small part of its cultural and technical heritage' (1984: 1). This insight has been obscured by the tendency for individual societies and nations to indigenize that which was originally imported or introduced from outside. How many Italians, for example, realize that pasta originates from China, and how many English-language speakers appreciate that the alphabet came originally from Phoenicia, centred on what is now the Lebanon?

This argument suggests that human history from way back has a far greater syncretic character than is typically realized. What are taken-for-granted features of everyday life often have very diffuse origins derived or borrowed from many different sources. Curtin illustrates this with the example of the English-language book. English, as a language, is of Indo-European origin. It developed in Western Europe in the hands of Germanic immigrants and became combined with elements from Latin that had come northward with the Roman Empire. The alphabet, as we have already noted, came from Phoenicea, while page numbers are Arabic, in the sense that Europeans learned them from Arabs, who in turn learned them from Indians, who had earlier invented positional notation. Curtin also points out that until the recent electronic revolution transformed printing, a book would have been produced with movable type, a system that has Chinese origins.

The challenge of finding convincing evidence of interconnection is, however, an enormous one. First, there is the difficulty of bringing together data from different regions of the globe spread across long tracts of time. This is magnified by the fragmentation of academic specialisms by discipline (history, archaeology, anthropology) and area of study (China, Islam, the Mediterranean). Beyond this, there lies the evaluative difficulty that the interconnections specified must be more than trivial ones. Charles Tilly (1984) has warned against the construction of overblown world-historical and world-systemic studies that treat *any* kind of interconnection as significant. If any such connection (for example, a visit by a European traveller to another continent, or the discovery of an artefact made in one region in another far away) is taken as significant, then, Tilly says, 'we will most likely discover ... the world has always formed a single system' (ibid.: 62).

Tilly's own antidote to the challenge of trivial interconnection is to specify a minimum criterion for interconnectedness. This is 'that the actions of powerholders in one region of a network rapidly (say within a year) ... visibly ... affect the welfare of at least a significant minority (say a tenth) of the population in another region of the network' (ibid.). The problems with this definition are twofold. First, it is linked with the identifiable actions of power-holders; second, it is very much attuned to rapid instances of change characteristic of the contemporary world. What this excludes are interconnections embedded more deeply in social life and which take longer to diffuse. Examples include the diffusion of business practices such as the trading of new products or the use of new commercial practices. These are less clearly linked to central power-holders such as emperors, politicians and generals, and may impact less rapidly than an invasion or a piece of legislation, nonetheless constituting, over the longer term, an interconnection.

While Tilly's definition of a significant interconnection is not entirely satisfactory, his general warning against the exaggeration of connections is well taken. What, then, does the evidence suggest about global inter-connection prior to the modern period, and how far back in time can an interconnecting thread be traced?

Curtin's account of the syncretic character of innovation in human history goes some way towards an interconnecting thread. Yet it remains compatible with the notion that individual nations or regions learn or borrow selectively from the more widely available stock of resources. The Chinese, for example, may have invented printing, yet they did not take up the printing of mass circulation publications in the same way as occurred in Western Europe from the Renaissance onwards. Alternatively, when the idea of windmill technology diffused from Islamic sources to the West via Mediterranean Islamdom, 'what passed was the basic idea and not the complex practice of building windmills in its particulars' (Hodgson, 1974, vol. 2: 363). Whereas the arms of the windmill spread horizontally among the Muslims, they became repositioned vertically in the Occident.

A valuable attempt to develop stronger notions of a global connecting thread has been attempted in accounts of what is seen as a 'Central Civilization' (Wilkinson, 1987). Wilkinson's argument centres on the bold proposition that 'Today there is on the Earth only one civilization, a single global civilization' (ibid.: 30). This originated in West Asia in Egypt and Sumer around 1500BCE. This core subsequently expanded to cover the entire globe, first through the Europe–Asia links and later through the incorporation of Africa and the Americas. In his commentary on this scenario, Frank (1990: 230) argues that this world-system had included 'most of the Asian–African–European' landmass by 600BCE and had incorporated much of the New World by AD1500.

For Wilkinson, the Central Civilization has been neither dominated by one form of economic system (be it capitalist, feudal, or peasant-based) nor been fully political centred or statist. It has never been fully capitalist, owing to the robust persistence of a succession of state forms, impermanent over long periods of time but grounded nonetheless on a variety of different modes of force, rent-seeking and coercive taxation. It has, on the other hand, never been fully statist because of the incapacity of particular states to survive over significant periods of time without reliance on private sources of economic power and resources. Thus 'the Central economy is at all times a mixed political economy, embodying trade and war, coercion and bargaining ... the balance shifts with time, scale, region, and commodity' (Wilkinson, 1987: 51). In a wider sense, Wilkinson's choice of the term 'Central' to characterize the development of this singular Civilization is deliberately designed to avoid any necessary reference to a particular socio-geographical locus of globalization. Given the complex and changing multilateral interconnections of the Central Civilization across history, it would be 'too parochial to label the civilization by the nomenclatures of any of ... the states that have successively dominated, or the regions that have successively centred it' (Wilkinson, 1993: 227).

This work by Wilkinson and Frank builds, in part, on the earlier studies of Marshall Hodgson (1974) on Islam. Hodgson argued for the existence of an Afro-Eurasian Oikoumene. He conceived this as 'the interdependent and more or less parallel development of four major complexes of civilised traditions', namely the Chinese, Indic, European and Nile-to-Oxus. The specific linkages between them related to commerce, art, religion and science. William McNeill, who had earlier thought of individual civilizations as being largely distinct (1964), has more recently come to support Hodgson's inter-civilizational approach (McNeill, 1990). Nonetheless, he gives pride of place in the dynamic of the Eurasian Oikoumene to different regions over time, Hellenic civilization holding the key role between 500BCE and AD200, the Indic region from AD200 to AD600, the Muslim world from AD600 to AD1000 and the Chinese from AD1000 to AD1500.

Such discourses of civilization have broken with a Eurocentric or Western approach in two ways. First, they have identified the centrality of non-Western sources of dynamism in areas such as trade, technology and science. Frank calls this a 'humanocentric' approach (1990: 157). For Mazrui (1990), it means recognizing that, for much of human history, the Chinese, Indian and Islamic worlds have been net exporters of innovations to others. This has been obscured by the rise of the West to become the leading exporter of innovation in the nineteenth and twentieth centuries.

Second, the civilizational discourses draw attention to the arbitrariness of associating geographic continents (or regions within them) with exclusive and autonomous centres of global development. In this sense, 'Europe', 'Asia' and 'Africa' are not to be regarded as continents with separate independent histories reflecting the distinctive nature or character of the continent. The peoples of the geographic continents do not have separate natures – some dynamic, others passive or conservative. The attribution of distinctive characters to continents, or to the Western and non-Western worlds, is, on the contrary, an invention of the human imagination, very often based on a highly selective or arbitrary interpretation of the evidence. This alerts us, once again, to the problem of representation discussed in Chapter 1. There is much merit in the argument that the historical understanding of globalization has been distorted by representations of 'Europe', or 'the West', as the dynamic force behind the development of a single world. This distortion has two main problems. First, the historical contribution of non-European regions to the history of globalization is marginalized. This leads to the ironic presumption that the non-Western world can only participate in the global by assimilating 'Western' practices, many of which actually originated outside the West.

Second, the very idea of the West is an elastic concept used to appropriate any development regarded as dynamic and desirable rather than being a social scientific term with an objective meaning. Two thousand years ago the intellectually and commercially dynamic Hellenic world spanned Mediterranean Europe, Asia and North Africa. This world thought of itself as Occidental more than European, but Occidental referred to the Eastern Mediterranean, that is, the Hellenic Occident, rather than to current notions of Europe as a continent distinct from Asia. As Delanty points out, 'For the peoples of Antiquity the divide between north and south was a more significant one than that of east versus west' (1995: 21). It was only far later in European history that representations of the classical past were reconstructed around the myth of a pure Western Europeanized legacy stretching from ancient Greece and Rome to the present (see the controversial discussion in Bernal, 1987).

On this basis, Christianity too originated in parts of the Middle East colonized by Rome (Turner, 2007) rather than within Europe in any conventional sense. It may then be regarded as an Oriental religion that was subsequently Westernized and Europeanized (only to be reorientated to Africa and Latin America in the contemporary global age). The original European indigenization of this Oriental import was so successful in organizational terms (Beyer, 2006) that Christianity was subsequently represented as the bulwark of Western civilization against Islam in the late medieval Europe (Delanty, 1995). Once again, a non-Western development is appropriated by powerful elements within the emerging West as part of its own distinctive way of life.

In spite of these problems, the idea of the West continues to function as the most influential element within the dynamics of globalization. The focus here is on the institutions of private capital and entrepreneurship, and the institutions of the nation state and the interstate system regarded in an – often idealized – sense as thoroughly open and democratic. This projection of the West is further highlighted by the drawing of sharp contrasts with 'others', who can be represented as both different and challenging. Islamic 'fundamentalism', in which economy and politics are subordinate to a religious world-view, continues to be cast in this role.

Where does all this leave the concept of a central global civilization?

On the positive side, this concept draws attention to significant patterns of interconnection and transfers in areas such as commerce, knowledge and technology across supposed civilizational divides separating West and East. These suggest early phases of archaic globalization took on a cross-regional character well beyond the more spatially limited idea of 'mini-globalizations', yet far from being spatially extensive across the globe. On the negative side, there is as yet no convincing sense that the supposed central civilization had a consciousness of itself as such. This is a rather disabling problem for any candidate for the status of a civilization. Indeed, during the archaic period civilizational fractures grew rather than subsided in the face of global linkages. What remains is a long-run set of interconnections, circuits of cross-regional mobility, and the periodic emergence of ways of seeing the world as a single space. These fall short of coherence as a singular civilization, but are nonetheless significant as forms of emerging world consciousness.

There are further challenges involved in understanding globalization when we switch our attention from the historical origins of structures and networks to look more explicitly at issues of cultural representation. What is at stake here is how people come to conceive of the world as a single place.

Understanding Globalization: Seeing the World as a Single Place

Roland Robertson (1992, 1995) includes images of globalization or world order, whether from religion, science, or political ideology, within his conceptualization of globalization. In this sense, globalization is not only about structures, institutions and networks, but also about the ways in which we think of social life and our place within it. Robertson goes on to argue that the idea of the world as a single community (be it in reality or in potential) goes back a very long time, reflected in notions such as the Kingdom of God on Earth (Robertson, 1992: 81). In more recent work, Inglis and Robertson (2004, 2005) provide a more elaborate account of early phases in the idea of a single world, drawn from ancient Greece and Rome.

Discussion focuses in part on the development of an ancient Greek 'ecumenical sensibility' (Inglis and Robertson, 2005: 14) stretching from the time of Alexander the Great in the fourth century BCE to the rise of Rome. This is linked with the outward-looking consequences of Alexander's Asian conquests and the Hellenization of populations in the Eastern Mediterranean and eastward. Such processes shift intellectual horizons from narrow Greek chauvinism to some sense of a general Hellenic universe. This intersected with Cynic and Stoic thought involving the spread of cosmopolitan ideals and practices. Broad horizons were also seen in Greek historiographies of 'world history'. These involved an interest in trans-local contexts rather than inward-looking parochialism. Such rather modern-sounding developments are also indicative of the implausibility of Great Divide arguments which assume modernity is only a few centuries old, and that the world before was embedded in traditionalism.

For the more recent period, Robertson provides a very useful 'temporal-historical' sketch of the globalization process. Beginning in early fifteenth-century Europe, he lists as relevant developments such as the Heliocentric (that is, sun-centred) theory of the universe, ideas about a common humanity linked with humanism and individualism, citizenship and, most recently of all, ideas of world citizenship and environmentalism. These are not only manifestations of globalization, but also, in a sense, causal elements within its emergence.

What all these developments have in common, according to Robertson, is that they contain within them ways of seeing the world as a single place occupied by a single humanity, sharing converging conceptions of rights and identities. This is not to deny that major counter-trends are also evident in this period of history, including the intensification of slavery and the development of racism, both of which challenge notions of a common humanity. Nonetheless, what Robertson seems to have in mind is less the reality of one world than the emergence of globalization as an 'imagined community'. This term, first applied by Benedict Anderson (1983) to the world-view of nationalism, seems equally applicable to globalization. Both involve images of a community composed of people most of whom will never meet face to face but who nonetheless possess a shared sense of common bonds intensified by changes to communications. What the printing press did for the diffusion of nationalism as an imagined community, satellite communication and the internet may now be doing for contemporary globalism.

Social actors have thought of the world as a single place for millennia. We do not have to scour more recent periods of change for the origins of world consciousness. Arguments like those that see the fifteenth-century European Renaissance as the decisive watershed, in such ways of thinking are vulnerable to the charge that they neglect earlier world-views derived from ancient Greece and Rome, as developed and mediated by the medieval Islamic world. Certainly, Heliocentric views of the cosmos, with which Robertson commences his sketch, were known to the ancient Greeks (Kopal, 1973: 2–3). Nonetheless, Heliocentrism was never the dominant world-view, being subordinated to the systems of Ptolemy and Aristotle, both of whom took the Earth as the centre of the universe. The alternative Aristotelian-Ptolemaic view of the Earth as a planet differentiated between distinct continents, and connected to the cosmos through spheres, continued to be influential right up to the renewed Heliocentric challenges of Copernicus, Kepler and Galileo during the sixteenth and seventeenth centuries, which themselves drew on earlier Islamic doubt as to the coherence of the celestial parts of the Ptolemaic system.

Even so, the Ptolemaic view did not inhibit thinking of the world as a single place, either in Europe or in the Arab world. In terms of the representation of space in cartography, for example, David Harvey (1989) argues that the rediscovery of the Ptolemaic map in fifteenth-century Florence represented a fundamental breakthrough in the construction of geographic knowledge of the world as a single global entity. Ptolemy's second-century AD geographical mapping based on coordinates of latitude and longitude created the possibility of both a cartographic and a spherical representation of global space. The subsequent development of cartographic representations of the globe by map-makers such as the Dutchman Mercator nonetheless had a strongly Eurocentric bias. Mercator's projection, for example, gives undue prominence to the northern hemisphere. Meanwhile, terrestrial globes soon became features of every European court as symbols of statecraft, and in the universities as accoutrements of learning. In more recent times, globes depicting the world became domesticated, serving as fashionable items of interior bourgeois furnishing, so much so that the significance of their way of representing the world as a single place has become taken for granted.

For Harvey, such intellectual changes cannot be regarded as free-standing causes of change but rather as responses to the demands of expanding capitalist commerce. This reminds us that an exclusive reliance on intellectual history may be misleading. Before disposing of the autonomy of changes in ideas altogether, it is necessary to ask whether or not there are more satisfactory ways of reformulating the significance of changes in representations of the world.

The pursuit of particular doctrines within intellectual history is an important exercise, but it does have its limitations. One is a narrow emphasis on scientific doctrines combined with neglect of broader world-views, which may be amalgams of metaphysics and mythology as much as what is regarded as science. Rather than picking out precursors of globalization within intellectual history, an alternative anthropological way of addressing the question may yield more insight. This starts out from the basic point that all human societies have, from prehistoric times, developed cosmologies that situate the life of tribes, or communities, nations, empires and individuals, within a broader, sometimes mythical realm composed (variously) of gods, monsters, natural phenomena such as rivers and mountains, animals and, of course, other humans. Such cosmologies, in the loosest and most general sense, may have a sense of unity, be it the unity of God's creation, the natural world, or the history of the social group. Yet this unity would scarcely qualify as an intimation of globalization – that is, of the world as a single place – because it lacks any of the substance of interconnection between human groups that is a basic feature of globalization.

Accordingly, it is not so much the sense of the world as a single place that matters as a sense of the interconnections that exist within that space. The long-run history of emergent understandings of globalization is therefore contained, as pointed out by the anthropologist Jonathan Friedman (1994), within the ways in which people think about the relationship between themselves and others. Friedman's body of work supports arguments about the long-run processes involved in seeing the world as a single space, but is taken in different directions to Inglis and Robertson.

For Friedman, spatial classification of the external world within some overarching sense of a finite and closed universe is a feature common, in his view, to Amazonian Indians, to African chiefdoms and to feudal Europe (ibid.: 44–5). Typically, the world is pictured as a set of concentric circles, the tribal or kinship group lying at the centre, around which are placed concentric circles representing increasingly non-local and often non-human segments of the world. These images are, in a sense, projections of the world as a single place, but the sense of interconnection between the inhabitants of the various circles is very weak. We therefore need some more tangible indicators of an emergent sense of globalization.

Friedman tackles this problem by exploring the social conditions under which such concentric cosmologies broke down to be replaced by clearer senses of the world as a single place based on inter-relationships and interdependency. He locates two major contributions to the process. One is the process of expansion and conquest by powerful interests, which creates civilizational centres and a sense of differentiation between centre and periphery. The other, inter-related mechanism is the set of processes whereby closed kin-centred worlds are eroded by developments such as cross-regional trade as well as conquest. Two major types of social structure that eventuate are centralized bureaucratic empires and commercial capitalist world-systems. It is these structures which generate cosmologies with a clearer sense of interdependency between the different elements that comprise the world as a single place.

Movement beyond the model of concentric circles is analyzed by Friedman in terms of two alternative world-views. In the first, the wider world is pictured hierarchically, positioning other peoples and regions in terms of their correct place in a hierarchy defined in terms of a varying criterion. This shift from a spatial to a hierarchical approach is seen to characterize both centralized bureaucratic empires and commercial capitalist states. The case of the Chinese empires represents the most static model, China being represented as the universal centre of an unchanging universe, surrounded by various types of civilized and uncivilized barbarians (ibid.: 63–4). A more dynamic and pluralistic example is that of early Arab cosmologies. These typically identify six zones beyond the Arab centre, each with certain attributes but none surpassing the Arabs. Thus the Chinese appear as the people of technology and artisanry, and the Persians the people of ethics and politics, while the Blacks are treated as a 'lower' zone, characterized merely by sheer numbers. All this contrasts with the Arabs, who possess the 'higher' gift of poetry (Yapp, 1992; Friedman, 1995: 61).

Similar hierarchical and often racist classifications appear in the commercial capitalist civilizations of ancient Greece and early modern Europe. Once again, hierarchies develop that differentiate the centre from the barbarians, savages, or, in the later period, infidels and Orientals that lie outside. In all cases, the shift from an enclosed concentric cosmology to a hierarchical classification reflects both the greater intensification of contact and interaction between different parts of the globe, and the pressing into service of representations of 'the other' that legitimate conquest, domination and racist superiority.

For Friedman, however, the intensification of interconnection associated with commercial capitalist expansion encourages further changes in the way in which the world is conceived of as a single place. There is thus a further shift from concentric hierarchy to evolutionism. The point about evolutionism, as he defines it, is that spatial classifications become subsumed into temporal classifications. That is, other groups, once seen as living out there in a space other than our own, become recast as groups whose otherness reflects their location within modes of human endeavour characteristic of our past. 'We' therefore stand for what is advanced and progressive, while 'they' represent an earlier, less developed stage of social life. Evolutionism does, however, offer the promise of advancement provided the institutions and techniques of advanced society are taken up by the less advanced.

The theory of a further shift towards evolutionism is sustained by comparing changes to world-views in two major phases in the history of commercial capitalist civilizations. These are, first, the commercial, imperial and intellectual expansion of the Athenian and later Hellenic world of ancient Greece in the period between roughly 800 and 200BCE, and second, the Western European expansion associated with the period between roughly AD1500 and 1750 embracing the Renaissance and the Enlightenment. The argument is that both exhibit a similar shift away from both concentric anthropocentric and hierarchical representations of the world to more evolutionary approaches. These are connected with a secularization of thought and the detachment of understandings of the world from both theology and nature.

Developments of this kind are evident, albeit fleetingly, in sixth-century BCE Greece, among writers such as Democritus and Hippocrates, and again in the period from the first-century BCE Roman Republic to the first century AD. For Friedman, 'the classical Mediterranean world reveals a succession of mentalities strikingly similar to that of Western Europe in the era of expansion' (1994: 60), culminating in the eighteenth and nineteenth centuries.

Summarizing Why Images of the World Matter

So what does all this mean for the understanding of globalization? Three points may be made here.

First, Friedman's work, building on a range of specialist studies of the ancient Mediterranean, Arab and Chinese worlds, alerts us to the long and complex historical emergence of views of the world as a single place. This process may usefully be traced further back than fifteenth-century Heliocentrism. Second, the analysis is both comparative and non-inclusive in extending the analytical framework well beyond the spatial and temporal setting of the expansion of the Western world since the sixteenth century. Third, it seeks to integrate together the long-run inclusive analysis of structures and institutions attempted by writers such as Frank with the analysis of world-views and representations of the world, the importance of which has been advanced by Robertson.

If representations of the world as a single place are to be integrated into the historical analysis of globalization, it is clear that some kind of distinction should be made between representations that somehow encourage globalization and those that do not. Put another way, the existence of many different views of the world as a single place is not, in and of itself, a causal influence on the further development of globalization. Many of the concentric representations discussed above, notably those of the Chinese, do not lend themselves to engagement with the external world. This does not mean that long-range inter-regional relationships with other parts of Europe and Asia did not take place in areas such as trade and technology transfer. What it does mean is that, in such cases, emergent globalism did not find its way into dominant representations of the world.

Conversely, the particular character of certain world-views may have exerted considerable influence on the direction taken in trends towards globalization. As Friedman points out, debate raged within sixteenth- and seventeenth-century Europe over the full humanity or otherwise of the newly found South American Indian populations (see also Mignolo, 2000). Were they to be regarded as barely human and thus fit for slavery, as claimed by the so-called 'civilizationists', or as no less human than Europeans and therefore entitled to the same rights? In the former case, representations of the globe as a single place see the population of that place as rigidly stratified and use this as a basis for a potentially globalized exploitation of labour through the commercialization of slavery. In the latter case, images of the world as a single place draw on notions of the unity of humanity as the basis for ideas that are today labelled as human rights, ideas that have fuelled both the transnational nineteenth-century anti-slavery movement and more recent moves to institutionalize a worldwide set of human rights.

The way in which images of the world as a single place are articulated may matter a very great deal to the kind of global interdependencies that are created. This particular argument is at variance with the excessively materialist approach of Marxist-influenced writers such as David Harvey and Immanuel Wallerstein, who explain systems of ideas or cultural representation in terms of the functional requirements of modes of production and the capitalist world-system respectively. The more general underpinning of the alternative argument is that the character of cultural representation cannot simply be read off from the nature of economic life.

The example of differing approaches to the understanding of South American Indian populations also reflects the ambivalence of globalization in relation to any single set of evaluative standpoints. Globalization as an idea is neither the monopoly of the economically powerful and imperially rapacious nor solely and exclusively a positive Utopia based on the inviolability of human rights and human community. Ideas of a single world may be hierarchically ordered and used to justify the most brutal social arrangements, but they may equally be strongly egalitarian.

Four Images of World Order

The foregoing discussion gives some anthropological and historical depth to a major insight of Robertson's concerning contemporary images of world order. While all images of the human world now conceive of it as a single place, the nature of such representations varies considerably according to the connections that exist between the component parts. In other words, the world is singular yet somehow differentiated and subdivided. One fundamental aspect of this differentiation is the existence and persistence of particular nation states. Some images of the world, it is true, take a 'strong' form, as in ideals of a single, integrated world community or the idea of single world government incorporating all parts of the globe in a single polity. These ideals still have considerable purchase among activists and visionaries. Yet for many others, including the sphere of practical politics, a weaker sense of global interconnections and levels of integration is posited, major boundaries between nations and localities persisting in spite of the development of global interconnection.

This argument is pursued schematically in Table 2.2 in terms of two types of distinction. On the vertical axis, images of world order vary according to the extent to which they represent principles of community (or *Gemeinschaft*) compared with a voluntary association of consenting parties (or *Gesellschaft*), a distinction introduced into sociology by Ferdinand Toennies (1955 [1887]). On the horizontal axis, types of world order vary according to whether they exhibit strong centralized bonds or weaker decentralized linkages.

This generates four major types of world-image. Along the community dimension, the strong version of global community without boundaries is contrasted with a world subdivided into local communities between which only limited connections exist. While the former includes religious utopias such as the 'Kingdom of God on Earth', the latter is reflected in anti-global, green and communitarian thinking about ecology. On the voluntary association dimension, the strong project of world federalism builds persistent local differences into a world polity in which rational agreements to cooperate are more important. Examples of this orientation are easier to find on a regional than strictly world scale, as in ideals of a federal Europe. This strong associational pattern, meanwhile, contrasts with a world of weaker

Table 2.2 Images of world order developed by Robertson

Principle of social organization	Type of interconnection	
	Stronger bonds	Weaker linkages
Gemeinschaft (community)	One single worldwide community. Belief in communal *unity*. Connection with religious or utopian dreams of an earthly paradise	World consists of *bounded communities*, such as nations or localities
Gesellschaft (voluntary association)	World government, in federal rather than communitarian form. Constituent parts of the world order agree to cooperate together	World composed of *bounded nation states*, who sometimes agree to cooperate together out of national *interest* rather than commitment to world government

Source: Adapted from Robertson (1992: 78–83).

types of associational linkage, in which nation states cooperate globally but only out of self-interest. This arrangement is the one which many would identify with the contemporary interstate system and the apparatus of international bodies such as the UN or World Bank, as they currently exist, as distinct from the Utopian projections sometimes placed on them.

This schema is an abstract way of distinguishing between the logic of contrasting ways of picturing world order rather than a set of stark contrasts to be applied mechanistically. Robertson stresses the need for flexibility in the way in which his schema is used, for several reasons. First, the generalized images may have sub-variants depending on the degree of equality or symmetry of status that exists within the global arena. What has been here termed the 'weak' or decentralized version of the global *Gesellschaft*, for example, may be conceived of in terms of contrasting patterns of participation available to nation states within trans-national organizations. The contrasts between powerful G20 nations, who also occupy key positions in the UN and the World Bank, compared with poorer and smaller developing nations, who generally occupy less central positions, indicates inequality between nations in terms of levels of access to organized global power and influence. Alternatively, more accessible forms of integration may be possible in areas where the symbolic equality of autonomous nations within the world order is more central, as in images of a family of nations of equal social and cultural worth. Some such image often underlies images of global cultural activities such as the Olympic Games.

Second, and more provocatively, Robertson argues that images of the globe as a single place implicate both those who evaluate globalism positively and those who are explicitly anti-global. Examples of the latter include movements that appeal to particularistic claims rooted variously in locality, religion, or ethnicity. Robertson's point is that these claims are today globally orientated rather than being the primordial manifestations of ancient historical allegiance. Robertson maintains that anti-global movements are globally orientated even where no direct or explicit concern with world order is evident, as among some fundamentalist American Christian groups. (Robertson, 1992: 35; see also 2003: *passim*).

Robertson's work on images of world order is of major significance to the analysis of representations of the world as a single place. First, it is a useful reminder that images of globalization are not restricted to utopian desires for one world or political movements for world government. Nor do such images necessarily imply homogeneity or equality between the various parts of the globe. Second, Robertson's emphasis on images of the globe and global order assists in opening up excessively economic or political accounts of globalization to wider issues of cultural representation and evaluation. For globalization is as much about ideals and values as economic development, about ideals of what the world should be as well as what it currently is or is thought to be. Such normative issues recur as we move forward in time to consider the historical sociology of globalization and its relations with Western modernity.

Globalization, the Great Divide and Alternative Global Histories

The historical perspectives on globalization sketched in the first part of this chapter are important for a number of reasons. One of the most important is that they break through a widespread sociological tendency to think of history in terms of what might be called a 'great divide' between traditional society and modernity. The work of Anthony Giddens represents a major contemporary reaffirmation of this 'great divide' approach.

Giddens argues that modern society is fundamentally different from what went before, and that the history of civilization is of far less significance than the recent history of capitalism. Whereas,

> the history of human 'civilisation' stretches back some 7000 years – so far as we know ... Capitalism is at most some 400 or 500 years old, yet

it has introduced social and material transformations of quite staggering proportions compared with the range of societal variations that existed previously. (Giddens, 1981: 164)

In further work, the dynamism of the contemporary world is linked more broadly with modernity; that is, a social process that subsumes capitalism in a broader set of features. Globalization is seen as having been made possible by modernization (Giddens, 1990: 55–78). Four major aspects of modernization are identified as being important: capitalism, industrialism, the surveillance capacities of the nation state and nationally based military power. These are associated with the recent history of the Western world in such a way that globalization is interpreted, up until the present, as a primarily Western phenomenon. It is therefore only in the future that globalization will involve signifi-cant inputs from 'non-Western settings' (ibid.: 175).

While elements of this approach, such as the significance of capitalism and industrialization to modern globalization, are vitally important, the foreshortened historical perspectives here simply fail to deliver any sense of the long-run processes that lie behind recent develop-ments, or the relationship between the West and the rest in the making of globalization. To say that modernization stimulates globalization fails to engage with the productivity of worlds Giddens regards as traditional. In so doing, it bypasses dynamic global initiatives of non-Western as well as Western worlds prior to the nineteenth century. Inputs from 'non-Western settings' in technology, knowledge, cross-regional trade and religion have been around for a long time. Tradition and ways of life embedded in localism certainly matter across history as limits to globalization. Yet archaic and proto-modern phases of globalization suggest either that there are traditional forms of globali-zation, or, more probably, that modernity and sociology itself go back several millennia rather than springing from the Industrial and French revolutions (Inglis and Robertson, 2004, 2005).

The failure of the ancient Roman Empire to develop a sustainable world economic system, as Wallerstein (1974), among others, points out, is testimony to the limits of 'archaic' global institutions, however modern or traditional they may seem. And it was not until the epoch of Western capitalism and industrial technology that the historic Malthusian challenge of population growth outstripping food supply was able to be addressed in principle if not in practice.

An alternative to Giddens' approach to the history of globalization, based on historically informed evidence about global structures and imaginings, may be assembled from the work of Roland Robertson and his associates (Robertson, 1992: 58–9; Guilianotti and Robertson,

2009). This provides a very useful supplement to the broader and more long-run global history suggested by Hopkins (2002b, 2000c) and Bayly (2002). But it also offers a far richer account of broad concepts like 'globalization' and 'modernization' that often appear as abstract forces rather than concrete social processes.

Recent Phases in the History of Globalization

Robertson, like many others, sees the period from 1500 to 1750 very much as a 'germinal' phase in the development of contemporary globalization. Of more concern to the discussion here are a further five phases, concentrated in the last 250 years, during the period when global connections have become far more intensified than before. Table 2.3 below utilizes this section of Robertson's schema, while adding further dimensions and themes to it. These phases, are not to be regarded as a rigid chronological sequence, but as ways of looking at the period from the mid-eighteenth century to the end of the First World War, Robertson identifies two phases: the first, from 1750 to the 1870s, is regarded as one of *'incipient globalization'*; the second, from the 1870s to the 1920s, is seen as the crucial phase of *'take-off'* into the establishment of a global society. These two phases are identified with a mix of political, economic, cultural and technological developments.

Table 2.3 Recent phases in the development of globalization

1. Incipient globalization	1750–1870s	Not as yet the dominant trend
2. Take-off into global society	1870s–1920	Characteristically modern features emerge (e.g., industrialization) and an international state system
3. Struggle for hegemony	1920s–60s	Conflicts over global leadership between strong nations and powerful ideologies
4. Uncertainty	1970s–2000	Uncertainties about the future of international relations after Cold War. Rise of radical Islam
5. Millennial	2001–present	Ushered in by 9/11. New fundamentalist conflicts. State focus on security. Cultural pessimism

Sources: Draws on Robertson (1992) and Giulianotti and Robertson (2009), supplemented by material from Holton (2005).

The phase of *incipient globalization*, involves the following:

- The development of more formalized international relations between increasingly consolidated nation states. Nation states consolidated their rights of self-determination in written declarations and constitutions (Weissbrodt, 1988: 6), while international relations between states were increasingly embodied in bilateral and multilateral treaties.
- An increase in the number of legal conventions and agencies concerned with the regulation of international relations, including war and communication (for example, the 1864 Geneva Convention for the Amelioration of the Condition of the Wounded and Sick in Armies in the Field, and the 1868 St Petersburg Declaration to prevent the use of incendiary substances in war).
- The establishment of the International Committee of the Red Cross in 1863 as the one of the first global non-government organizations (NGOs).
- The growth of social movements, notably labour and socialist movements, stressing internationalism alongside nationalist movements.
- The beginning of the era of international exhibitions.
- Progress towards the achievement of a more concrete sense of a single humanity, through moves against slavery, condemned in the 1814 Paris Peace Treaty between Britain and France, and articulated at the 1840 World Anti-Slavery Convention.

Robertson's next phase of *take-off into global society* comprises the following:

- The development of world-time, replacing a myriad of local times. Twenty-four nations meeting in 1884 established Greenwich as the zero meridian and divided the world into 24 time zones (Kern, 1983: 12).
- The consolidation of four interlinked trends in Western modernity:
  - national societies, reflected in the spread of the nation state as the typical political form
  - autonomous individuals, reflected in the growth of institutions of citizenship and consumer markets
  - a single international society
  - a singular conception of humankind, which includes all rather than perpetuating the hierarchies of racial exclusion.
- A sharp increase in the number and speed of global forms of communication (for example, the telegraph, telephone – invented in 1876 – and radio), together with invention of the key global transportation innovation: the aeroplane.

- The first international novels, symbolized by Jules Verne's *Around the World in Eighty Days*, published in 1873 (Verne, 1873).
- The inclusion of a number of non-European societies, including Japan, into 'international society'.
- The development of international competitions – for example, the modern Olympic Games, begun in 1896, and the Nobel prizes, which commenced in 1901.
- The First World War.

If this sketch has a weakness, it is the curious neglect of economic aspects of globalization in favour of the political and cultural. The take-off phase, in particular, should be supplemented by developments such as:

- the institutionalization of the Gold Standard as the framework for global monetary exchange;
- the massive expansion of capital export from Western countries;
- the origins of multinational companies.

Robertson continues his historical sketch onwards from 1920, noting, among other trends, the gradual re-emergence of the non-Western world in the ongoing development of globalization. In the next phase, between the 1920s and the 1960s, labelled *'The Struggle for Hegemony'* (Robertson, 1992: 58–9), the following key processes and events took place:

- Disputes and wars about which nations had hegemony over globalization, including the relative decline of Britain and the rise to post-war dominance of the USA.
- The establishment of the League of Nations in 1919, and the renewal of global political organization through the UN in 1945; a rapid increase in UN membership with colonial independence, bringing non-Western voices to the fore.
- Increased reference to the interests of humanity as a whole in the light of the Hiroshima and Nagasaki atom bombs, and the Holocaust against the Jews.
- Cold War conflict over conflicting conceptions of modernity and global order.
- Crystallization of a sense of *the* Third World and of non-aligned countries poised between the superpowers.

In the penultimate 'uncertainty' phase, the following trends are identified:

- The end of the Cold War and bipolarity, in favour of a shift towards a more fluid but uncertain international system.

- An accelerated expansion of global communications, notably through electronic technology, allowing virtually instantaneous transfers of information around the globe.
- Civil rights becoming a global issue, reflected in expanding reference to human rights.
- Concern for humanity as a whole, enhanced by concern for the environment being seen as an intrinsically global issue, as symbolized by the Rio Earth Summit in 1992.
- The number of global institutions and movements rapidly increases. The establishment of key global social movements such as Amnesty International (1961) and Friends of the Earth (1969) dates from this time.
- An increased trans-continental migration of people, and an expanded challenge to monocultural nation states in the name of multiculturalism and poly-ethnicity.
- The explosion of difference around gender, sexuality, ethnicity and race eroding any universalistic conception of the individual.
- The uncertain impact of Islam, which may be interpreted either as a deglobalizing trend towards localism or regionalism, or as a reglobalizing movement challenging the credentials of Western approaches to globalization.

Such trends are once again only a sketch, but they do begin to reintegrate non-Western elements into the picture. These later phases in Robertson's global history show the same attention to influences from both above and below as we saw in the earlier periods. Their major limitation is again the curious submerging of economic aspects of globalization. This list should thus be supplemented by the following:

- The key role of the Bretton Woods institutions, notably the International Monetary Fund (IMF) and the World Bank, in restabilizing the post-war economy on economically liberal market-orientated principles.
- The rapid expansion of foreign direct investment from core Western countries, much of it concentrated in the triad comprising North America, Europe and East Asia.
- The increasing consolidation of the power of multinational companies and the development of cross-national strategic business alliances.

The fifth 'millennial' phase (Giulianotti and Robertson, 2009) attempts to characterize the world after 9/11, which many social actors see in pessimistic and apocalyptic terms. Its components include:

- 'Darkening cultures of fear' and insecurity linked with increased global political risk

- Ubiquitous fundamentalism in Jewish, Christian and Islamic worlds
- Nation state focus on security and surveillance of populations
- Personal involvement in self-mediatization through revelation in electronic media.

This 'phase' can be seen as introducing a radical cultural and political turn to the uncertainties of the previous phase. However, like some of the earlier phases in the schema, this one needs to be strengthened in a political-economic sense, with reference to the global financial crisis and the heightened risk profile of global capitalism.

Concluding Remarks

This chapter covers a great deal of historical territory which may be unfamiliar to many. Its purpose has been to explore the ways in which historical perspectives may shed light on processes of globalization, and to give some kind of perspective about what is really new in the contemporary world and what has a far longer history behind it. And in this process of historical analysis, the dynamics of globalization have been linked at many points in the last 500 years with the dynamics of nation-building and the nation state. The conclusions that may be reached on the basis of this survey are as follows.

First, globalization has a long history. The many processes involved include long-distance trade, expansive political empires and in the modern period the nation state, religion and knowledge, technology transfer and migration. The significance of individual items from this list may have waxed and waned over time, and some (e.g., trade) may have expanded while others (e.g., empire) have contracted. Each also has also had its limits, as we see from periods of economic closure and protectionism in relation to both trade and immigration.

Second, the long-run character of global history does not mean that globalization is the end-point of history, driven by some kind of underlying tendency for human society to expand across borders. Much of the history of globalization is episodic, with advances and reversals, rather than a steady ever onward and upward progression.

Third, globalization does pre-date the nation state, but it is doubtful whether it will also produce its demise. Both territory and borders supervised by nation states matter a great deal to the modern history of globalization, sometimes as limits to global expansiveness, but often, paradoxically as engines of global expansion. This paradox lies at the heart of this book, and will be further developed in subsequent chapters.

Third, there are multiple phases and processes of globalization, rather than one singular format and logic. From a historical as well as contemporary viewpoint we may speak of globalizations in the plural rather than globalization in the singular.

Fourth, in spite of variations in forms of globalization, it is arguable that this complex set of global assemblages, has certain of the characteristics of a central global civilization. This is not, however, founded on any kind of highly structured world-system around a singular logic such as capital accumulation. It looks rather more like a set of global networks and flows that are partially interconnected, but also characterized by conflict and resistance. This is clearly manifest in the phenomenon of 9/11. While indicative in some respects as a war of civilizations between the West and radical Islam, it is also striking how both parties operate within and draw upon similar global connections, whether in terms of communications technology, movements of peoples, or global alliances of supporters. 9/11 is, then, in some sense a battle within the 'Central Civilization'.

Fifth, there is a balance to be struck between continuity and change in forms and processes of globalization. The long history of features like cross-border trade or inter-regional religious expansion should not obscure very recent changes. These include the intensification of globalization in recent years in terms of growth in the movement of capital, peoples, technology and communications. Virtually instantaneous electronic communication has radically changed the relationship between space and time, inherited from the past. Change matters too, alongside continuity.

Lastly, the importance of taking a longer-run historical perspective is that it does not simply emphasize global continuities; it places the babble about the breathtaking novelty of so much globe-talk into a more accurate perspective. For it also draws attention to at least two anthropological generalizations about human society. The first is Philip Curtin's point that no human group has developed from within its own resources more than a small proportion of its current repertoire of practices and stock of ideas. The second generalization is that humans have always been a travelling species, characterized by periodic physical movement as well as travel within the imagination. The net effect of these two points is to suggest that inward-looking stasis and immobility is not, as it were, the default setting for humanity. Globalization is rather to be seen as an endemic feature of the human condition, in the sense of inclinations to look or move outwards for other ways of living, surviving and prospering. This has been obscured both by the methodological nationalism that takes separate nation states or peoples as the most fundamental unit of social analysis, and by the

Great Divide assumption that we have mostly all been localists until recent modernity ushered in the possibility of a global world.

In this historical chapter, care has been taken to present globalization as a multi-faceted combination of interacting economic, political and cultural processes. In the following chapters the focus shifts to more detailed accounts of such processes, beginning, in Chapter 3, with economic globalization.

3

The Global Economy

'Man Buys the World.' This headline appeared in *Business Week* magazine on the occasion of the acquisition by the international entrepreneur Rupert Murdoch of the full assets of Hong Kong-based Star TV (*Guardian*, 24 July 1995). Murdoch, whose business career started when he inherited the Murdoch family newspaper empire in Australia, is, at the time of writing, head of News Corporation, a diversified global media conglomerate spanning film, television, cable vision and print media as well as satellite broadcasting and information technology industries across four continents. Familiar names such as *The Times* newspaper of London, Twentieth Century Fox Films and Television, HarperCollins, the world's largest English-language publisher, as well as Star TV – broadcasting by satellite and cable to 53 Asian countries – are all part of this empire. Since the first edition of this book, Newscorp has purchased the *Wall Street Journal* and expanded further into Latin America, through Sky satellite TV and Fox cable TV available in 17 countries, and into India through regional extensions of Star India TV. In 1985, Murdoch renounced Australian nationality for American citizenship in order to pursue media acquisition in the USA, thereby surmounting legal restrictions on foreign media ownership. The Corporation itself left its original Australian domicile in 2004 for incorporation in the USA.

The Murdoch anecdote illustrates some of the ways in which concentrations of economic power and control over information transcend political boundaries for both businesses and individuals. Yet even the personal power of Murdoch, seen in the use of print and visual media to influence politics, has its limits. What was originally a family-based enterprise has become a global corporation with a declining proportion of shares owned by the Murdoch family, as other major investors take large shares, such as John Malone, the US cable vision entrepreneur, and al-Waleed bin Talal, the Saudi investor.

Taken literally, the Murdoch-inspired headline is, of course, exaggerated. The scale and competitive intensity of global economic activity is such that no one person could take over a single industry, let alone the entire world. This much is obvious. In any case, it is private *corporate* power, represented by multinational or trans-national entities such as Royal Dutch Shell, HSBC Bank, Toyota Motors and Microsoft, as much as the activity of particular entrepreneurs that lies at the heart of concerns about the demise of the nation state. Their control over access to capital investment and new technology gives them considerable leverage over even the most powerful governments anxious to attract employment-generating and taxation-generating investment.

These giants of globalization operate on a scale that exceeds the gross domestic product of most of the nations of the world. Data available for the year 2000, reviewed by Steger (2003: 49), provide telling examples. Then, General Motors' sales were a little larger than the GDP of Denmark, twice that of Ireland, three times that of Pakistan and almost four times that of Hungary.

This intensification of economic globalization raises many important issues, not least of which is the spectre of the concentration of economic power in a few hands, beyond the jurisdiction of democratically elected governments. Sklair (2001), drawing on evidence from the Fortune 500 list of global companies, talks of the emergence of a trans-national capitalist class (see also Carroll and Carson, 2003). The members of this small group are active not only within corporations, but in policy circles involving academics and politicians, such as the World Economic Forum or the Bilderburg group, both of which meet annually to discuss global strategy. Sassen (2007) has further developed the idea of global classes, identifying three distinct formations. These involve a dominant trans-national 'professional' and 'executive' class, a class composed of networks of public officials, including civil servants, judges, immigration officials and police, and, lastly, a class of disadvantaged resource-poor workers and activists (ibid.: 168–9).

For the majority of individuals, and unlike Rupert Murdoch, opportunities for mobility in search of wealth and influence are more circumscribed. They are limited both by shifting patterns of international investment and demand for labour in the first place, and by restrictions on population movement imposed by nation states in the second. These restrictions involve tighter border policing, and rules on the kinds of immigrants deemed suitable for intake and settlement. Yet world migration is on the increase, with the total stock of international migrants increasing steadily from 155 million in 1990 to an estimated 213 million in 2010 (United Nations, 2008), representing about 3 per cent of the world's population. This increase reflects the continuing salience of global movements of labour alongside the mobility of capital.

In parallel with the figure of the global entrepreneur is the equally important figure of the global migrant. Alongside the well-known Rupert Murdoch, we may place Hajji Sulieman, a Pakistani migrant working for a multinational company in the Gulf region (Werbner, 1999). In addition to being an economic migrant Sulieman is also a devout Muslim and member of a trans-national Sufi sect. Whereas some 'trans-national' migrants remain embedded within their existing cultural groups, Werbner argues that others realize the cosmopolitan possibilities inherent in their conditions of employment, through openness to others. Sulieman learnt Japanese, the language of his employers, but also English and Arabic. He also observed the customs and ways of life of other groups, including Hindus, Arabs and Bangladeshis, and has developed cross-cultural friendships. He also went on the pilgrimage to Mecca. Economic globalization, as the story of Sulieman indicates, is not simply a top-down process of Western-centred elite dominance, nor is it immune to the cross-cutting influences of culture and social relationships. Inequalities of power nonetheless matter a great deal to the dynamics of global development.

The Recent Intensification of Economic Globalization

Processes of globalization, constituted through evolving social structures, actively made in the relations between existing and emerging social groups, are, as we have seen, not new (see also Holton, 2005). Global change has nonetheless intensified in recent decades with the rapid expansion of the ratio of trans-national to purely domestic activity and with technological changes that facilitate communications and virtually instantaneous transfers of information and finance across borders. These are charted in more depth in Chapter 4.

The intensification of economic globalization is also extremely topical, as seen in the global financial crisis. Here shocks to the global market system originating in the US home mortgage sector have had major reverberations not simply on Wall Street, but throughout global financial markets (Wolf, 2010). Major institutions had not simply lent imprudently without due regard for risk, creating an unsustainable upward-moving financial bubble. In addition, they had devised unregulated financial instruments, such as collaterized debt obligations, which they sold to each other. Shocks, such as the failure or impending failure of major banks or the impending bankruptcy of nation states like Greece, have been instantaneously transmitted through the labyrinth of debt obligations throughout the globe. No nation has been immune to the resultant crisis of confidence and collapse of credit markets, which, for a while, brought flows of credit into industrial corporations and a myriad of small to medium-sized businesses to a halt.

Sassen (1996) has spoken of the loss of national political sovereignty created both by familiar concentrations of corporate power, and by less familiar private regulatory processes. These include the private debt-rating agencies like Moody's and Standard & Poors, who calculate the credit-worthiness of businesses and governments. The global financial crisis proved this form of private regulation severely defective in that the debt agencies had failed to inhibit risky types and levels of private lending by lowering the credit-worthiness of those institutions most at fault. The fee income accruing to credit agencies across time depends, as Crotty (2009) points out, on corporate willingness to submit credit ratings applications to particular agencies. This creates a perverse incentive for agencies to magnify the credit-worthiness of financial institutions, and of the institutions in which they in turn invest, in order to maintain and promote the market for their services. Such perverse incentives are further compounded by the hitherto unregulated bonus culture of financial institutions in which income to traders depends on the volume and immediate profitability of transactions, regardless of risk or longer-term financial success – let alone the stability of the financial system as a whole.

These considerations are very far from being an obscure technical matter. This is largely because failures in credit regulation and the resultant losses in wealth and confidence adversely affect both the financial stability of corporations with negative effects on employment and investment, and the fiscal freedom of governments. The latter problem arises because governments have felt it necessary to divert massive amounts of public money to the financial system to restore trust and stability This in turn has raised doubts about the credit-worthiness of governments among holders of government bonds, leading to increases in the cost of borrowing, thereby limiting funds available for other public purposes, in both the short and longer terms. In this respect, neither concentrations of economic power nor elite financial networks prevented the global financial crises of 2008–10. Powerful nation states organized in the G20 or EU have tried to fill the void left by market failure, but the fiscal, political and social stability of the most indebted countries like Greece and Ireland have led to social as much as financial crisis.

While such broad trends are clear, there are a number of misconceptions or exaggerations current in much of the broader commentary on economic globalization. First, as we have already discussed, there is the idea that the global economy is entirely new. Second is the emphasis on mobility, change and transformation, at the expense of any understanding of the ways in which economic globalization is institutionalized and regulated. Third, there is the fashionable but superficial view that the nation state has been both overtaken and marginalized by globalization. This chapter is designed to highlight the weaknesses of such approaches. It proceeds by first identifying some of the main contours of economic globalization, with particular reference to the operations of multinational enterprises and a range of economic networks. Attention then shifts to a wider consideration of the range of institutions seeking to regulate and influence aspects of the global economy, the nation state included.

Some Contours of Economic Globalization

A major distinction is worth making at the outset between an international and a trans-national economy. An international economy may be thought of in terms of exchanges between national economies carried out by economic actors and institutions based within particular nations. Typically, raw materials, goods, or services produced in one country are consumed in another. The expansion of world trade between national economies is a key indicator of this process. Much of the expansion of the international economy in the nineteenth and early twentieth centuries took this form and was further associated with processes of international migration. International flows of capital, often in the form of loans from the major Western nations, were also significant. As late as the 1950s, 'the major international flow was world trade, concentrated in raw materials, other primary products, and resource-based manufacturing' (Sassen, 1994: 11). This system, encompassing both manufacturing and primary production, involved both the developed capitalist world and developing countries.

A trans-national economy, in contrast, while incorporating international trade of this kind, has additional features. These include the development of trans-national processes and institutions. The recent integration of the world's financial markets through information technology, allows virtually instantaneous transactions across political boundaries on a vast and unprecedented scale. By 1989, trading in foreign exchange alone averaged $650 billion per day; that is, 40 times the value of world trade (Frieden, 1991). By the late 1990s, daily volumes exceeded $1,000 billion or $1 trillion. The comparable figure for 2007 was $3 trillion, to which must be added an expanding trade in interest rate and non-traditional foreign exchange instruments of another \$2.1 trillion (BIS, 2007).

Alongside labour mobility, the central features of a trans-national economy are continuing foreign domestic investment (FDI) and extensive circuits of capital investment, production and marketing. For Sklair (2001: 81–4), who has researched the Fortune Global 500 corporations, a definite shift is evident from the 'global reach' characteristic of an international economy to 'global shift', characteristic of a trans-national one. In the former 'reach' implies a national state-centred home base to which international branches and subsidiaries are accountable. In the latter 'shift' implies a global rather than nationally based strategic focus, including global production strategies, global branding and business norms such as world's best practice. This kind of 'shift' sees business increasingly being conducted on a global scale in a range of interconnected and shifting locations according to trans-national calculations of optimal profitability. This typically involves one or more of the following: foreign direct investment in production outside the country of origin, the articulation of specialized production or service provision from a wide range of national sources in an integrated global production or service delivery strategy; and the development of strategic business alliances across political and industry boundaries. One effect of this is constant shift in the location of employment. This kind of trans-national economy has become more characteristic of economic globalization since the 1960s.

Within the new trans-national economy individual nations are increasingly dependent not only on trade, but also on flows of capital from outside. These are seen as necessary to achieve economic growth, gain access to new technology and maximize employment. The increased demand for foreign investment has also been associated with processes of deregulation of capital transfers and with opportunities created by the privatization of former public monopolies in sectors such as power supply and telecommunications. Yet nation states are far from absent as key players within this economy. States play a major role both individually through national processes of market regulation, infrastructural development and welfare expenditure, and collectively through the planning and coordinating processes of the G7, G8, G20, Group of 77, IMF, World Bank, World Trade Organization and EU.

In the mid- to late 1990s it was still possible to say that the development of a trans-national economy over previous decades was founded on the developed world, linking the core areas of the USA, Western Europe and Japan. These regions and countries had large markets, generated huge sums of capital available for investment and drove much of the technological innovation process, especially that which involved information technology. They were also home to the world's largest banks. According to UN data for the second half of the 1980s, around 80 per cent of all FDI inflows were concentrated in the developed countries (UNCTAD, 1993: 16).

By the end of the first decade of the twenty-first century this situation has changed radically with the rise of a group of major countries – Brazil, Russia, India and China. Known collectively as the BRICs (a term first used by Goldman Sachs in 2001), these four economies had, by 2007, expanded to comprise 15 per cent of the global economy (Goldman Sachs, 2007: 5). This advance is evidenced by high economic growth rates and in terms of the establishment of large global businesses.

The growth rates of the BRIC economies far exceeded those of the established economies during the first decade of the twenty-first century. Pride of place goes to China, whose growth rate between 1980 and 2003 was the highest in the world at an annual rate in excess of 10 per cent and export growth even higher (Dicken, 2007: 45). Since 2000, to take another growth measure, China's per capita income has risen at 8.4 per cent a year, as compared with 1.8 per cent in the USA (Rowthorn, 2008: 49). Until recently India's growth in per capita income has been less spectacular, but is still significant at 4.3 per cent. In Russia, meanwhile, notwithstanding massive social turbulence, after a decline in GDP of 37 per cent during the Yeltsin presidency in the 1990s, growth rates of 6.8 per cent have been achieved under Putin between 2000 and 2007 (Goldman Sachs, 2007: 29). Brazil's GDP growth rate of around 2.7 per cent in the same period makes it the least impressive BRIC. In the main, however, the BRICs' growth rates far exceed the 1.5–3.0 per cent figures achieved by the other major economies.

While the growth rates achieved by China, India and Russia are not sustainable over the very long term, and while some growth is orientated to non-traded goods in the domestic economy, they do begin to signify a relative geographic shift in the global economy. This has also proven relatively robust during the global financial crisis. The BRICs were not immune from this, but nonetheless, with the exception of Russia, seem to have weathered it better than the USA, Europe and Japan (Goldman Sachs, 2009: 1–2).

Evidence drawn from comparative national growth rates indicates world's economic geography well beyond the trilateral links between North America, Europe and Japan, dominant in the late twentieth century. But more is required to indicate how the mechanisms of economic globalization are involved. Foreign direct investment, foreign trade and global business organization supply many of the key elements here. Over the last 20 years, the expansion of the Chinese economy has drawn in huge amounts of foreign capital, and this has helped to shift the global FDI inflow pattern back towards the developing countries. Its positioning in the global economy is reflected both in the absorption of large volumes of capital and raw materials, while expanding its exports, and investing in overseas companies. Supported by state monetary policy that prevents an upward movement of the yuan against the dollar, the massive balance of payment surpluses involved have led to the purchase of vast quantities of US government bonds. This Chinese willingness to invest has allowed the USA to run trade and expenditure deficits, thereby underwriting the global economy.

The expansion of the BRICs, and other examples of economic development in South Korea and South East Asia, has not, however, been replicated everywhere. Large areas of sub-Saharan Africa and other parts of Asia remain in great economic difficulty with high levels of poverty and illiteracy. Many of these countries implemented reform programmes based on economic deregulation and reduction in public expenditure during the 1980s at the behest of the International Monetary Fund and World Bank. Such measures were promoted as the only way out of poverty and growing indebtedness to Western institutions. Yet, 20 years later, many of the same countries were still in as bad if not a worse position, and were now labelled hyper-indebted poor countries (HIPCs) (Sassen, 1994: 24–6). They include countries like Benin, Ethiopia, Madagascar, Niger and Senegal, which have received little increase in foreign investment in spite of deregulation. Worse, the burden of servicing government foreign debts remains high as a proportion of export revenue. This indicates the reality of a global poverty trap, something only partly relieved in 2006 by the cancellation of public debt held by foreign interests for the 18 poorest nations.

Understanding these sharp economic contrasts between the BRICs and the HIPCs requires some analytical care in terms of the depiction of global economic contours. Above all there is an obvious demise in clear-cut distinctions between an advancing Western world and a Third World trapped in poverty and exploitation. The category of 'Third World' is no longer helpful because of the vast contrasts in development within developing countries. These contrasts apply, even in spite of periodic crises, like those that occurred in South East Asia between 1997 and 1999, or the recent global financial crisis. Yet it remains the case that large sections of the world's population are indeed trapped in poverty, illiteracy and poor health, characteristics that apply *both* to many nations *and* within some of the more successful BRICs, such as the indigenous populations of Brazil, or regions like Kerala within India.

We now move to consider the institutional forms of the global economy.

The Multinational Enterprise: Global Organization of Production and Consumption

The most tangible institutional form within which this new pattern has emerged is the multinational enterprise (MNE). Since 1950, international trade has grown considerably, yet the value of production by multinational companies exceeds that of world trade itself (Dunning, 1993: 107). This reflects the fact that production of goods and services outside their original boundaries accounts for a large proportion of the total sales of MNEs. This proportion varies from around 35–40 per cent for companies originally based in nations with large home markets (for example, the USA), to upwards of 80–90 per cent for MNEs such as the Swiss-based Nestlé or Dutch-based Philips, where home markets are much smaller. Most FDI and a good deal of technology transfer between nations is carried out by MNEs.

The history of the MNE is instructive in clarifying the dynamics of the recent development of economic globalization. Trading organizations operating across political boundaries go back a long way in human history. However, the origins of MNEs go back to the period from 1870 to 1900 when enterprises began to set up foreign branches and become involved in FDI (Corley, 1989). Many contemporary multinationals, such as Ford, IBM and General Motors, began their own multinational operations in the period from 1900 to 1930 (Dassbach, 1989). The number of MNEs expanded more rapidly still after 1950. Multinationals originating in the USA and Western Europe were first in the field, joined in the 1970s and 1980s by the rise of the Japanese.

The more recent rise of the BRIC economies has created an expanding presence of MNEs from other countries. The Forbes Global 2000, in October 2009, included 13 BRIC MNEs in its top 100, alongside 45 from Europe, 24 from the USA and 11 from Japan (Forbes Global, 2000, 2009). The largest of these were banks, such as ICBC and CCB from China, and oil and gas companies like Gazprom from Russia, PetroChina and Petrobras-Petroleo Brasil, all within the top 30.

The image of the typical multinational is often associated with corporate giants in industry or raw material extraction and processing. This is somewhat misleading, since MNEs are also present within the rapidly growing service sector. This includes banks and insurance companies, accounting, advertising and consultancy bodies, together with internet search and other communications service providers such as mobile phone companies. At the time of writing, HSBC, Goldman

Sachs, Bank of China, AXA Group, Vodafone and Google comprise significant parts of the multinational presence within the service sector.

A fundamental aspect of MNEs within the global economy is clearly the growth of information industries. These typically link together production and service provision in a network of interconnected activities. Microelectronics, informatics, digitalization and telecommunications not only stimulate the global economy through productivity growth (Castells, 1993, 2001), but also change the basis upon which business is conducted. The virtual exchange of information, in particular, minimizes the constraints of geographic distance upon exchange, allowing financial markets to operate across a 24-hour time window, and consumer market information to be linked back to production processes in real time. Even more fundamental than the shift from industry to services, then, is the development of what Porat (1977) has called the 'information economy', based on 'time-space compression' (Harvey, 1989).

A crucial organizational feature of the information economy is the rise of network organization, which for Castells (1996) represents the new dominant form of organizational life, superior to both markets and hierarchical corporations (for a critical appraisal of this argument, see Thompson, 2003 ; Holton, 2008). Thus network firms operate through inter-firm networks, partly regulated by network states, to constitute network societies. This organizational form is superior because it combines the flexibility of markets and the coherence of corporations, while avoiding corporate bureaucracy and market anarchy.

Information technology has thus not only created new MNEs, such as Microsoft, Sun Microsystems and Apple, but also enhanced the capacity of other multinationals to operate across geographical and political boundaries. For Sassen (2006: 328–77), such digital networks have set free sub-national scales of economic life centred on global cities which are themselves connected at supra-national scales through global markets. The spatial location of multinational power, she believes, is now centred on global cities, such as New York, Tokyo, London, Frankfurt and, more recently, Shanghai (Chen, 2009; Sassen, 2009). These contain the global or regional headquarters of many MNE corporations together with the business networks within which financial, banking, business consulting and advertising are concentrated.

Such cities typically have a long history as economic centres. What has happened recently is a relative decline of older, urban centres of global economic power associated with manufacturing areas, such as Detroit or the Ruhr, and a growing importance of producer service centres, linked as much with each other as with their respective national hinterlands. Added to such cities, of course, are *new* information-based regions such as Silicon Valley in the San Francisco area and a similar area to the north around Seattle.

Why then has this wide range of MNEs developed? The answers to this question depend, in part, on the advantages that accrue (or are perceived to accrue) to businesses which take up trans-national investment and business partnerships, as against the exporting of domestic production. Dunning (1993: 109), in his major study of the globalization of business, identifies four general reasons for MNE activity: *market-seeking, resource-seeking, efficiency-seeking* and *strategic asset-seeking*. He argues against any general theory of MNE activity, such as the search for cheap labour or market access, and in favour of a multi-dimensional approach in which one or more reasons may be relevant. MNE strategy depends on the type of industry activity involved, complementarity with existing activities and the competitive position of the firm *vis-à-vis* other enterprises. For example, mining multinationals may be more likely to engage in resource-seeking, while firms facing high-cost technological investments in a competitive environment may seek to command strategic assets, such as new technology, in partnership with major business partners. Access to cheap labour may be important to certain manufacturing industries involved in the assembly of prefabricated parts, including automobiles or electronics, as well as in processes requiring limited skill, such as garment and shoe manufacture. Many Nike shoes for the US market, for example, are made by contractors in low-wage South East Asian countries like Vietnam, and the subject of widespread criticism (World Bank, 2009). Cheap labour is, on the other hand, far less relevant where greater levels of skill and education are needed, as in high-technology businesses and many aspects of financial services and consulting. Economic globalization, therefore, draws on both, rather than intrinsically preferring cheap labour.

The shift from an international to a trans-national form of global economy also involves qualitative changes in the strategic orientation of businesses. Instead of seeing foreign activities as simple subsidiaries or as a series of bilateral linkages to the home base, a trans-national orientation encourages genuinely global strategic activity. What this means, in the case of global production, is that MNEs may choose to subdivide the production process across of a range of locations, often in collaboration with other manufacturers. Relative costs and access to particular technologies already used producing cars affect locational preferences. In the case of the Opel Agila, available from 2000 onwards, for example, while sold by a General Motors subsidiary, the car was a badge-engineered version of the successful Japanese city cars, the Suzuki Wagon R and Suzuki Splash, manufactured as small city cars first in Hungary and then in Poland. It was, however, marketed by General Motors under a number of names including Vauxhall in the UK.

Contrary to perceptions of their monolithic strength, MNEs are not so powerful in relation to each other that their market position and economic viability are guaranteed. Niall Ferguson (2009: 350), drawing on research by Leslie Hannah (1999), notes that of the world's largest companies in 1912 – most of them multinationals – 29 per cent were bankrupt by 1995, 48 per cent had disappeared and only 19 per cent were still in the top 100. Such trends, which have continued into the twenty-first century, are partly the product of intensifying global competitive pressure, exacerbated by periodic global financial crises in the Great Depression between the wars and the recent global financial crisis, which saw the collapse of Lehmann Brothers and the near demise of the Bank of America. Nation states have not had the regulatory foresight to prevent such crises, and lack the resources to prevent many episodes of corporate failure.

Greater global competition, it should be emphasized, does not inevitably produce crisis. Other more typical responses include the takeover of poorly performing businesses by others, or the divestiture of segments of particular corporate businesses where competitive pressures are too great. In manufacturing, competition from cheaper Japanese products was the reason why the giant multinational General Electric abandoned consumer electronics in the latter part of the twentieth century. Yet the company itself has recently diversified into other sectors, including wind power and, since 2004, communications media through involvement with NBC, and remains in 2010 the second largest global business. Agile strategic management matters a great deal.

Another major response to increased inter-firm competition and the increased costs of technological or organizational change is the development of strategic business alliances or networks (Dunning, 1993; Todeva and Knoke, 2005). These take a variety of forms from formal corporate alliances to pursue agreed joint strategies using joint resources, or more informal cooperation through networks of business associates to gain market advantage through improved information, enhanced learning, or marketing collaboration and cross-selling.

A recent example in manufacturing over the last decade is the cross-national alliance between Nissan of Japan and Renault of France. Both carmakers, by the end of the 1990s, were experiencing challenging competitive conditions on a scale difficult for them to respond to. Prior to their alliance Renault faced problems breaking into markets beyond Europe, while Nissan had huge debts, was extremely bureaucratic and lacked good automobile design. Through collaboration in technological development, design and marketing, this alliance, by 2008, had become the third largest global carmaker and had a significant market presence in the USA, Europe and Asia (Renault-Nissan, 2010). Outside manufacturing, a successful example of strategic alliance in marketing occurs in airline marketing where developments like the One World or Star Alliances between airlines linked with code-sharing and booking arrangements stimulate cross-selling of tickets and other travel services.

A word of caution is necessary at this point, to avoid the presumption that businesses must develop cross-national business alliance to meet extremely competitive global conditions. An alternative, relevant to the new technology sector, is to rely heavily on internal research and development, meaning that innovative technology, protected by intellectual property patents, need not be shared with others. The case of Apple's iPhone is instructive here. Unlike some earlier new technology products of the previous generation like the CD player, developed jointly by Sony and Phillips (Shibata, 1993), iPhone technology was developed by Apple engineers alone, concentrated in the business's Californian headquarters (Vogelstein, 2008). Apple did utilize a strategic business alliance in developing the new phone, but this was not for technological reasons; it was more to do with marketing. Thus the alliance made with the American telecommunications giant AT&T (or Cingular, as it had recently become) in 2005, conferred upon them sole-carrier status in the USA for five years, with rights to sell iPhones in their stores. This exclusivity deal helped Apple achieve rapid take-up when the product was launched in 2007, without ceding any control or influence over the product to AT&T. From AT&T's point of view it brought many new customers, to set against the costs of them developing one new feature – the visual voicemail – as well as the levy on AT&T's iPhone revenue payable to Apple. This example, based on a strategic alliance within the USA rather than across borders, shows that global alliances are not always necessary, especially when high R&D expenditure within business is combined with a large home market.

The worldwide success of products like the iPhone is sometimes taken to mean that MNEs are so powerful that consumers have no choice but to buy their products. This may be combined with a second assumption that technology is a virtually unstoppable force pulling all other interests, including consumers and the welfare of nation states, in its wake. How far these assumptions are accurate is, however, debatable.

Global Marketing and the Consumer

Corporations may select from several alternative orientations to global marketing. One is that of *standardization*, whereby the same product with the same characteristics under the same brand name is sold in a range of different markets. This has several advantages, including economies of scale in production and the enhancement of brand loyalty through the achievement of reliability in the character of the product wherever it is purchased. Up until recently, the McDonald's fast-food operation marketed hamburgers in basically this manner. The use of standardized ingredients meant that a Big Mac would look and taste the same in Los Angeles, Moscow, Sydney, or Madrid. A similar approach characterized the thinking of Coca-Cola. Kline (1995) cites the comments made in 1992 by Coca-Cola's senior vice president and director for global marketing:' There is global media now ... and there is a global teenager. The same kid you see at the Ginza in Tokyo is in Piccadilly Square, in London, in Pushkin Square, at Notre Dame' (109).

Widespread perceptions that this was a general model for global marketing led to the theory that globalization means homogenization (Levitt, 1983). It also led to the spectre of the McDonaldization of the world (Ritzer, 1993) and to parallel concerns that globalization means Americanization (this specific issue will be picked up again in Chapter 7).

Standardization remains a major element of much global marketing. Global branding and universal advertising themes delivering standardized products remain, for example, a major element in the global youth market. As Kline (1995: 110) points out, Coca-Cola, Levi-Strauss, McDonald's and Disney 'have become the source of endless campaigns designed to enfranchise youth in the globalizing democracy of the market'. This emphasis on the youth market has intensified in more recent years, including the personal electronic communications technology market with the MP3 player as well as the iPhone. These are not simply stand-alone products, but elements of global youth lifestyles; not simply consumed but performed.

At the same time, many MNEs have come to realize that consumers are not entirely standard, and that tastes and demands vary across nations, cultures, regions and localities. Usenier and Lee (2009: xi), writing at the end of the first decade of the twenty-first century, note that corporations, even those with strong brands like Pepsi-Cola, L'Oréal or Nestlé, 'do not follow traditional textbook recipes, their practice is always much more adaptive to, and respectful towards local contexts'. This realization has grown in part as a result of consumer resistance to standardized products and marketing campaigns. For example, the original Barbie doll, developed as an American television toy and then marketed globally, sold less well in Europe, especially Britain. The existence of trans-national variations of this kind led the toy manufacturer Mattel to develop product and marketing changes, including a UNICEF Barbie doll (Kline, 1995: 124–5). Such shifts may reflect consumer resistance to a particular product, but they are not in and of themselves evidence of effective resistance to consumerism itself. All that the MNE may need to do in such situations is modify the product.

Consumer resistance can, however, prove more intractable, reflecting the fact that local consumption cultures are often highly resilient to new global influences (Jackson, 2004). One example of consumer resistance occurred in Japan in the 1950s and 1960s. At this time, US manufacturers of breakfast cereals and other foodstuffs, such as Kellogg and General Foods, found it hard to persuade the Japanese to abandon their traditional breakfast of rice, fish and seaweed, as well as other dietary practices. Nonetheless, by the close of the 1970s, the situation was changing, teenagers adopting fast- and frozen-food preferences and rice gradually being replaced by bread. Even so, such developments have not led to the final abandonment of traditional diets in Japan and other parts of East and South East Asia in favour of homogenized Western taste. This is illustrated by the recent launch by Kraft Foods, one of the largest food multinationals, of a whole-wheat biscuit for the Chinese market, in three local flavours – red date (seen by the Chinese as good for the blood), black sesame seed and peanut (both of which are regarded as good for the kidneys) (Wang Fanqing, 2010).

Standardization continues to have many attractions for consumers, especially when associated with powerful brand images of consistency, reliability, symbolic success and competitiveness in process and design. Yet it clearly has significant cross-cultural limits too. Global producers have not succeeded in creating standardized global consumers whose tastes and behaviour may be manipulated at will. Variations in consumer behaviour affecting the acceptability or otherwise of particular goods and services may depend on a range of cultural factors as well as differential incomes. An example of this is the requirement that McDonald's operations in Israel abandon the company's standardization routines in favour of a Kosher system that recognizes Jewish religious practices. Research indicates that the expectation of increased standardization in marketing has not taken place in any straightforward way. Cultural resistance and variations in consumer taste have led to significant elements of localization and regionalization (Boddewyn *et al.*, 1986; Tai, 1997). The emergence of *niche and micro-marketing* by MNEs (encapsulated in the term 'glocalization') represents an alternative global marketing strategy to standardization. Niche marketing may also be used by small and local as much as large global corporate producers.

One enabling factor in niche marketing has been the increasing availability, after 1990, of information technology that permits constant feedback about variations in consumer behaviour to corporate producers. A highly significant example of this is the Benetton clothing company's use of information systems across the range of countries in which they sell goods to analyze weekly variations in retail sales patterns in different markets (Giroux, 1994). Rather than insist on standardization in apparel market profiles according to style, colour and volume per head, information technology allows market variations to be fed back into the production and design process in determining production mixes, the size of product runs and distribution patterns. The overall effect is to create a greater global flexibility in matching supply to highly complex patterns of demand. Knowledge and information are thereby at an increasing premium.

Flexibility in production and marketing strategies is thus an increasingly significant characteristic of the highly competitive global environment. Producers can no longer expect to remain indefinitely in the same industry or the same market sector. This reflects not simply uncertainties arising from the complexity of consumer behaviour in different cultures and across time, but also the increasing penetration of every market by other producers. Within this context, the development of flexible specialization has been seen by theorists of capitalist development as some kind of sea change in the nature of economic life. For Piore and Sabel (1984) the shift represents a move beyond the large-scale standardized production strategies associated with Henry Ford (labelled 'Fordism'), to post-Fordist flexible specialization based on computer-assisted design, production and marketing in shorter production runs, often met through subcontracted production carried out by small producers. Outsourcing of specialized services in areas such as information technology or human resources may also be seen as a further example of corporate decentralization. For Lash and Urry (1987) this shift is seen as similar to one from organized to disorganized capitalism. The latter term is not a synonym for chaos but a way of referring to the growth of decentralized or decentred patterns of economic activity. While organized capitalism was centred on the large-scale industrial giants of the leading Western nations in sectors such as iron, steel and automobiles, disorganized capitalism is more economically and spatially mobile, characteristics enhanced by new information technology (Castells, 2001).

We have emphasized both the power of MNEs and some limits to this power. Such limits apply to the capacity of MNEs to sustain a competitive advantage *vis-à-vis* each other and to their relationship with consumers. While significant asymmetries of power are evident between producers and consumers, standardized marketing strategies do not always work, sometimes failing. In this sense, economic globalization promoted by MNEs is not always an all-powerful juggernaut, nor is it necessarily a harbinger of the McDonaldization of the world.

It would be foolish to exaggerate the power of MNEs but equally shortsighted to underestimate it. Their centrality within the global economy is evident in the scale of their operations, measured both by the value of their operations and in terms of their geographical scope. It is also evident in their command over many new technologies. This should not simply be seen as power over innovatory wealth-generating assets. To do so would underestimate the integral part played by MNEs in a range of activities, including research and development, technology transfer through licensing, the setting of industry standards for goods and services, and control over many aspects of the development and delivery of information through advertising and through private ownership of the mass media. In so doing, multinational enterprise has become a major political and cultural force, as well as an economic one.

The Wider Institutionalization of the Global Economy

MNEs are crucial players in the global economy. The disproportionate emphasis usually given to their dominant role does, however, create the impression that the global economy is more tightly organized through freestanding corporations than is really the case. Four general considerations may be listed at the outset, which, taken together, suggest a rather different account of the organizational shape of the global economy.

First, MNEs have become increasingly involved in inter-firm collaborations or strategic business alliances. In the process, principles of vertical corporate hierarchy have become less important than the networks or chains through which inter-firm relationships take place. Second, other more informal types of global business network have arisen, dependent on personalized ties of family and ethnicity rather than formal corporate bureaucracy. Third, the global economy contains a significant anarcho-capitalist sector connected in large measure with organized crime. Fourth, the global mobility of labour is largely dominated by informal micro-level decisions by individuals, families and kinship groups. The net effect of these four characteristics is to suggest a model of the global economy based less on organization than on networks.

Organizations and Networks

An important analytical shift has recently taken place from a primary concern with the involvement of corporations and states in processes of economic development to a broader concern with the organizational and normative shape of global economic life. The focus is less on the dynamics of global capitalism, or on state-centric accounts of development, and more on fine-grained accounts of how particular global markets and organizations actually function (Henderson *et al.*, 2001). One feature of this organizational perspective is a growing emphasis on the importance of networks of cooperation, exchange and trust.

From this perspective, multinational enterprises remain central players in the global economy, but increasingly as part of cooperative 'alliances' or 'chains' that link firms together rather than as freestanding hierarchies operating separately. One striking example of this perspective is the idea of global commodity chains (Gereffi and Korzeniewicz, 1994; Gereffi, 1996). Such chains link together sets of firms, households and states, such that no individual corporation has unilateral control over the chain. Cooperation between automobile companies whereby producers share technological and organizational competencies is one such example.

A growing body of research emphasizes the emergence, alongside this kind of producer-driven chain, of chains that are buyer driven, in the sense of being dominated by retail chains such as Wal-Mart or Target. This has occurred in sectors such as clothing, toys, shoes and various electronic goods (Gereffi, 1994). Buyers (or retail capitalists) drive production, which is often organized through complex subcontracting arrangements with producers. Complex inter-firm chains may involve large producers, subcontractors, wholesalers and retailers, as well as banking and other financial service providers. Some of the largest chains of this kind occur within Japanese business networks such as those centred on the Mitsubishi or Mitsui groups (Gerlach, 1992). The net effect is to create great flexibility in flows of resources and information, which gives considerable advantage in competitive global markets.

What is not entirely clear in all of this is how firms relate to the 'specific social and institutional contexts at the national level' wherein most firms arise (Henderson *et al.*, 2001: 15). Are they simply the structural effects of chains, or can firms develop independent strategies that may be specific to particular national contexts? These and other problems have resulted in a conceptual alternative to global commodity chain analysis, based on the idea of 'global production networks'.

These integrate firms and national economies, or at least, parts of them (Henderson, 1999).

A second, less formal type of global economic network, centring on personalized ties of family and ethnicity, is the global business diaspora. These networks are often of significance where business conditions are uncertain and unpredictable, and where MNEs decide it is too risky to get involved. This may arise as a result of political instability, chronic social unrest and dislocation, or an absence of secure property rights. Problems of this kind have sometimes been overcome, as in parts of Latin America, by alliances with authoritarian social and political interests, including the military. This option has been far harder to achieve elsewhere, as in many parts of the former Soviet Union, where organized crime has stepped in. In other cases, such as contemporary China, invitations to invest on the part of an authoritarian government, which lacks the capacity to coordinate and deliver a stable set of administrative rules, has also in the past deterred many MNEs.

Lever-Tracy *et al.* (1996) point out that the spectacular growth of the Chinese economy in the period after 1985 undoubtedly depended on foreign investment, but that, as things stood in the early 1990s, only one-fifth of this derived from American, Japanese, or European sources. A far greater role had been played by Chinese diaspora capitalists from Hong Kong and other parts of East and South East Asia, including Taiwan, Singapore, Malaysia, Indonesia and Thailand. These have typically operated on a personalized basis through family and friend-ship networks rather than through the formal bureaucratic structures of MNEs. Personalized networks generate trust, which is at a premium where property rights are insecure and reliable formal legal arrange-ments for commerce largely non-existent. For Kotkin (1993), diaspora groups such as the Chinese, Jews and Indians have come to represent *global tribes*, combining geographical dispersal with cultural networks and economic adaptability to new and changing conditions.

The scope for global economic networks involving diaspora groups of common ethnic ancestry operating across national boundaries is not simply a product of the advantages of ethnicity in a context of uncertainty. It also draws, according to Lever-Tracy *et al.* (1996: 6–7), on developments in technology and consumer demand. Innovations in microelectronics, for example, have cheapened costs of production in manufacturing, lowering the costs of entry for new producers, while also undermining economies of scale. Similarly, consumer demand, as we have seen above, has become more diverse, leading to the expansion of specialized markets in which local knowledge and contacts may be as important as global corporate strength. None of this has, however, inhibited expanding FDI from outside China, which has expanded in importance in the last two decades, with an increasingly prominent role played by MNEs. By 2003, China had attracted the largest number of foreign affiliates of MNEs of any country in the world (Sassen, 2009: 8–9).

Another informal component of the global economy involves what might be termed anarcho-capitalism; that is, activity expressly based on the evasion of formal visible structure of business organization and legal regulation. Based around illegal or clandestine activities such as drugs, armaments supply and criminal extortion, this type of activity clearly depends on global networks of an informal kind able to evade legal and business regulation (Freemantle, 1986; McDonald, 1988). At the same time, it may have an interface with the formal legal side of economic activity through money-laundering and unofficial deals with nation states (Mills, 1986), including activities such as arms procurement.

The scale of global anarcho-capitalism is not easy to quantify, but it cannot therefore be dismissed as marginal. Rather, its impact is concentrated in particular nations and cities. In the late 1980s, for example, it was calculated that cocaine exports represented 10–20 per cent of Columbia's legal exports, 25–30 per cent of Peru's and 50–100 per cent of Bolivia's (Lee, 1989: 60). Meanwhile, a US Congress source estimated that the Medellin syndicates at that time themselves held $10 billion worth of fixed and liquid assets in North America, Europe and Asia (ibid.: 61). For the late 1980s period, this scale of assets is dwarfed only by the world's largest 50 banks and top 30 insurance companies, and the biggest manufacturing and mining MNEs (see the discussion of UN data in Sklair, 1991: 48–9). More recently UNESCO (1999) data suggest that around 50 per cent of the rural population in central Asian republics like Uzbekistan grow drugs on their land. Global cities like Miami, New York and Hong Kong play a significant part in the distribution of drugs through the unofficial global economy. According to the 2009 World Drug Report issued by the UN's Office for Drugs and Crime (UNODC, 2009), the value of the global illegal drugs trade is now $320 billion, which is not far short of the annual legal global arms trade.

Moving beyond networks of capital, it is clear that global migrant workers have played a considerable part in key sectors of the global economy, by meeting local labour and skill shortages, and in stimulating economic growth. Global migrants have been disproportionately concentrated in a range of sectors including automobiles, building, clothing production and services. They are thus not always clustered in sectors that are directly linked with the operation of multinational companies. Undoubtedly, many of the manufacturing workers in multinational car plants around the world are global migrants, such as Turkish 'guest workers' who have worked for Ford in Germany, or Italian- or Greek-Australians employed by Ford in Australia. Less visible perhaps is migration between developing countries, for example that between Asian countries such as Pakistan and the Philippines to the oil-rich Gulf states, much of it involving manual and service employment, with little direct MNE involvement.

As with diaspora capitalism, much labour migration does not operate spontaneously but takes place within networks. Chain migration within family, extended kinship, or close-knit, village-based groups plays an important role in maximizing information about opportunities elsewhere while minimizing the disruption costs to those who eventually emigrate. This cost-minimization consideration has even been built into the immigration intake regulations of countries such as Australia through family reunion schemes. These are built on the assumption that the family rather than the receiving government will bear the bulk of the financial and social costs associated with international migration. Chain migration of this kind assists economic migrants in seeking out employment within a global economy characterized by mobility of capital and consequent shifts in the location of employment. In addition, such networks may tie into the business of ethnic diaspora by providing new injections of kin-based labour. Alternatively, migration may be more short term and contract bound in nature but again dependent on networks organized directly by potential employers or through intermediaries. Women are particularly vulnerable to physical and sexual exploitation and violence, either where they become attached to private families, as in the domestic service sector in Europe, Asia and the Americas, or where they become locked into unregulated or illegal employment such as prostitution or outwork.

In all of this, the highly visible presence of nation states in formulating immigration intake targets and policing illegal migration represents only the formal part of the more complex multi-centred process of global labour migration. Economic networks, both legal and clandestine, are evident here, as with global capital movement. Processes of economic globalization cannot thus be understood simply by reference to the more formal organization side of corporate and governmental decision-making.

Institutional Regulation of the Global Economy

It is commonplace to regard economic activity as fundamentally driven by economic interests, through relationships between economic institutions such as markets, businesses and labour-supply networks. This is the familiar setting within which land, capital, entrepreneurship, technology, knowledge, skill and labour power are deployed. While belief in the 'economic primacy' model is widespread, it has been challenged by political science, economic sociology and international relations. A major difficulty with it is the presumption that economies are somehow self-constituting and self-reliant, such that economic activity happens first, as it were, leaving states or governments to intervene subsequently should problems arise that markets appear unable to resolve. This presumption is not altogether unreasonable, since it is a characteristic of market economies to operate with a high degree of differentiation between economy and society. This kind of differentiation does not, however, dispose of the objection that governments and cultures enter into the constitution, reproduction and regulation of economic life (Polanyi, 1957; Holton, 1992).

In the case of public bodies, embracing government and non-governmental organizations, this may occur through securing stable and secure property rights for private interests and through the construction of frameworks of rules and procedures that minimize crisis or economic dislocation and maximize orderly expansion. They may also involve infrastructural investments, including human and physical capital commitments, which are neither profitable nor appropriate for private interests to undertake. Such public initiatives need not depend on direct state investment and planning but on strategies that are designed to provide incentives for private capital rather than standing in its place. Consequently, when we talk of the regulation of economic activity, this refers to a broad set of activities, including some that are often designated 'deregulation' in political discourse. Free trade, for example, requires deregulation in matters such as the ending of tariff barriers, but forms of regulation are still evident in the sets of rules and rights that the various parties to regulatory arrangements establish to institutionalize stable regimes for trade in general as well as particular types of trade such as agricultural products or information technology. From this perspective, regulatory institutions are a constitutive part of the global economy rather than external constraints.

The construction of a global regulatory framework over the past 50 years began with the Bretton Woods system (see Table 3.1). This involved the IMF, the World Bank and the General Agreement on Tariffs and Trade (GATT). Other significant bodies include the Organisation for Economic Co-operation and Development (OECD), which assists governments in policy analysis and better policy-making, as well as UN organizations like the International Labour Organization (ILO) and the Food and Agricultural Organization (FAO). Finally, regional

Table 3.1   The Bretton Woods system

Aim	Institution	Programme
Stable exchange rates and orderly adjustment of balance of payments problems	IMF	Financial support packages conditional on national economic adjustment (for example, cuts in public spending)
Economic development	World Bank	Provision of loan capital for public projects, conditional on an approved public framework
Expansion of world trade	GATT	Negotiation of tariff reductions
Full employment	National governments	Demand management based on fiscal policy

Source: Draws on Vines (1996).

forms of trans-national governance have been significantly extended, notably through the establishment and expanded functions of the European Union (EU) in areas like monetary and competition policy.

The Bretton Woods system was fundamental for the post-war regulation of global economic activity. Between 1929 and 1945, the world had been afflicted by the Great Depression, economic nationalism, Stalinism, fascism and then the Second World War. As the war came to a close, initiatives were begun again to restabilize both world politics, through the UN (successor to the ill-fated League of Nations), and the world-economy. The institutional framework that emerged from the Bretton Woods Conference of 1944 may be seen as an amalgam of international and national modes of regulation. Nonetheless, the various aims listed in Table 3.1 are clearly interdependent, in the sense that national measures to achieve full employment are not independent of the regulatory system surrounding balance of payments patterns, the availability of development capital and the conduct of world trade.

The original Bretton Woods system lasted, in a strict sense, until the 1970s. In the preceding 25 years it undoubtedly contributed to the restabilization of the global economy in general and to the dominance of a market-orientated global capitalist economy in particular. Neither worldwide economic nationalism nor world depression returned, initial capital shortages were largely overcome, and world trade and global investment rapidly increased. This apparently 'golden age' of the post-war boom received its first shocks in the 1970s with the breakdown of the fixed exchange rate system – usually regarded as the 'collapse of Bretton Woods' – and the 'oil price crisis' of 1973.

One of the fundamental mechanisms of breakdown was the globalization of international capital flows that far exceeded the value of World Bank development capital. Trans-national capital markets were, in large measure, incompatible with the Bretton Woods emphasis on fixed exchange rates and the sparing use of devaluation to correct national balance of payments crises. The combination of fixed exchange rates and national monetary policy levers to fine-tune interest rates and prevent capital outflows proved ineffective in a world of mobile capital and increased economic flexibility. Greater levels of fluctuation in exchange rates are thus a concomitant of the globalization of capital.

Post-Bretton Woods

The global regulatory framework since the demise of Bretton Woods retains some of the older features and institutions, but regulation has grown more complex and more diffuse (Braithwaite and Drahos, 2000). The IMF and World Bank remain in place, while the GATT regime was more formally institutionalized in the World Trade Organization (WTO), in 1995. These three regulatory bodies are responsible, respectively for monetary policy and financial stabilization, development and poverty-reduction, and international trade and trade dispute resolution. Beyond them a host of other regulatory and deliberative bodies exist with responsibility for particular sectors or functions. These include the Bank for International Settlements, dealing with global banking transactions, the International Standards Organization, responsible for technical standard-setting, and the International Telecommunications Organization, which deals with questions of telecommunications development and standards. And beyond this, inter-governmental cooperation on a global scale, has developed, first through the G7 and G8 meetings of the wealthiest economies and, latterly, in the expanded G20 forum.

The regulatory landscape since the end of the formal Bretton Woods system, reveals two main phases. The first in the 1980s and 1990s has been termed the 'Washington consensus' (Williamson, 1990). This is best summarized in the mantra 'Stabilize, Privatize, Liberalize'. This was directed mainly at the developing world, and both promoted and enforced by the IMF and World Bank. The second phase, has arisen in the first decade of the twenty-first century, dependent very much on deficiencies in the Washington consensus model, and criticism both from outside and within the Washington consensus institutions. The search for alternative and more effective institutional regulation has been influenced by a wider range of global voices and interests. Yet it is not entirely clear whether this phase has any kind of coherence as Rodrik (2006) points out in his argument that Washington consensus has been replaced by Washington confusion.

Some of the most powerful criticisms of the Washington consensus model were that it didn't produce the growth and development objectives that were promised. From the 1970s onwards analysts pointed out that stabilization and privatization measures in developing countries reduced public sector supports for populations without generating the kind of growth benefits that would reduce poverty. In most cases of programme aid the conditions attached (technically labelled conditionality and structural adjustment) have required changes in the recipient country's policies. Areas affected have included cutting levels of public spending, including public employment and social welfare provision, fiscal policy relaxation cutting taxation levels and an end to industry policy in favour of privatization measures, cuts to trade tariffs and to price support for local producer-support schemes. Devaluation of currencies has also been regularly proposed, increasing the burden of public debt. In addition, the IMF has required debtor governments to develop export revenue through an open-door policy of attracting foreign investment, and including the winding back of peasant agriculture in favour of production for global markets. While some have argued that conditionalities of this kind were rarely imposed inflexibly (Mosley *et al.*, 1991), critics of this overall strategy (Brett, 1985; Jackson, 1990; Bello, 2009) point to a litany of ensuing problems, including increased poverty, political conflict and social demoralization, food shortage due to the collapse of peasant farming, and increasing public indebtedness.

Looking back from the early twenty-first century, the World Bank, in its 2005 report *Economic Growth in the 1990s: Learning from a Decade of Reform*, admitted to significant problems with the previous global regulatory system. Development formulae such as 'Stabilize, Privatize, Liberalize' did not necessarily work. During the 1990s this had become clear with the stalling of development in Latin America, continuing crisis in most of sub-Saharan Africa and major difficulties facing post-communist Europe. While Uganda, Tanzania and Mozambique were seen as possible successes of the formula, this seems overly optimistic, given their continuing economic fragility in the twenty-first century. Even more interestingly, however, the global economic advance of countries like China and India seemed to be based less on thorough-going adherence to the Washington consensus and more on a mix of market and public state initiatives (Rodrik, 2006). These included significant trade protection, industry policies and loose fiscal and financial policies. The report also argues for context-specific policy packages because what may work in one place may not work elsewhere if underlying conditions and institutions are different.

This report offers a significant rethink, yet it represented only one current within the World Bank. Meanwhile some in the IMF, were, at the same date, pursuing a very different line of argument. This argued that development failures were in part produced because the Washington consensus reform agenda had not been pursued sufficiently radically. Even this was not, however, a uniform IMF position. Hence Rodrik's diagnosis of Washington confusion.

One of the underlying intellectual threads in the evolution of post-Bretton Woods thinking is that freeing markets from growth-limiting restrictions and inefficiencies underestimates the importance of the institutions and national or regional contexts involved. This is broadly a variant of the argument that politics and political institutions matter, and this in turn directs attention back to *both* forms of government associated with nation states, and to forms of governance. While 'government' refers here to the formal institutions of the state, involving legislation, executive power and the judiciary, 'governance' refers to the processes involving wider elements in society who wield power, influence and authority over policies and decisions concerning public life, and economic and social development, often in partnership with government.

The Global Economy, Global Regulation and the Nation State

Economic life has proven far easier to globalize than politics or culture. Yet the challenges of economic life to produce development, growth in human welfare, while helping to support social cohesion, human security and environmental sustainability, are far too profound to be left to the economy as the supposed engine of social improvement. This is why politics matters in a proactive manner actively reshaping society, including the economy, rather than in a reactive sense to do with the redistribution of the fruits of growth. Yet the role of nations and other kinds of state-like or public bodies within the global arena has become very complex. In the next chapter we look at the nation state as a formal body and the challenges of globalization to national sovereignty. In the remainder of this chapter we look more at governance rather than government, less at issues of national sovereignty and more at the governance of the global economy.

There are two broad ways of conceiving of patterns of governance in the global economy. One is to focus on centralized domination, whether by a single or a small group of powerful interests, a characteristic associated with empire (Harvey, 2003: Petras and Veltmayer, 2007). The leading actors are few, and patterns of inequality of power and influence great. The other is to focus on multilateral processes of governance involving multiple actors (Braithwaite and Drahos, 2000). In this case inequality may still be significant, but it is likely that multilateralism is potentially more open to a wider set of voices and to bargaining for advantage rather than physical coercion. Multilateralism may be more likely to generate norms of inclusion, though not necessarily fully cosmopolitan ideals of world citizenship. These two conceptual pictures are meant as sociological ideal-types, having the capacity to tease out the logics behind social processes, as well as identify imperfect forms of domination or multilateralism when judged by the abstract concepts of governance depicted here. Reality may contain elements of both as well as hybrids of the two.

A second related consideration is that the agenda of regulation has not been wholly dominated by liberal capitalist objectives over the entire post-war period, even though economic liberalism is the single most important element in the framework. Additional concerns for social justice, environmental regulation and human rights have become more rather than less significant over time. They have expanded the agenda for global politics far beyond economic management, while adding new voices from below to debates over global regulation, themes to be addressed in the remainder of this and in following chapters.

Economic Regulation and Intellectual Property Rights: A Case Study

The nature of global economic regulation may be pursued further through the telling example of economic property rights, more especially intellectual property rights. The 1994 Trade-Related Intellectual Property Rights (TRIPS) agreement that emerged from the Uruguay round of GATT is particularly instructive in this respect. This agreement, mandatory on all GATT signatories, required governments to take a greater role in enforcing existing intellectual property rights, mostly held as patents by MNEs, as well as allowing new rights (the following analysis being based on Drahos, 1995; Braithwaite and Drahos, 2000). Many patents would be valid for 20 years, generally longer than before, while certain new areas, such as plant variety protection or micro-organisms, would henceforth be subject to the same property rights as would apply in sectors like communications technology and pharmaceuticals (Sell, 2004). This regime would, moreover, be enforced through networks of surveillance in terms of monitoring and reporting requirements placed on states, as well as continuing monitoring by MNEs.

Not surprisingly, the USA was the major advocate of TRIPS. This emerged as a result of at least two developments. The first was the concern of MNEs such as Microsoft and Pfizer over the pirating of their products, thereby lowering profits through the evasion of property rights. The second pressure, largely exerted by politicians, was the fear that the USA was losing its competitiveness and power in the global system. The net effect was the successful deployment of US power simultaneously to skew market rules in favour of multinationals and to regain some political bargaining power for the USA as a nation state.

The regulation of intellectual property rights is crucial for several reasons. The first concerns the growing importance of intellectual property in the science- and knowledge-based industries that are a very dynamic element within the global economy. Another major point of significance is that the intellectual property rights regime that TRIPS created has major significance for political and social as well as economic life. Politically, it constrains the sovereignty of nations to deal with intellectual property rights in a manner that places national benefits over global ones. Socially, it constrains weaker and poorer nations from affordable access to the fruits of intellectual advances in areas such as patented plant types and patented medicines, where patent-holders can charge monopoly profits for the life of the patent.

The clash between global patent protection and social welfare came to the fore in debates and conflicts over HIV/AIDS medications of great potential in poor countries of Africa, where the incidence of infection was extremely high. The crux of the problem has been that access to relevant medication was ruled out because of high-cost pricing allowed by TRIPS, but that low-cost production to supply cheaper medicines was ruled out by TRIPS as a violation of the intellectual property regime that protected patent-holders. This conflict of interest between MNE self-interest and public health represents one example of a broader crisis in global health. Here death and morbidity persist on a massive scale even though much poor health is preventable given medical knowledge and technology (Labonté and Schrecker, 2009: 1).

While the signing of TRIPS represented a triumph for US corporate interests, its implementation has proven problematic, as the HIV/AIDS debate over access to pharmaceuticals reveals. Braithwaite (1995: 121) goes further, arguing that the US success was itself based on multilateral negotiation rather than unilateral domination. The adherence to TRIPS among the agricultural producing nations of the Cairns group was, for example, dependent on the USA agreeing to sanction the liberalization of agricultural trade. Nonetheless it was in subsequent years that its practical limits became clearer. One manifestation of resistance was to be found in those who ignored TRIPS-based requirements. An example was the South African government's decision to licence generic drug production of anti-viral drugs under patent for use with HIV/AIDS sufferers. While global pharmaceutical companies started legal action against this, they subsequently withdrew this under massive public pressure (Matthews, 2004: 78–80), though the South African government subsequently withdrew the planned drug programme.

At a governmental level, meanwhile, countries such as Brazil, used the threat of licensing production of patented drugs to leverage large discounts from MNEs in patented drug prices necessary for public health (Sell, 2004: 375). Measures like these occurred against a background of increased public awareness of the issues at stake stimulated in part by NGOs like Médecins Sans Frontières and Ralph Nader's consumer movement in the USA. In this way the full implementation of TRIPS has been mitigated by conflicts between the competing priorities of trade policy on the one side and public health on the other. This case study has a more general implication, namely that market-centred regulation does not solve all social problems and may obstruct them. It also shows that corporate power has not gone unchecked, especially where both government and non-government actors are involved.

Economic Regulation: An Unequal Multi-actor System

Global economic regulation, as the case of intellectual property rights makes clear, involves a complex set of actors and interests. These are implicated in relationships that are often highly unequal in terms of power and influence, yet inequality of power is not set in stone, nor is opposition or resistance fruitless. This is demonstrated in limited reforms to the scope of TRIPS. It is also to be seen late in 1998 with successful opposition to the proposed Multilateral Agreement on Investment. This would have limited the scope of nation states to impose conditions on incoming foreign investment. Success in achieving global labour standards that protect against low wages and abuse at work, have been far harder to achieve. It is also clear that in cases of successful opposition to powerful global economic interests, this has depended on differences of view among global players, including powerful nation states, as much as anti-globalization protest (Mandle, 2003).

Inequalities among global players remain. Multinational business has generally been successful in pressing for trade to be regulated in such a way as to open up markets to penetration, but it has been far more difficult for underdeveloped countries to have regulatory arrangements put in place that protect them from the dumping of dangerous pharmaceuticals or hazardous industrial waste. Similarly, while the WTO supports free trade in commodities, which is of particular benefit to those able to export products and services, it has generally opposed the free movement of labour, which might be of far more benefit to many developing countries. All this is not, of course, to deny that there are powerful groups in developing countries, whether at a governmental level (evidenced by the rise of China and India), inter-governmentally (in the case of OPEC), or in relation to the recent growth of MNEs outside the US, Europe and Japan.

Across the second half of the twentieth century, the global regulatory institutions were also slow to incorporate a broader set of interests and voices in their forums, representing the developing world. In the aftermath of decolonization, as Krasner (1985: 3) argues, post-colonial nations, 'want power and control as much as wealth'. This has been slow to materialize, especially for the smaller and poorer nations. Until recently the IMF and World Bank were dominated by the Western interests that established and financed them. For much of the post-war period, developing countries looked elsewhere for support, mainly to the UN General Assembly and associated UN agencies. This led in 1964 to the foundation of the UN Conference on Trade and Development (UNCTAD) as a counterweight to the market-orientated policies of the Bretton Woods bodies. At the first meeting of UNCTAD, the so-called Group of 77, representing 77 developing nations, was established to coordinate the Third World push for change in such areas as exploitation by MNEs and Third World debt relief for the poorest nations. This led, in turn, by the early 1970s to a greater awareness of North–South conflicts over the direction of the global economy, and the development of a new global economic agenda around the challenges in building a New International Economic Order (NIEO). In the Brandt Report, *North–South: A Programme for Survival*, prepared by the Independent Commission on International Development Issues, it was pointed out that the 'North' (in about 1980) had a quarter of the world's population and four-fifths of its income, while the South contained three-quarters of the world's population living off only one-fifth of its income (Brandt, 1980: 32).

North/South differences have persisted into the twenty-first century, even though the idea of a uniformly poor developing world has become outmoded by successful economic advance by the BRICs and some smaller nations, including much of South East Asia. This has impacted on the work of global regulatory bodies and, especially, the World Bank. Whereas the original Bretton Woods institutional regulators were focused on the past spectre of protectionism, exchange rate instability and a return of economic depression, the new regulatory agenda now includes global poverty reduction, the impact of trade policy on labour standards health and the environment. Economic and social objectives are now intertwined.

Meanwhile officials, economists and planners, from countries other than Europe and North America, now play a greater role within regulatory bodies. Most recently of all the enlargement of the inter-governmental bodies identified as the G7 or G8 to G20 status now brings countries like China and India into major global deliberative bodies, dealing with issues like the global financial crisis.

The multiple actors now involved include not only national governments with a variety of interests, MNEs and trans-national regulatory bodies themselves, but also NGOs. This multi-actor system is very far from being a pluralist democracy composed of interests with roughly equal power. The governments of rich countries and large multinationals clearly have organizational and legal resources superior to those protesting issues such as global pollution or lax food standards. The politics of economic regulation is nonetheless subject to complex processes of contestation and negotiation rather than unilateral dominance. Above all, no single interest is sufficiently powerful to dominate the regulatory agenda.

Braithwaite and Drahos (2000), in a major study of global business regulation across 13 different sectors, open up a way of studying regulation that is sensitive to both inequality and complexity. Each sector differs somewhat both in the actors involved, the principles at stake, the patterns of power and influence at work and the ways in which conflicts are resolved. Much regulation is achieved through the development of rules and standards, which may be imposed by coercion, mutually agreed, or the outcome of rewards and sanctions. Economic coercion is stronger in some areas such as trade, or intellectual property, but of minor significance in others such as the environment or telecommunications, where mutual agreement in the form of mutual adjustment of interests is more prominent. Similarly business influence, the policies of particular states, the influence of scientific opinion, or public pressure from below vary in their significance, with the environment being an example of greater pressure from below, together with scientific input and selective state support from Europe, whereas business and states, notably the USA, have taken a more dominant role in trade regulation.

Regulation through these complex processes can amount to a race to the bottom, as is evident in the search in many unskilled labour markets for lowest-cost locations. However, it may equally involve ratcheting-up of standards, as in nuclear and drugs regulation as well as in some environmental areas (ibid.: 518–23). Here norms such as continuous improvement or best available technology have made an impact on practice. Yet the global stalemate at the time of writing over climate change regulation indicates that the momentum behind the ratcheting up of limits to greenhouse gas emissions may well have faltered. Similarly, Braithwaite and Drahos' identification of financial regulation as an arena of higher regulatory standards looks problematic in the light of the global financial crisis, exacerbated by the lack of regulation of newer global financial instruments.

Conclusion

In this chapter, the main contours of globalization have been outlined, looking both at economic processes and organizational forms. As compared with the situation in the late 1990s, reviewed in the first edition of this book, some continuities are evident, but some newer trends are also apparent. Capital mobility, foreign trade and cross-border migration remain central to the dynamics of the global economy. So too does technological change and organizational innovation. The spatial importance of global cities is also striking. Meanwhile, global inequalities remain very significant, though these are being transformed by the changing spatial distribution of global economic development.

Major changes in the last 10–12 years include the spatial extension of global economic development of the BRIC economies, together with associated regions such as South East Asia. These affect patterns of inequality between developing countries, which are not solely influenced by the power of Western economic interests. In all of this, a sense of global shift is replacing global reach and, with it, a greater shift to a global as distinct from international economy.

The other major change of recent years is in the continuing extension of global regulation beyond the confines of the deregulatory Washington consensus. This is partly a response to failures in purely market-based nostrums for successful development, and partly a reflection of the growth of economic power outside Europe, North America and Japan. This shift has been further dramatized by the global financial crisis, which revealed additional flaws in processes of unregulated financial transactions, required market reliance on public finance against the central tenets of *laissez-faire* and the relative robustness of China and India compared with many Western economies.

The nation state, especially those that have power and resources, has been a major player in the recent intensification of economic globalization. This is seen both in the richer Western economies and in the very recent rise of China and the BRIC economies. Nation states have generally supported their large corporations in their global ambitions in a period characterized by deregulation of global trade and investment. They have also participated in global regulatory arrangements to try to achieve a more friendly global business environment that does not penalize the particular business interests of their own nations. Yet, for all this, many see the sovereignty of nation states being undermined as economic transactions that move across borders intensify. So is the nation state finished? A more detailed study of such questions will now be provided in Chapter 4.

4

Is the Nation State Finished?

It is sometimes said that the nation state is fast becoming outmoded by economic globalization. Integrated global finance markets shift billions of dollars around the world daily in a manner that influences national economies through its impact on foreign exchanges, interest rates, the stock market, employment levels and government tax revenues. Meanwhile, powerful multinational enterprises are able to transfer investment across political boundaries, control the terms of technology transfer, and negotiate favourable tax and subsidy deals with governments. Global business strategies are themselves enhanced by radical changes in information technology and telecommunications. These flows of investment, technology, communications and profit across national boundaries are often seen as the most striking symptom of global challenge to the nation state.

The challenge of globalization to the nation state is not, however, simply a matter of economic processes that cross borders with powerful effects on social development and human welfare. As we have seen in the previous chapter, economic globalization involves not only flows of finance, capital investment, technology and labour, but also an expanding web of trans-national regulatory institutions. Many of these may have started out as inter-governmental bodies or bodies sanctioned by national governments, but, over time, their autonomy from national governmental control has increased even though an elite of nation states remain powerful regulatory players (Braithwaite and Drahos, 2000). It is possible, therefore, to speak both of 'regulatory globalization' (ibid.: 571–8), and 'regulatory capitalism' (Levi-Faur, 2005; Braithwaite, 2008) as core elements within the global order.

Much of this is centred on the growth in the regulatory capacity of bodies such as the IMF, World Bank, WTO and OECD, and, on a regional scale, the EU, as well as nation states, staffed by 'regulocrats'. These institutions instigate or guide an expanding set of declarations, conventions and international legal instruments to which governments have become signatories, in the economic sphere and many other areas of public policy and law.

This chapter links together the contours of economic globalization and global regulation, with the wider fate of the nation state in an epoch of globalization. Is it finished as an institution, as many first-wave theorists of globalization presumed (see Holton, 2005, for a more extended review of the various waves of globalization theory). And if so, is the world becoming deterritorialized? Or is the nation state evolving as Michael Mann has argued (1993, 1997), losing some functions but gaining others? And is this perhaps reflected in active state support for global competitive advantage in many nations? Is there a large degree of compatibility between global markets and states, rather than a necessary and radical incompatibility (Weiss, 1998; Held and McGrew, 2002)? And do neo-liberal global restructuring processes require states, rather than finding them redundant?

Defining the Nation State

In pursuing these questions, some initial attention should be given to what is involved in the concept of the nation state. This is obviously a hybrid word, linking the idea of 'nation' with the idea of 'state'. While the former refers to what might loosely be termed a 'people' – that is, to a cultural entity often defined in terms of ethnicity – the latter refers to a set of institutions through which public authority is exercised within a particular bounded territory.

Although the connection between the two is conventionally regarded as a necessary one, this is largely a reflection of the formative experience of European nation state building, founded on the normative concept of rights to national self-determination. This has helped, first in Europe and later in the colonial world, to legitimate the idea of 'one people – one state'. This normative principle is not, however, reflected in the basis of many existing nation states, which, for one reason or another, contain a mixture of peoples or ethnicities. (For further elaboration, see Chapter 6.) In such cases, the identity of the nation has often become a matter for dispute and, sometimes, national fragmentation. Even in such instances, however, the nation state is more than a state apparatus, requiring that attention be given to the intersection of politics, culture and economic change.

If the nation state is thought of in this dual or hybrid sense, then the question of the relationship between nation states and globalization becomes larger and more complex. Two large issues stand out. The first is the challenge of maintaining state sovereignty in relation to the cross-border character of the global economy and global regulatory processes. The second problem, that of the national integrity of a people, brings into focus questions of political and cultural identity. These are influenced not only by the internal cultural composition of the nation and the strength of nationalism in various forms, but also by global trends such as culturally diverse labour migration, the globalization of culture industries such as music and film, and the cultural impact of trans-national regulatory bodies in areas such as human rights and citizenship. An underlying question here is how far the nation state remains anchored in national identity, or whether nations, as culturally distinct entities, will be eroded by cultural and political as much as economic processes.

The focus here is solely on the first of these two questions, leaving questions to do with political identity, nationalism and global cultural changes to subsequent chapters.

Variations and Commonalities Among Nation States in Relation to Global Challenges

Some initial caution is required in dealing with any general proposition about the nation state that is taken to hold for all of the nearly 200 states that currently exist. Clearly nation states vary in size, wealth, natural resource endowment and power. To speak of the impact of globalization upon the nation state, as if this were a unitary process that took the same form for every nation state, large and small, rich and poor, is therefore highly misleading. Variations in the capacity of nation states to respond to global challenges depend both on accumulated wealth, existing business networks and connections, available institutional and technological resources, fiscal strength, political stability and, in some cases, military power.

Such characteristics are unequally distributed across the world's states. Thus the USA, which has positive resources and assets on all of these criteria is not a nation state of the same order as countries like East Timor or Mozambique, which are far smaller, poorer states with very restricted assets, and largely negative historical experiences arising from colonization and occupation. This does not render all small or poor states, and social actors within them, passive victims. A telling counter-example is the banking innovations in Bangladesh, associated with the foundation of the Grameen Bank to supply micro-credit to the poorest members of the population in support of local development (Hossain, 1988; Schreiner, 2003). But it does make it much harder to develop and negotiate an effective place for poorer countries within the global order, especially in settings where large sections of the population are starving, lack access to electricity and lack literacy.

Such variations make a general theory of the relationship between globalization and the nation state very difficult. There are nonetheless some common features which nation states share to do with difficulties in regulating cross-border mobility. Physical movements of goods or peoples have generally proved less difficult for individual nations to regulate, monitor and tax than has the electronic transfer of funds or information. All states, however, face common challenges from the illegal importation of drugs, illegal immigration and tax evasion, which are all features of global society. Every state, however powerful, also has to come to terms with external global processes that make capital, technology and educated professional labour highly mobile and refractory to the interests and demands of any particular nation.

As a very general proposition it may be said that most nation states favour some kind of positive linkage with the global economy for the potential benefits that are likely to ensue. Economic self-reliance or autarky, as practised in post-war Albania, is no longer an option. Such benefits are felt to involve a higher level of growth in output, investment, employment and income than would otherwise be possible. There are, however, significant differences between states both in terms of the limits they would wish to set to market processes, and in terms of the capacity to negotiate effectively either with multinational enterprises (MNEs) or global regulatory bodies like the IMF. The main analytical question here, as we saw in Chapter 3, is how far poorer countries really benefit from neo-liberal deregulation, given lack of bargaining power. This question will be further explored in the second part of this chapter.

Problems in regulating global processes from any particular national standpoint also arise as a result of variations in regulatory standards, and the uneven and often ineffective policing of activity that crosses several jurisdictions with different regulatory standards. This lends itself to global evasion of controls, through devices such as tax havens and the construction of corporate structures that are impenetrable to national scrutiny. In some cases too it is expedient for some government agencies and powerful political figures to tolerate uneven regulatory arrangements, so as to have access to clandestine channels of activity, operating outside conventional regulatory processes that are within the view of public scrutiny. The case of the Bank of Commerce and Credit International (BCCI) is particularly instructive in this respect.

BCCI, founded in 1972, had grown over the subsequent two decades into an entity with $20 billion in assets and branches in 70 countries. Created by a Pakistani banker, its corporate structure involved a Luxemburg-based holding company with two main subsidiaries, one in the Cayman Islands, the other in Luxembourg (Kapstein, 1994). Designed to evade scrutiny, these two jurisdictions offered banking secrecy and virtually non-existent regulation. No consolidated accounts of the holding company were ever prepared, and Luxemburg authorities found it impossible to exercise any control over a body 98 per cent of whose operations were in other jurisdictions. It has been said that BCCI was constituted to be effectively 'offshore' in every jurisdiction in which it operated. It was on this basis that the bank provided a lucrative basis for deposits of both Western capital and Middle Eastern petro-dollars as well as an even more lucrative money-laundering operation for international drugs and arms dealers. Clients included General Noriega of Panama. Expansion into the financial centres of London, Hong Kong and New York, despite the concern of regulatory authorities, was facilitated by lawyers and lobbyists, including Bert Lance, briefly director of the Office of Management and Budget in the Jimmy Carter administration. Although finally closed by the combined efforts of regulators in 1991, BCCI had for 20 years capitalized on both the inability of nationally based regulators to cooperate effectively and the existence of lax regulatory standards in a number of jurisdictions.

Yet the BCCI case is by no means typical of the relations between nations and trans-national economic actors. One reason for this is that the global economy is a good deal less anarchic than this case study implies. This reflects the value of order and coherence in economic transactions for most parties. Trust matters where parties wish to create business relationships that endure across time. Most global markets exhibit forms of self-regulation through a variety of means. These range from networks of trust and information flow among participants, through quasi-legal processes such as *lex mercatoria*, a system of trade dispute resolution (Appelbaum *et al.*, 2004), to the formal processes of credit-rating whereby private bodies like Moody's & Standard and Poor's decide on the credit worthiness of both corporations and sovereign governments (Sassen, 1996). Such mechanisms exist in addition to the regulatory institutions of nation states, regional bodies like the EU and the global bodies discussed above.

Variations in the capacities of nation states to regulate cross-border transactions are an important element when we come to consider contrasts in the impact of globalization on individual nations. As already indicated, the position of powerful players such as the USA, and other G8 nations such as Japan or Germany, together with the recent BRIC nation states like China, contrasts markedly with the poorest nations of Africa and Asia. Effective regulation requires strong legal and fiscal systems, administrative experience and knowledge base to design and implement controls over cross-border processes. In addition, the larger, wealthier and more powerful nation states exert considerable influence within trans-national regulatory organizations such as the World Bank or WTO, of which China recently became a member. Meanwhile, within the EU, an ever-larger group of diverse nation states are able to draw upon regional resources and regulatory institutions to respond to cross-border challenges. Compared with all of this, poorer nations often lack a secure legal system, an effective tax base and administrative systems and hence possess very little bargaining strength or regulatory capacity beyond their formal juridical independence as nations.

Another factor influencing divergent national relationships with globalization is that while some nations are the home base of MNEs, most are not. Those that are differ from all other nations, in that much of the profit made elsewhere may be expected to be repatriated to the country of corporate origin. The link between most multinationals and a particular national jurisdiction is often obscured by talk of cross-border transactions and the mobility of capital (Hirst and Thompson, 1996). Although shareholdings in many MNEs have become trans-national, most MNEs have headquarters within a single nation, hold annual shareholders' meetings within that nation and cultivate close relations with the government of the country in which they are domiciled. In sectors such as banking, telecommunications and the media, they are often also subject to national controls limiting foreign ownership. Balancing such restrictions are the power and influence exerted by MNEs within the nation of domicile. The strategy of most MNEs on most issues is to utilize this power and influence to obtain a favourable regulatory environment and the support of governments for their global activities rather than to evade regulation in a footloose manner. Governments, meanwhile, welcome the investment, financial returns and international prestige that such relationships bring.

These preliminary observations pose some awkward questions for those who predict the demise of the nation state under the impact of globalization. MNEs do not typically operate outside the jurisdictions of nations. Rather, they depend on state structures to guarantee stable property rights or at least predictability in determining many of the rules of the game under which they operate (Krasner, 1985). In addition, states may also provide infrastructural support and favourable fiscal treatment. Given that MNEs depend or rely on nation states in this manner, it might well be supposed that the nation state is alive and well rather than in decline. Theorists of the robustness of the nation state point to its continuing role in many aspects of economic and social regulation and its involvement in the revival of nationalism, evident in many parts of the globe. This alternative view, as we shall see, has much to be said for it. Yet the destabilizing impact of globalization is not so easily dismissed. This applies particularly as it concerns conventional ideas and practices of national sovereignty.

Globalization and the Sovereignty of the State

The question of sovereignty is a controversial issue within political science and the study of international relations (for a useful review of the issues, see Thomson, 1995). One of the major difficulties with the argument that national sovereignty is under attack from globalization is the presumption that there was once a golden age when states possessed some kind of absolute control over their territory and the movement of resources, people and cultural influences across their borders. This presumption is very much a myth. National sovereignty, as it has evolved over the past 300 years or so, has always been more conditional than the myth implies. This is partly because the sovereignty of any one nation has usually depended on recognition by other nations within the interstate system, and partly because states have never been able, even if they wanted to, to achieve absolute control of transnational movements of people and resources across borders. The very obvious presence of borders and sometimes walls or fences around territories, is not in and of itself evidence of their solidity and lack of permeability.

If national sovereignty has never been absolute and unconditional, some care is needed in assessing the argument that contemporary processes of globalization undermine national sovereignty. If absolute sovereignty never existed, what exactly about sovereignty is being undermined? This difficulty does not, however, dispose of the argument that globalization challenges national sovereignty. Two points may be made in reply.

The first is that limits to national sovereignty on the part of transnational processes and actors are certainly not restricted to the contemporary post-1945 world. In addition to limits set by the interstate system, it is important to note that economically derived restrictions on sovereignty also pre-date the post-war period. Globalization has been built up over hundreds of years, through the development of world markets and an international division of labour. MNEs have been around for 100 years, while banking and trade have exhibited a trans-national character over millennia. In the past two centuries, private international bankers, for example, have periodically influenced the terms upon which nations responded to fiscal or military crisis by conditions placed on credit, whether in France in 1870–1 or Britain in 1931.

Recognition of these historical parallels with the present is perfectly compatible with arguments about continuing contemporary global challenges to national sovereignty. Such present-day arguments need not necessarily depend for their cogency on dubious assumptions about a golden age of sovereignty in the past. On the contrary, it is possible to speak of significant continuities over time in attempts by nations to regulate and control the mobile flow of economic resources across political boundaries, and in bargaining or conflict between nations and the more powerful economic actors over the regulation of this kind of activity.

This emphasis on continuity in the conditional nature of sovereignty should not, however, obscure the rapid intensification of cross-border transactions in the latter part of the twentieth century. This process has impacted not only upon the pre-existing, mostly Western, nations of the pre-1939 world, but also on the vastly expanded number of newly independent post-colonial states established between 1945 and 1980. The global interdependence of national economies, polities and cultures is not by any means a product of the post-1945 world (Thomson and Krasner, 1989). Yet the process of interdependence has undoubtedly accelerated in the past 50 years (Keohane, 1995). This has impacted on the sovereignty of both historically well-established and more newly established states in the developing world.

It is in this historically qualified sense, to be more fully developed in this chapter, that contemporary globalization may be said to pose intensified challenges to the conditional forms of national sovereignty that nations, both old and new, have inherited from the past. In this chapter, we shall pursue the impact of globalization on national sovereignty, identifying both the reasons for the robustness of the nation state within the global economy and the changing and more conditional nature of national sovereignty.

Absolute sovereignty may well be a historical myth, but it is still popularly said that the sovereignty of the nation state is being undermined by globalization. This applies whether the threat is perceived to come from multinational enterprises or trans-national regulatory bodies. Protests against the interference by outside groups in domestic affairs are widespread. Nonetheless, protest is rarely against outside interference in principle. Rather, different kinds of interest group are likely to protest against different aspects of global 'interference' while welcoming others. As Alston (1995: 7) points out in an analysis of Australian responses to globalization, business groups have supported the GATT/WTO type of global trading rules in support of free trade while often opposing global environmental treaties. Similarly, opponents of the penetration of MNEs into national affairs often welcome international human rights treaties and conventions. This suggests that widespread rhetoric about the negative consequences of globalization is often combined with a less obvious but equally significant acceptance of some global trends as helpful to the realization of nationally based socio-economic objectives. But where does all this leave the question of sovereignty?

Contemporary ideals of national sovereignty have a complex and gradual history drawing on ideas and institutions that developed between the sixteenth and nineteenth centuries (Osiander, 2001). Seventeenth-century European discussions of political theory and international law are one important moment in this evolution. Writers such as Bodin and Hobbes developed theories of sovereignty that focused on the necessity of vesting power in a single centralized unified entity, generally a monarchy. In a very familiar argument, Hobbes saw this as necessary to constrain the war of self-interest between individuals. Without sovereign power, life would, in Hobbes' much-cited phrase, be 'solitary, poor, nasty, brutish and short'. Equally, however, the prospect of a unitary Leviathan state raised the spectre of despotism; that is, the creation of a predatory oppressive regime, unchecked by institutional regulation. This creates what Martin Wight (1992: 35) calls the Hobbesian paradox; that is, the need for sovereign power to check anarchy but the equal need to protect society from autocratic or despotic forms of power exercised by sovereign states.

Seventeenth-century discussions of sovereignty raise a further issue, namely the distinction between internal sovereignty within a given territory and external sovereignty evident in relations between states. While Hobbes was aware of both dimensions, he tended to concentrate on the former. This created a situation whereby national sovereign power might resolve internal war, only for war to break out in the international arena. Hobbes' main contribution here was to assume that national sovereigns would be able to protect their subjects. In one sense, international warfare, from the European Thirty Years War of 1618–48 to the present day, suggests a major flaw in this argument. The national populations of even the strongest states have not proved immune from the anarchy of interstate warfare. Hence, while many later International Relations theorists presumed sovereignty was grounded primarily in military power, it is more plausible to regard it as the product of mutual empowerment by states of each other (Osiander, 2001: 280).

Clearly, the external aspects of national sovereignty, as they have developed in the interstate system since the seventeenth century, depend on some sense of commonly agreed rules governing political reciprocity between sovereign states. Contrary to its much-vaunted reputation as the source of the modern system of sovereign states, the Peace of Westphalia of 1648, as Osiander (2001: *passim*) shows, said very little about sovereignty. It was far more concerned with stabilizing relations between the politically autonomous entities within the Holy Roman Empire. This has been obscured by the triumphalist retrospective accounts of nineteenth-century nationalist writers, seeking to find origins for the ideas of sovereignty that had come to the fore in their own times. These depended far more on the successful industrial and technological changes of the Industrial Revolution, together with the French revolution and the idea of national citizenship (Gellner, 1983). These gave national sovereignty its modern form, linked with both enhanced capacities to administer territories, while connecting sovereignty with notions of democratic self-determination. It is this conception of sovereignty which globalization is taken to challenge, rather than any legalistic outcome of the Peace of Westphalia.

The evolution of international law is, nonetheless, connected with this wider context. From the seventeenth century onwards a sense of the legal immunity of states from prosecution in the courts of another state for actions performed in pursuance of national policy becomes manifest. States, meanwhile, came conventionally to be seen as the appropriate parties to international law, before which they have juridical equality. In Oppenheim's (1905) formulation, international law is and should remain 'law between states only and exclusively'.

While such principles are reaffirmed in the UN Charter (Art. 2(1)), they have not gone unchallenged. Held (1991, 1995) has argued that there has occurred a shift away from exclusive emphasis on the claims of states, with the emergence of claims in the name of humanity and the world order pursued, in large measure, through the judicial processes of the International or European Courts of Justice and the European Court of Human Rights. Here, both states and individuals may and do take action against states in the name of broader transnational principles.

The earlier work of the League of Nations in relation to treaties with national minorities went some way towards challenging the exclusive monopoly of states within international law. However, the major watershed in undermining the exclusive juridical rights of nations to pursue their sovereign interests in foreign policy were the Nuremberg war trials after the Second World War. The judgement of the International Tribunal was that where state laws, such as those underlying the German holocaust, were in conflict with international humanitarian rules, state laws should be disobeyed wherever scope existed for the exercise of moral choice (Cassese, 1988). By affirming circumstances in which the rights and obligations of individuals take precedence over those of the nation states of which they are members, the Tribunal took a step of major historical significance in the creation of a trans-national legal and political system where nation states no longer have an exclusive monopoly of sovereignty within international law.

Yet there remain significant limits in the extent to which international law, or the regional law of the EU, has proved able to constrain the actions or usurp the ultimate autonomy of nation states. Trans-national legal bodies generally lack the ultimate capacity –military or otherwise – to force recalcitrant nations to participate in or accept the outcome of judicial process.

In the case of the UN, for example, as Held (1995) points out, members are automatically parties to the Statutes of the International Court of Justice (ICJ) but need not accept the Court's jurisdiction (ibid.: 96). Suter (1996) calculates that only around a third of UN members accept its jurisdiction (247). Many authorities cite as a prominent example of non-recognition the case brought by the Nicaraguan Sandanista government against the USA in 1984 for the mining of its harbours and the support given to insurgents. The US response was first to challenge the ICJ's competence in the matter and, when this failed, to refuse to accept the Court's ruling. In an earlier case in 1973, New Zealand and Australia took France to the Court over atmospheric nuclear testing in the Pacific (Templeton, 1996: 52). While France refused to accept the Court's jurisdiction, it did thereafter cease atmospheric in favour of underground testing. This may reflect the greater importance of international public opinion over legal enforcement, whereby nations choose to regulate themselves rather than being coerced to change direction.

It is arguable that European attempts to establish systems of trans-national law have proved more effective. One such attempt in the human rights area stems from the European Convention for the Protection of Human Rights and Fundamental Freedoms, ratified in 1950 to come into force in 1953 (Weissbrodt, 1988: 14). Under the convention, individuals as well as states may petition the European Commission of Human Rights. If the Commission believes that the Convention has been breached, cases may be referred to the European Court of Human Rights. States and individuals involved may also take cases to the

Court. By 1986, all 20 members of the then Council of Europe recognized the court's jurisdiction, and over 100 cases had been dealt with. These challenged states over matters recognized in the Convention, such as guarantees of a fair public trial, or freedom from torture or degrading treatment.

The European Court of Justice developed a wider remit. It is concerned in large measure with determination of the legality of the powers claimed and exercised by the central EU institutions, notably the Council of Ministers. Unlike most of the trans-national political institutions centred on the UN, the EU has the right to make laws in certain areas, such as trade, which it may impose, if necessary, on members through regulations and directives. The Court also takes appeals on the legality of individual member governments' actions towards its citizens in relation to foundation treaties of the EU, formerly the EEC and EC. Member states must comply with the Court's rulings on these matters. This has led, for example, to changes in British law regarding sexual discrimination and equal pay (Held, 1991: 220).

Beck and Grande (2007: 42–6) argue that the European Court of Justice has extended notions of European sovereignty in a quasi-entrepreneurial manner. While the Court's original status as a body to administer justice depended on European treaties signed by national governments, it was the Court that elevated those treaties to the status of constitutional law. This created a further momentum in developing the treaties' cosmopolitan potential, whereby European law can trump national law, because it is recognized as having a higher authority. Although uncertainties over the future direction of trans-national European institutions abound, it appears that recent shifts in regional European law have made greater inroads into national sovereignty than is evident in international law, enforced through the UN system.

It is nonetheless arguable that such shifts as have occurred in international law have not entirely undermined the interstate system of national sovereignty. New norms of international law, such as human rights, are at best emergent and at worst still very much visions of a possible future, yet (if ever) to be implemented. While the formal juridical challenge of international law to national sovereignty has mostly been held at bay, what usually counts for more is the extent of practical sovereignty that states can exercise over a range of economic, social and political matters in relation to powerful global economic as well as political forces. This question of what might be termed the 'conditionality of sovereignty' is, however, hard to pursue, while issues of sovereignty continue to be enveloped in the myth that national sovereignty is, and has always been, absolute.

It has been argued that nostalgic conceptions of absolute sovereignty are especially inappropriate in an epoch of intensifying globalization. As Keohane (1995) argues, the nature of national sovereignty in the seventeenth century developed under conditions of relatively low interdependency between nation states. These conditions no longer apply. The far higher levels of interdependency that apply in the late twentieth century, with large flows of capital, labour, technology and information across boundaries (Williams, 1993), have emerged within changing rules of sovereignty that are increasingly more conditional, negotiable and complex.

Sovereign statehood never existed in an absolute sense. Even so, it is an institution whose meaning and conditionality have continued to evolve and change, this having taken place unevenly in different regions of the world. What characterizes the late twentieth century is, according to Keohane, not a shift to idealistic institutionalism in global politics, along the lines of the failed inter-war League of Nations, but rather the development of a mixed system of 'multilateral cooperation and tough inter-state bargaining' (Keohane, 1995: 176). This reflects the simultaneous expansion of global regulatory organizations and national assertiveness in the pursuit of interests. Within this framework, 'Sovereignty is less a territorially defined barrier than a bargaining resource for a politics characterized by complex transnational networks' (ibid.: 177).

For sovereignty to survive in any form, it is necessary for states to remain institutions with capacities to act that are of potential benefit to particular sets of interests. These capacities may involve a range of areas ranging from economic rule-setting, industrial relations regulations and fiscal policy, to capacities that involve effective taxation systems and infrastructural policy. There are, finally, functions that involve the legitimization of particular institutional arrangements. An example of this function is where states possess the capacity to speak for the national interest involving matters of national identity and the cultural integrity of the nation. These may be deployed to mediate controversial issues such as foreign takeovers of major companies or increases in culturally diverse immigration levels.

The types of interest involved may include domestic organizations such as businesses, labour organizations, consumers and those with interests in the cultural integrity of the nation. Such groups may, singly or in alliances, pressure the state to secure freer or more protected trade, to ratify or reject international treaties and conventions, and to expand or contract flows of immigrants. Simultaneously, external interests such as MNEs, international regulatory bodies such as the IMF and the WTO and international non-governmental bodies such as Amnesty

International or Greenpeace International may press for various changes to national policy-making, affecting issues such as controls over foreign investment, fiscal policy, or human rights practices.

How these pressures work out, and how consistent they are with conventional notions of democracy, is a complex matter. As Held (1991: 201) points out, most conceptions of liberal democracy have generally assumed state sovereignty 'subject only to compromises it must make and limits imposed upon it by actors, agencies, and forces operating within its territorial boundaries'. This assumption is, rendered highly problematic by globalization, inasmuch as trans-national regulatory bodies are not governed by the majoritarian procedures of liberal democracy.

Relations between national and trans-national interests may involve negotiation and the search for common or complementary interests. However, they may equally mean conflict and sometimes coercion where interests differ (Martell, 2010). A major factor here is the under-lying structure of interdependency, whereby the various external interests are dependent on elements of state support, while state insti-tutions are dependent on various resources from without. The limits to models based on bargaining are twofold. First, there is the limit set by irreconcilable conflicts of interest. Second, there are limits set when asymmetries of power between particular external interests and the state are so great that domination replaces bargaining. While the fundamental 'asymmetries of power' model is widely canvassed in world-system theory, there is considerable evidence in favour of the alternative approach suggested here. This draws on Keohane's analysis of bargaining and on notions of the possibility of complementarity of interests between MNEs and nation states.

Global Capitalism, MNEs and the Nation State

Notions of bargaining and the development of common interests between MNEs and the nation state conflict with widely held beliefs that global capitalism is not merely corrosive of the nation state, but also obstructive of national political autonomy over economic and social policy. This in turn has implications for national sovereignty. Whereas analysts such as Beck (2003: 54) see a deterritorialization of governance, as a result of the 'global power of meta-business', an alternative argument sees national territories and polities as having a continuing significance. The contours of business–state relations therefore demand more subtle analysis.

An important version of the deterritorialization claim is that economic globalization undermines the capacity of nations to pursue or maintain welfare states, based on the redistribution of resources to those unable to secure a decent life from market transactions. Instead, what is seen is downward pressure on wages and the dismantling of social supports for the poor, together with the privatization of social services, like health and education (Babb, 2005: 205–8). The argument here depends not only on the actions taken by MNEs, but also, in a broader sense, on what is seen as the underlying logic of capital accumulation operating through markets and the global governance of the IMF and World Bank.

Under these conditions, it is claimed that national forms of redistributive politics according to social need are undermined by market-driven capital accumulation imperatives. Welfare states and socialist polities tend to limit the power of capital and reduce profit. This supposedly renders them either liable to erosion through a revived politics of economic rationalism or to neglect through the flight of capital elsewhere. In both cases, investment and employment levels would suffer and increases in social dislocation and uncertainty would ensue. These kinds of spectres, it is said, create great pressure on politicians acting in the present to limit welfare and other kinds of redistributive spending. The assumption is that increased globalization means increased competition, and increased competition requires cuts in welfare spending (Flora, 1987; Pierson, 1991; Scharpf, 2000). This entire scenario may be regarded as a worst-case reading of the impact of economic globalization on the nation state.

This argument certainly has some credibility. Economic globalization within an increasingly interdependent world undoubtedly rules out economic autarky, while the mobility of finance and capital, under largely flexible exchange rates, exert limits on national decision-making (even for the most powerful nations) over matters such as interest rates and levels of taxation. It is also the case that recent decades have seen the collapse of the 'most historically important counter-multinational alternative-international state socialism' (Carnoy, 1993: 47). Whether this leaves nation states with little alternative but to 'fall deeper into the waiting arms of technology-bearing, capital-laden multinational firms' (ibid.: 48) is, however, more debatable.

In the first place, it is by no means clear that economic globalization does require the end of the welfare state, redistributive reform and active state industry and infrastructure policies to be replaced by convergence around a market-orientated national politics, regulated in a manner that suits only MNEs. One of the major arguments against the 'end of the welfare state' view is the lack of policy regime convergence. Clear variations may be found in forms of national state strategy and policy. While the USA has remained steadfastly hostile to social democratic welfare policies, many European countries such as Scandinavia and post-Thatcherite Britain have not (Held and McGrew, 2002: 47). This lack of convergence suggests there is no singular 'logic of capital' process that requires a diminution in social expenditure to allow increased economic openness to world markets. While the neo-liberal tenets of the Washington consensus did very often demand social and economic deregulation for developing countries, even here there is no clear convergence around economic liberalism alone, as the counter-case of China demonstrates.

There is a significant evidence base to support those sceptical of the end of the welfare state thesis. Cameron (1978), for example, found that exposure to foreign trade did not create negative effects on welfare state spending. In more extensive recent research on 14 industrial countries between 1966 and 1990, Garrett and Mitchell (1996) report that, for this group of nations at least, greater exposure to international trade and foreign capital penetration exerted no downward pressure on welfare state expenditure. The emphasis here on measuring income transfers, such as pensions, rather than education or health spending was designed to focus on those forms of spending seen as less directly relevant to meeting the challenges of economic competitiveness.

Garrett and Mitchell explain their findings in two ways. First, globalization increases levels of insecurity for large sections of the population, heightening political expectations of redistributive social support. Second, welfare spending does not necessarily lead to capital flight because countries with greater social stability offer a better environment for investors than more unstable milieux. In addition, the connection between globalization and welfare spending is greater in countries with strong labour movements and weaker right-wing parties. Political differences between nations matter. All this does not mean that the welfare states or industry policies remain unchanged in an epoch of globalization, nor that periodic crises beset particular welfare regimes. Rather what it indicates is that there is no necessary connection between globalization and crises in the autonomy of nation states.

This argument is magnified in significance by the resort back to state support by many global capitalist institutions during the recent global financial crisis. This was also accompanied in many countries by stimulus packages which increased social expenditure supports. Deregulation was abandoned for reregulation. While this might turn out to be short-lived, the crisis certainly undermined much of the political legitimacy of unregulated markets.

A second area of debate relevant to the relationship between economic globalization and nation states, involved the large global corporations. Here it is not clear that critics are correct in saying that nations in general lack bargaining power in dealings with MNEs and trans-national global agencies. To say that nation states cannot ignore multinational enterprise is not to say that MNEs are typically beyond the scope of nationally based negotiations concerning the terms of their operations or beyond any kind of national regulatory control or influence.

MNEs certainly make decisions on the basis of optimizing the private profitability of the corporation rather the economic health of particular nations. Such decisions include whether and where to locate investment, how to articulate flows of resources and semi-finished products within the global operations of the corporation, what intra-firm prices to charge and where to generate profit within the organization. Such decisions apply especially to MNEs with multiple investments in different countries linked together in a global production strategy that sources components from locations different from those where, for example, car bodies are manufactured and/or where car assembly is completed.

The decisions made in such circumstances affect individual nations in multiple, intersecting ways. Agreements made by states to support inflows of private capital affect national growth rates, employment levels and government taxation receipts. Effects that have been observed include a reduction on limits to capital flows and a lowering of taxation on capital (Held and McGrew, 2002: 55). Once deals are done, moreover, private corporate decisions about intra-firm flows of resources and profits affect a nation's balance of payments and levels of national income. The optimization of corporate interests within such a system may well take precedence over harmonization with national interests.

Another set of disadvantages may occur where MNEs are unwilling to share firm-specific intellectual property and technological and managerial skills with national competitors (Carnoy, 1993: 62). The more fundamental types of research and development are generally not located outside the home base, though this situation has begun to change. The policies of the MNEs' home-based governments, especially the USA, often serve to compound this situation in areas such as intellectual property rights and controls of certain types of sophisticated technology transfer (for example, in aerospace and weapons systems). All of this threatens to create a dualistic system in which information-rich corporations dominate nations who lack intellectual property advantages. Such nations are either shut out entirely or must pay high royalties to MNEs for access to selected areas of information technology.

Dilemmas Facing the Nation State

The dilemma for the nation is that economies may stagnate without MNE involvement, but the price for bringing them in may be too high in terms of loss of control over economic affairs or in relation to opposition from domestic economic and political interests. Economic globalization may thereby reduce the influence that governments can exercise over the economic activities of their citizens, while not in any way guaranteeing social consensus among citizens on the desirability of global penetration into domestic economic affairs. Nonetheless, not all nation states face this dilemma, especially the most powerful, which are home to MNEs and which use government policy to support their worldwide operations. The reconstruction of the post-war global capitalist economy, to take a leading example, depended very much on the military and political support of the USA as a superpower. Gilpin (1975: 41) has argued that multinationals prospered because they were 'dependent on the power of, and consistent with the political interests of, the United States'. This power was instrumental in the restabilization of Europe and Japan, which were to become major sites for the operation of American MNEs as well as home bases for expanding European and Japanese multinationals.

How far the scenario of eroded national autonomy in the face of economic globalization applies cannot be resolved in a general way that fits all cases. This is not simply because nation states differ in power, but also because there are gains as well as losses from economic globalization.

Nation states may draw additional resources from inward foreign investment, allowing the state to maintain and enhance rather than limit public policy development. This is well illustrated in the case of Ireland in the 20 years between the mid-1980s and the mid-2000s. Now regarded as one of the most economically globalized countries in the world (Lockwood and Redoano, 2005), Ireland's economic history as recently as the 1980s saw a profound crisis, manifested in increased unemployment and out-migration and severe fiscal pressure on public resources (Allen, 2000; Inglis, 2008). This led not to the imposition of neo-liberal deregulation by powerful interests alone, but to a social partnership of government, capital and labour. The strategy that ensued combined increased openness to further inward foreign direct investment with lower business taxes, with increased educational expenditure to generate a more skilled labour force, and new forms of collaborative national governance to underwrite social cohesion. Positively supported too by EU regional development support, such arrangements underlay a rapid expansion in economic growth after 1990, which lasted until the recent global financial crisis. Notwithstanding continuing problems, including significant social inequality and political corruption, and the impact of the global financial crisis, this case indicates how a small highly globalized national economy was not steam-rollered by global corporate interests that invested in the country. Even the dire fiscal crisis for Ireland in 2010–11 had domestic as much as global causes.

An underlying reason why MNEs do not necessarily undermine national sovereignty is that they are dependent on nation states for a range of supports (Martinelli, 1982). These include secure property rights, the quality of the public education system, management training, protection and the investment in infrastructural items such as transport systems and telecommunications. In addition, the long-run stability and legitimation of a market-based system as both efficient and somehow fair is also important. Carnoy (1993: 89) argues that national governments receive a pay-off from such public investments in that local productivity growth arising from inflows of global investment provides 'greater political space'. Increased fiscal returns provide a basis for increased public resources potentially available for other ends, if not wasted in corruption. The enhancement this autonomy gives states rests not only on pressure to solve problems left unresolved by the market, but also on the basis of domestic political opposition to MNEs. This may come from local producers or interest groups that feel threatened by their operations – for example, organized labour or environmentalist groups. As a result, a range of policies has emerged to limit MNE autonomy, including controls on inward investment, incentives to domestic industry and product standards for environmental protection.

In this argument, MNEs and the nation state need each other, and the relationship between the two allows for significant elements of bargaining between them. Such power as the nation state possesses in this kind of model derives from failures of the market to resolve issues such as economic stability and the legitimacy of a social order, based primarily on capitalist property rights. This approach is a useful one, but it fails to consider wider aspects of the modern nation state that are not explicable simply in terms of the vicissitudes of the market and the capitalist economy. In other words, states may exist for reasons other than the problems and conflicts generated by capitalism. Martinelli's argument is, in this sense, excessively functionalist in that it presumes that whatever the state does must in some sense be functional to problems of the global capitalist economy.

Are there State-Based Alternatives to Corporate Capitalism?

Further weaknesses in general theories of multinational dominance relate to assumption of some kind of coercive relationship between MNEs and national governments – whether that takes the form of direct pressure or a more indirect process to do with the 'logic of the situation'. By this is meant a sense that there is no alternative to agreeing to the terms that corporate interests and global institutions like the World Bank demand. Looking at this from the vantage point of a theory of pure coercion, the argument is that governments could act differently by organizing investment and economic planning on a national basis, but are constrained to do so by the power of multinationals backed up by the ideology of economic liberalism and free trade and, in cases such as Allende's Chile, by US-backed political destabilization.

In one sense, this argument about viable alternatives that have been closed off draws on an old socialist or communist dream of the possibility of operating planned command economies outside the global capitalist system. In the recent past, Fidel Castro's Cuba has been one of the few surviving governmental homes of this kind of thinking. Contemporary experience, on the contrary, is that *some kind of engagement* with the global capitalist economy and global markets is unavoidable. This is not just an unavoidable fate, but, in fact, a process that may bring benefits as well as disadvantages and a process that can be shaped, in a number of ways, by nation states.

There is another sense, then, in which there are alternative strategies facing national governments. These involve MNEs as major players, but not necessarily as unilaterally dominant players. This kind of national autonomy is clearest in the case of economically advanced nations. Bailey *et al.* (1994), in their review of relations between MNEs and governments, point to major limitations on inward foreign investment, most notably in post-war Japan. Despite a slow trend toward liberalization, the evidence is that Japan has only eased barriers against foreign multinationals when circumstances were deemed to be in Japanese interests. Liberalization remains controlled through a system of administrative guidance that itself reflects the key role of government policy in Japanese capitalist development.

More liberal approaches to inward foreign investment are evident in other places, especially in Britain and the USA. Elsewhere, especially in France, governments, while tending towards liberalization, have nonetheless intervened selectively to block both foreign takeovers of, and joint ventures with, French businesses (ibid.: 64–75). This in turn reflects widely articulated French concerns about problems such as the foreign ownership of key industrial sectors as well as perceived adverse effects on MNE penetration on employment and the economic vitality of regions. This argument about national variations is confirmed by Reich's (1989) study of contrasting national responses in Western Europe to the regulation of foreign investment in the automobile industry.

In all of this, the terms upon which MNEs operate are subject to negotiation and sometimes veto wherever governments have decided that the balance of costs might exceed that of benefits. It is nonetheless increasingly the case that governments regard national interests and those of most MNEs to be broadly complementary. This is scarcely consistent with a picture of unilateral domination, although this is not to say that undue MNE pressure is not sometimes put on politicians and other business leaders. Bribery is one way that this occurs; it has a continuing history in recent phases of globalization from the scandals of the Lockheed and ITT bribery cases in Japan in the 1970s (Martinelli, 1982: 92) to very recent cases of Daimler Motors, who admitted to bribery in 22 countries (BBC, 2010a), and Rio Tinto, the mining giant, in negotiations with Chinese steel makers (BBC, 2010b).

Multinationals and the Third World

An earlier generation of critics tended to emphasize the victim status of Third World economies and governments in relation to multinationals. For the poorer countries, it was argued that small sets of MNEs could dominate an entire nation, as in the case of fruit companies in Central America or copper mining firms in parts of Latin America. The more general argument proposed by Frobel *et al.* (1980) was that a New International Division of Labour (NIDL) had been created based upon the systematic exploitation of developing countries. This involved cheap labour, minimal skill transmission from MNEs to local workers and a lack of long-term commitment to sustained investment. Governments in this scenario exercised little bargaining power. Instead, their role was to maintain authoritarian labour market policies that suited the exploitative economic regime. The prospects for democracy were even worse, insofar as political elites and multinationals have a shared interest in political authoritarianism.

This victimology of Third World domination by Western MNEs, backed up by market-orientated regulatory institutions such as the IMF, has come under critical attack for a number of reasons. First, the success of a number of countries in East and South East Asia, and parts of Latin America, such as Brazil, in breaking out of dependency and asserting their autonomy has, as discussed earlier, undermined any notion of dependency as a permanent condition. China, India, Brazil, South Korea and Mexico now have MNEs of their own. This in turn challenges the very concept of the Third World as a homogeneous group of underdeveloped nations unable to exercise any kind of sovereignty. Second, and following on from this, comes evidence of the complex bilateral nature of the interaction between developing states and external trans-national actors such as MNEs. This bilateral complexity is currently manifest in the processes whereby iron ore prices are negotiated between China and MNEs such as BHP Billiton and Rio Tinto.

It has been pointed out that the principle of juridical sovereignty of states, inherited from the pre-1939 interstate system and reaffirmed in the Charter of the UN, means that all states have the capacity to regulate their domestic polity, to set rules and so forth. The decisive point here, however, is not so much the existence of formal rules about MNE activities that developing states may, from time to time, establish, as the effectiveness of such rules. Krasner (1985), for example, argues that the capacity of such states to bargain varies according to their size, relative military capacity and wealth, and the type of economic activity involved. For example, states with a significant home market, such as India, may bargain more effectively over the terms of MNE entry than those without.

Krasner also argues that states, even those in developing countries, may strike better deals with MNEs involved with raw material extraction than with those involved in manufacturing (ibid.: 183–5). Providing developing states are rich in marketable raw materials, they are in a stronger position to bargain about the terms under which these are extracted than about the terms under which manufacturing investment is brought in. This is because raw material-focused MNEs may have few alternative sources of supply and because, once established, it is hard for extraction-based MNEs to threaten to exit. Manufacturing-based MNEs looking at production sites may have a range of alternatives to choose from, while such operations are easier to exit from.

In addition, some aspects of technical expertise and market knowledge are easier to acquire (for example, in sectors such as mineral extraction) than in the high-technology aspects of manufacturing, where MNEs closely guard intellectual property rights. This is one reason why developing countries have done better in sectors such as oil production, where the developing countries of OPEC now play a major role, than in manufacturing. In 1970 MNEs owned 94 per cent of crude oil production; by 1980 this had fallen to less than 50 per cent. Whereas

MNEs in the 1940s and 1950s controlled Middle Eastern oil production through concessions imposed on weak states (for example, Standard Oil of California (now Chevron) and Texaco dominating Saudi Arabia, and BP dominating Iran), this concessionary regime has been replaced by the OPEC system, which represents a greater rather than lesser measure of sovereignty for those nation states who are members.

A somewhat different line of argument about Third World domination by MNEs is that a relatively small proportion of multinational investment has gone to developing countries, reflecting the fact that MNEs are not solely driven by a search for low-cost labour. This pattern may have been true of the last quarter of the twentieth century, although the 1980s and 1990s continue to see some countries and regions expand economically on the basis of low labour costs, such as the *maquiladora* industries in Northern Mexico or cheap labour production in the region around Bangkok, and in many other parts of South East Asia. Nonetheless, within the broader context of the information economy, there is declining scope for national competitive advantage based purely on low-wage factories producing for world markets. Massive inflows of investment have occurred between 1990 and 2010 in countries like China and India, involving both low-wage occupations and those using more skilled labour, as in the Indian IT sector.

The significance of this discussion for present purposes is not to attempt to resolve general questions about the economic impact of MNEs but rather to evaluate the extent and limits of autonomy that developing countries may possess in relation to MNEs. In the light of new evidence reviewed above, there has recently been a reappraisal of earlier arguments that nation states remain weak or powerless victims in the face of MNE dominance. In earlier work Castells (1993: 27–8) identified three strategies open to governments in an era of MNE penetration. These involve (a) traditional international trade in primary products within the existing division of labour dominated by advanced countries, (b) import-substitution industrialization, attempted in Latin America in the 1960s and 1970s and (c) the largely Asian export-orientated manufacturing strategies of the 1980s. The latter involved either manufacturing exports from domestic firms as in South Korea, Hong Kong and Taiwan, or exports from MNE operations outside the country of origin, as in Singapore and Malaysia. By the late 1990s, as we saw in Chapter 3, China had begun its own growth spurt under politically guided state initiatives through regulated markets, and other BRIC nations such as Brazil and India had done so as well through somewhat less regulated policies. From an early twenty-first-century perspective this strategy has proven more successful than the other two options, and has seen the beginnings of a new strategy (d) involving developing country MNEs operating beyond the home market. Such successes, notwithstanding periodic financial crises, indicate the possibility and viability of government autonomy in the setting of national goals and the implementation of national strategies among developing societies.

Whether in the advanced economic nations or in the developing world, the older model of MNE dominance over nations seems too simplistic. It may be conceded that governments have few alternatives but to deal with MNEs if they wish to optimize levels of economic growth, employment, and government revenue. Many of the terms of the bargain are, however, up for negotiation and governments hold some cards, especially if they can deliver high levels of political stability, as well as infrastructural and fiscal support. Even within the developing world, there are many settings in which the nation state is far from dead or powerless, especially where development alliances between government and local capital are possible.

The discussion of multinationals and the nation state was designed, in part, as a critique of views that announce the demise of the nation state under the impact of the global economy in general and of multinational business in particular. Certain aspects of national sovereignty, but not the institution of the nation state itself, have undoubtedly been eroded by economic globalization. The reasons for the resilience of the nation state may be partly a response to problems or inadequacies of the market as an all-encompassing social institution, inadequacies that may have grown in significance in the contemporary epoch of globalization. It is, however, useful to place this contemporary state of affairs into a wider analysis of the historical development of the nation state, conceived of as a multi-functional institution involved in military, political and social, as well as economic affairs.

The Historical Dynamic of the Nation State

Has the nation state become some kind of social constant over the period since the seventeenth century and the emergence of modern political institutions? The arguments in this chapter have been critical of the idea of absolute sovereignty and its supposed erosion by globalization. Yet one should not rule out the possibility that nation states, embedded within interstate systems of conditional sovereignty do display certain continuities in political autonomy right up to the present, through the most recent modern phases of globalization. What is unclear, nonetheless, is how far those continuities have extended to the functional areas in which states have become involved.

Michael Mann (1993) has pointed out that most of the key functions of the modern state developed subsequently to sovereign powers in foreign policy. Prior to the eighteenth century, in his view, states did comparatively little apart from conduct war and diplomacy, and administer overarching forms of internal repression. While this argument underestimates the political economic scope of seventeenth-century mercantilism, the thrust of Mann's general argument stands. In short, 'the sovereign nation state is very young' (1993: 116), most of its powers and capacities being forged and consolidated in the eighteenth and nineteenth centuries, as far as Western Europe is concerned. Meanwhile, the twentieth and early twenty-first centuries have seen what Roland Robertson refers to as the universalization of statehood as a political form, in the aftermath of the break-up of dynastic empires and successful revolts against colonialism.

In the European case, Mann points to the consolidation of the state's military powers in the eighteenth century. The state's role was expanded during the nineteenth and early twentieth centuries with the extension of citizenship rights and the provision of economic and social infrastructures for industrial society in areas such as communications and mass education. During the twentieth century further extensions of welfare state function have been combined with macro-economic planning activities. While neo-liberalism within Western nation states has significantly reversed some of the latter developments in the past two decades, state activity is still expanding in other areas, as in the social regulation of personal relations affecting men and women, children and abortion. Meanwhile, nationalist feeling, or at the least a strong identification with the national community, remains highly significant.

Mann's argument, then, is multidimensional, emphasizing a range of state functions, in contrast to one-dimensional emphases on the sovereign power of nations in relation to one another. His underlying point is that the modern state fuses a range of functions together within a 'single caging institution' (1993: 118) and that this institution is still in a sense maturing rather than being in the last gasp of senility and decrepitude. While certain state functions may grow or recede in importance, the institution itself is in healthy shape.

One further indicator of this is the general reluctance of states to submit conflicts with other states to the dispute resolution processes of trans-national authorities such as the UN (Held, 1991: 212–13). This reluctance derives from states' continuing assertion of the sovereign right to make war. This represents a further illustration of Mann's emphasis on the military powers and capacities of the nation state.

There are, however, two reservations to be made about this overall judgement on the continuing resilience of the nation state. The first concerns the question of regionalism. European regionalism and the EU, of which the vast majority of Western European nations are members, is indicative of new, although not historically unprecedented, developments that affect states within its territory. While member nations have voting and certain veto rights, the EU, as was argued earlier in this chapter, has developed significant areas of trans-national sovereignty of its own, in such matters as trade liberalization and product standardization, the single European market, requiring the free movement of goods, and persons across national boundaries, and monetary union. Consensus across such issues is by no means complete, reflecting continuing areas of national resistance (for example, by Britain on the issue of a European currency). A considerable degree of constraint on the sovereignty of member nations has nonetheless been obtained by consent. This indicates that the nation state, however mature, holds no monopoly over economic policy or legal functions.

Mann goes on to argue that, beyond these economic areas, the European nation states retain effective political sovereignty in most areas of social policy, public order, communications infrastructure and the regulation of personal life. This suggests to him that European regionalism has largely been constructed to promote the interests of European capitalism against the challenges of the USA and Japan, leaving the individual nation states with a broader range of functions that do not necessarily stem from problems arising from the operations of markets or global economic competition. It is arguable that the less highly developed regional trading blocs of NAFTA and APEC reflect the same kind of concern to promote regional economic interests rather than any more profound shift to trans-national political organization.

This economistic approach to European regionalism has merit, but it is equally arguable that the EU has moved some way beyond economic policy-making. This is reflected both in the human rights and regulation of personal life issues discussed by Weissbrodt (1988) and Held (1995), and also in the Social Chapter, concerned with social justice and welfare. Mann's defence of the resilience of the nation state is, at least in respect to Europe, somewhat exaggerated.

A second reservation about any theory of the robustness of the nation state concerns its applicability outside Europe. While the post-colonial world has seen a massive expansion of statehood outside Europe, this has not always proved institutionally stable. There are undoubtedly a number of examples of successful state formation, as in China and South East Asian countries such as Indonesia, Malaysia,

Singapore and Thailand. In such cases, success has been based on a mix of strong economic and cultural infrastructures in civil society, together with strong modernizing state institutions.

At the other end of the spectrum, however, there is evidence of post-colonial state collapse, as reflected in Rwanda and Somalia. Here, the Hobbesian problem of order has overwhelmed state structures with few infrastructural capacities, largely as a result of internal ethnic or communal divisions rather than global capitalism. Most other state structures rest somewhere in between these two types. Here, state elites typically struggle to construct the capacities to secure internal social order and economic development in the face of disputes with neighbouring states, as in the Iran–Iraq war, ethnic division, seen in central Asia and poverty, which is a highly generalized condition. At the same time, many also experience problems of excessive military expenditure and predatory authoritarianism, reflected in corruption and human rights abuses.

While multinationals and trans-national regulatory bodies may some-times collude in or compound certain of these problems, they are by no means the underlying source of such problems of ineffective state formation and a weakly constituted civil society. Such problems may rather be traced both to colonial and pre-colonial history, and to the rapid process of decolonization after the Second World War. Jackson (1990), in particular, argues that decolonization created what were, in many cases, essentially 'quasi-states'. These emerged in a radically altered post-war interstate system. In this, post-colonial statehood depended on the international recognition of juridical statehood alone, rather than on effective claims to exercise statehood on the basis of the capacity to exercise effective power. Whereas statehood in past history depended on interstate as well as intrastate power struggles, in which some actual or would-be states survived and others succumbed, for Jackson, the post-war epoch of egalitarian rights of national self-determination has created post-colonial states that 'are not allowed to disappear juridically … [and which] cannot be deprived of sovereignty as a result of war, conquest, partition or colonialism as frequently happened in the past' (ibid.: 23). The result has been the creation of weak states, recognized juridically and admitted to equal formal membership of the club of nations on the same basis as others, yet unable to exercise substantive sovereignty in the sense of taking full advantage of their formal sovereign independence.

The recent juridical robustness of the nation state is reflected in statistics of state creation and disappearance assembled in Thomson and Krasner (1989). Table 4.1 indicates a contrast between a pre-1939 pattern of disappearance as well as creation, and the post-1945

Table 4.1　The creation and disappearance of states (1816–1973)

Time period	States created	States disappearing
1816–76	24	15
1876–1916	12	1
1916–45	16	7
1945–73	81	1

Source: Adapted from Thomson and Krasner (1989: 207).

process of state construction. While the table takes the story up to 1973, further phases of state formation have taken place with the collapse of communism and the development of post-communist states.

There is little doubt, then, that effective nation state hood remains the political form to which most developing countries, and many minorities within Western states, aspire. This in turn reflects the wish to have some kind of autonomy and effective sovereignty. Such aspirations may be found among peoples or nations that lack states, such as the Kurds or Chechnyans, as well as in national minorities within Europe, such as Basques and Scots. The general conclusion, therefore, is that while the state institutions and capacities of developing countries are often weak and undeveloped, effective nation states possessing elements of sovereignty in domestic affairs still remain a major goal. This aspiration is as robust in the developing world as the fact of effective state capacity is in Europe, the USA and the advanced economic countries.

Conclusion: The Nation State and Multiple Challenges to State Sovereignty

This chapter set out to investigate how far the nation state and its sovereign institutions are rendered redundant by processes of globalization. Is the nation state finished or does it have a future and, if so, around what issues and functions?

The broad argument of this chapter is that while the nation state has been radically challenged by a number of globalization processes, its historical dynamic is very far from being played out. To be sure, the world that nation states inhabit is changing and globalization is a major source of change. Globalization is altering the roles and relationships of nation states with each other, as well as with other organized interests within the global political system. Such changes may involve the erosion of traditional ideals of absolute state sovereignty within particular boundaries, yet they dispose neither of the idea of sovereignty as state autonomy from external coercion nor that of sovereignty as a bargaining resource that political elites may use in negotiation with external interests.

This process of shift towards ever more conditional forms of sovereignty may be analyzed following the work of David Held (1991: 212–22) as comprising the four main elements outlined in Table 4.2.

Table 4.2   Challenges to state sovereignty

1. The global economy	Multinational companies Global capital markets
2. Trans-national bodies	Economic regulatory bodies – for example, World Bank, GATT/WTO United Nations European Union
3. International law	Legal conventions recognized by national courts and states United Nations and European conventions and charters
4. Hegemonic powers and power blocs	NATO and former Warsaw Pact

Source: Data from Held (1991: 212–22).

With the end of the Cold War (Holm and Sorensen, 1995), the fourth of these components has become far less salient to the global polity. Superpower conflict no longer constrains national sovereignty in the way it once did. Nonetheless, NATO is far from dead, as the Balkans crisis in the mid-1990s proved. What Held calls 'the internationalization of security' remains a significant issue. This tends to limit national sovereignty, whether of nations whose armed forces may be committed to NATO missions, those nations that may become the target of such missions, or those third parties who may wish to support target nations. At the same time, the limits to sovereignty are generally inversely proportional to the military capacity of those involved, especially on the NATO side. For the most part, and under peacetime conditions, however, it is the first three challenges that represent the greatest limits on national sovereignty.

We now extend this discussion further to consider the place of the nation state within the emerging global polity. While the nation state is far from finished, there is good reason to doubt that states hold the monopoly of power within the politics of globalization. A number of theorists now see globalism as a multi-actor system rather than an interstate system; but who are the main actors, how do they interrelate and what new types of global political interdependency are emerging? Is 'world government' a genuine possibility, or are moves towards a global polity still dominated by bargaining between parties for whom self-interest still overrides cosmopolitanism.

5

Global Governance: Towards a Global Polity?

Introduction

The nation state is very far from finished, and clearly represents a major focus for political organization. This is not because ideals of absolute national sovereignty are a viable alternative to globalization. Nor is it because nation states are the predominant political institution, of far greater importance than either global or regional institutions. What has changed is that global politics is increasingly a multi-actor rather than a wholly state-centred set of processes and institutions. Rather nation states are an irreducible part of a more complex political world. Other parties and interests in this world include international organizations like the World Bank and the United Nations Educational, Scientific and Cultural Organization, multinational enterprises and a diffuse set of non-government organizations (NGOs), networks and forums of public debate.

One way of capturing this wider non-state world is through the idea of global civil society (Kaldor, 2003; Keane, 2003). Its components include professional and scientific organizations like the Medical Lobby for Appropriate Marketing and the International Accounting Standards Committee, public forums like the World Social Forum and, perhaps more prominently, social and cultural activists and social movements like Médecins sans Frontières and Amnesty International. They also include religious movements who seek to engage with global politics. And beyond this lie political norms that extend far beyond ideas of the national interest and national citizenship to include human rights, environmental sustainability, global security and the creation of religious community.

One of the major problems with the term 'global civil society' (as for many other key terms) is the conflation of analytical issues with moral or normative ones. Analytically it refers to social processes and institutions that somehow subsist beyond states and markets, roughly akin to a 'third sector'. Normatively, the term is associated with the moral desirability of particular political values and institutions. In this sense, it is often either valued as a carrier of reconstructed democratic politics suitable for a global age, or criticized as an illegitimate usurping of political agendas by unelected activists. One symptom of the conflation of analysis and moral values is a tendency by supporters of global civil society to exaggerate its unity, coherence and indeed 'civility'. A tendency here to surround the idea of global civil society with a romantic and positive moral glow has been punctured by Keane (2003). He notes that many processes, institutions and movements inhabiting global civil society or the third sector are uncivil, illiberal and authoritarian. Alerted to this danger, however, the idea of global civil society is nonetheless analytically helpful in drawing attention to a major set of relatively new players striving to challenge exclusively state-centric global political processes.

Because the multi-actor system that has ensued extends beyond states, it necessarily extends beyond government into the world of governance. This distinction, already discussed in Chapter 3, is between a focus on the formal institution of states (the legislative, executive and judiciary), on the one hand, and the wider processes through which different interests (including business, labour, the professions and NGOs) share power and influence. In exploring the global polity, therefore, earlier expectations that globalization might mean world government or a world state, as discussed by H. G. Wells (1933) have largely been replaced by an alternative focus on 'global governance'.

This world of multiple actors is also a world of complex interaction between the politics of multiple scales of global, regional and national politics. Two very different examples of this may be cited. The first is the attempt by Greenpeace and other activists to use protest ships to disrupt Japanese whaling, pressuring world opinion to secure tighter regulation through the International Whaling Commission. The other contrasting example is 9/11, the Al-Qaeda-inspired attack on the Twin Towers in New York, a symbol of global capitalism and US power. Neither involves a diplomatic or parliamentary encounter. But each encapsulates multi-actor engagement around leading political issues of the day. In the whaling case we see a major international NGO in conflict with the nation state of Japan in the context of an international regulatory regime in which scientific opinion and moral concern for animal welfare are major norms in conflict with national self-interest. In the second, religion and politics are fused in a successful radical Islamic assault by a network of believers on the most powerful nation state in the world.

In this chapter we look more closely at the emerging features of the global polity, defined in its widest sense. This centres on struggles for power and influence, including the ideas and norms that inform politics, as well as the organizations – formal and informal – through which such struggles are expressed. The discussion explores how far and in what ways the global polity has moved beyond a state-centred focus, and in what senses this represents a global or trans-national set of arrangements. Before this, attention is given to some broad thematic questions about the emergence of the world or globe as a political object, including issues of communications and knowledge.

A Short Historical Sociology of the Global Polity

The global polity has always been a multi-actor system – before the development of nation states, during their emergence since the eighteenth century and in more recent times during the renewed global upswing after 1950. In the long history of globalization, outlined in Chapter 2, cross-border political interactions were usually associated with empires which included city-states and regional cultures, often tied together by ethnicity, military and administrative elites, and religious movements, as well as traders and merchants (Hopkins, 2002a; Hutchinson, 2005). 'Global' politics (not as yet global in geographical scope) involved regional warfare between empires, as well as the creation of new mechanisms of resource extraction and population settlement. But it was also associated with outward-looking religious and cultural aspirations as occurred in the cross-regional trans-continental expansion of Islam and Christianity.

In all of this, the initiatives for the development of global political connections were top-down and elite-driven. It was not until the eighteenth century that the elements of an alternative approach grounded in a sense of emerging global public opinion began to be seen. For the philosopher Immanuel Kant, towards the end of the eighteenth century, a sense of global interdependence between peoples was emerging, such that an evil or wrong done in one place was felt everywhere. This Kant linked with the idea of a universal moral community, which might serve in turn as a basis for cosmopolitan as distinct from national law. He also called for some kind of 'League of Nations' to bring this into effect.

This speculative and somewhat intuitive argument was advanced in a period of increased long-distance trade, travel and colonial expansion, when communications and knowledge were extending rapidly across borders. It is from this period onwards that more self-conscious moves towards what might now be called a global polity emerged. Yet senses of the public and a public social sphere (Habermas, 1989[1962]) were, nonetheless, also very much tied up with the national and regional politics of Europe. With the Enlightenment and challenges to monarchical power and authority, increasing recourse was made by both monarchs and their opponents to 'the public' as an alternative source of authority (Ozouf, 1988; Price, 2008). For Peters (1995), a transformation was underway in understandings of political democracy from ancient Athenian assemblies of people, to mass-mediated senses of an imagined public, a literate public brought together by newspapers and pamphlets. While this argument draws on Anderson's celebrated work on imagined national communities (1983), it may clearly be extended, as Robbins (1999) points out, in a more global rather than exclusively national direction. Certainly by the early twentieth century, as Price (2008: 20) outlines, communications technologies such as the telegraph, newspaper and mail delivered by ever-faster transportation stimulated a rapid extension of global consciousness.

Described in various terms as 'universal' or 'international', this has generated both global norms such as human rights reflected in the Geneva Conventions, and institutions such as the eventual League of Nations and United Nations. We now speak explicitly of 'the international community' though this rhetoric is not without a self-serving element linked with the nation states and ideologists who deploy it against their political enemies.

As part of this process the emergence of democracy, greater literacy and wider political publics is an important theme. One aspect of this was the opening up of political print media through specialized journalism for a wide readership. The nineteenth-century emergence of war correspondents and the twentieth-century development of foreign correspondents (Hannerz, 2004) both helped to create civil as distinct from state-centred sources of information and hence widened access to news, including global news. Yet this could not overcome governmental domination of political communications at moments of great crisis, such as the outbreak of wars between nations. This prefigures what is today called the 'global democracy deficit', where citizens, even if better informed, feel marginalized by the elite politics of nations and regions, let alone global political processes.

More recent changes in global communications and information technology impact upon political events and broad currents of global politics. The development of satellite broadcasting technology, for example, has contributed to a simultaneity in the coverage of political events, in which events in one part of the globe can be watched simultaneously on television in all other parts. This occurred during the Gulf War of the early 1990s, when the timing of major events in the war was staged at prime-viewing times in Western capitals, especially in the USA. War could be both brought into the living-room as a global spectator event and managed to promote the public relations objectives of the protagonists, both American and Iraqi.

The technological capacity for simultaneity is part of the expanding capacity of global communications to convey information. Such flows of information cannot be regarded as neutral and objective transmissions of fact, as critics of the global media point out (Stam, 1992). What counts as newsworthy is the product of standards of selectivity on the part of broadcasters, as well as of strategies of news management adopted by powerful interests such as governments and MNEs. Writing of Gulf War media coverage, Stam speaks of the invitation of viewers to become spectators in the technological dominance of the Western military (ibid.: 102–3).

Whether television transmission of world events amounts to top-down ideological manipulation, as proposed by some media critics, is, however, debatable. This is because producer management of issues is not necessarily able to control the way in which news is interpreted by those who receive it. Much TV news is undoubtedly managed selectively, yet there are, on the other hand, other sources of information, including alternative news services to the dominant Western news agencies and TV channels. Alongside Reuters and Associated Press, CNN and BBC World, may be found Inter Press Service (IPS), specializing in the 'Third World', Mathaba.Net focusing on Green News, and Al-Jazeera, based in the Middle East and Asia as well as London.

Szerzynski and Urry (2002, 2006) look less at who controls various mass media and more at how the 'world' or 'globe' is represented. Specific communications technologies, they argue, influence how social life is imagined and acted upon. Television, they argue, is saturated with global images. These range from representations of the earth as a generic global environment, through images of wildlife as indicators of the state of the natural environment, and images of the 'family of man' enjoying global commodities, to images of 'global people', whether as celebrities or experts (Szerzynski and Urry, 2002: 466–7). In interviews conducted in northern England they explored the cultural and political significance of all this for the extent of everyday cosmopolitanism. While few claimed to be 'citizens of the world', many who identified with their nation also thought they had wider moral obligations in areas such as the welfare of the world's children or disaster relief. These fed on televisual images and personalized symbols and activities, whether to moral exemplars such as Nelson Mandela and Mother Teresa, organizations such as the Red Cross, or events such as Band Aid. Put another way, the world can be imagined at a distance, and such processes clearly influence the vernacular politics of everyday life, which may be largely distinct from the formal politics of international governance.

It is arguable that global communications changes, including the wider availability of the interactive information sources through the internet as much as television, has been to expand popular access to and awareness of world events. To this extent, overt political events in a single country or city become globalized, in that the rest of the world can soon hear of them. The Moroccan sociologist Fatima Mernissi (1993), for example, reports on the reception of major European events, such as the fall of the Berlin wall and of the Romanian Ceausescu dictatorship, in North Africa:

> I remember the day when a fishmonger in the Rabat medina left me standing with a kilo of marlin in hand while he rushed to the neighbouring shop which had a TV set, to hear the announcer report the capture of Nicolae and Elena Ceausescu. (Ibid. 3)

Mernissi claims that this event and the fall of the Berlin Wall, as reported in global media, were interpreted and welcomed by many Moroccans as universal symbols of the collapse of despotism, with implications for democratic struggles within Morocco. These democratic impulses were not, however, reported in the Western press, which narrowed its coverage to an obsessive search for examples of anti-Western fundamentalism for the Islamic 'other'.

As Mernissi reports it, the Rabat fishmonger, having seen the exciting events, bought a television set for himself, largely to receive global news. Westerners, regarded hitherto as brutal colonizers, had become slightly more credible as a result of recent political upheavals as forces for good. Then came the Gulf War and massive disillusion with the West. Two weeks after the start, the fishmonger sold his television and donated the money to the Red Crescent to buy supplies for Iraq. This story reflects both the global impact of communications technology in widening access to information and the capacity of television viewers, in this case Moroccan merchants, to make their own judgements about the meaning of events rather than being dominated by Western television newscasting strategies or military news management.

Finally, more explicit mention should be made to the internet. This has been connected with a range of processes from globalization and the network society (Castells, 1996), to the emergence of a new virtual democracy of active citizens (Negroponte, 1995). It is certainly tempting to emphasize the radical potential of interactive rather than top-down forms of communications technology. The internet easily crosses borders, yet is hard to censor. And there are some celebrated instances of the internet facilitating political mobilization from below through a widening interconnection with broader 'publics'. This concerns the 1994 local Zapatista uprisings in the Chiapas district of Mexico, the wide use made by supporters of the uprising in publicizing the Zapatistas' cause to world opinion through the internet.

Olessen (2004), in a detailed study of this set of events, identifies five ever-widening circles of support and interest. These start out from Chiapas residents, who pass information to a second circle of information gatherers in Mexico and the USA. This includes networks of political activists around groups such as Global Exchange, a human rights organization, and SIPAZ (International Service for Peace), linking activists in North America with Europe. The third circle comprised websites that picked up and publicized the story, and the fourth those consistently interested in the events but not as activists. Fifth and last were those with a transitory interest such as politicians and officials. The point of all this was that publicity made it hard for this local event to be ignored or repressed and aided the Zapatistas in gaining some of their demands.

Greater popular awareness of world events represents a change in the conditions under which major political actors operate. As recently as 1914, in an era before television, radio and mass diffusion of the telephone, the governments of the major states were still able to dominate domestic opinion in relation to decisions about going to war. Other parties could be represented as the aggressor, and there were virtually no alternative sources of popularly available information. Contrasts in popular access to global political information between 1914 and the contemporary world should not be exaggerated. Independently sourced information that challenges prevailing official views remains scarce and usually has actively to be sought out. Yet, however imperfect flows of information may be, governments can no longer take either domestic or international political decisions in an information void, filled solely by their own propaganda.

Much of this is due to the expanded presence of global civil society aided in large measure by new communications technology. This does not mean that global civil society has come to rival the power of the wealthier and larger nation states. As Held and McGrew (2007: 153–4) point out, most trans-national movements and NGOs lack the economic and political resources of nation states. Their impact may be thought of more in terms of the 'soft power' able 'to shape others' interests, attitudes, agendas, and identities' (154), rather than the 'hard power' of states over the allocation of resources (Nye, 2004).

Technology may have helped expand the number of interests able to disseminate information, as well as expanding access, but is this the same thing as informed access to knowledge, consistent with the idea of government by informed discussion? Should we be so optimistic about the information revolution? Many are sceptical as to whether the internet necessarily empowers citizens, partly because this medium fragments political discourse as much as unifying scattered users (Papacharissi, 2002).

The issues of growing complexity and overload in information flows, available to citizens and to governments alike, have also been raised by Sartori (1989) and Ionescu (1993). Problems here stem not only from new communications technology and increasing global interdependence in economic and political life, but also, according to Ionescu (ibid.: 224–5), from limits to the cognitive capacity of science to produce an accessible understanding of the causal processes of the natural and social worlds. The debate over climate change and appropriate policy responses, such as the technically complicated emissions trading system, would seem to fit this argument very well. The effect is to produce under-comprehension and cognitive incapacity.

The complexities of global interdependence set cognitive limits to political capacities to understand and explain what is happening within global society. This may constrain capacities to respond with the wisdom of understanding, but it does not necessarily constrain action on the basis of moral judgement or assertions of political will. A good deal of the actions of politicians representing nation states within the global polity may take this form. Yet beyond this, there has also been a shift towards the establishment of organizations based on non-elected expertise and knowledge as well as institutional autonomy from individual nation states, though not necessarily from political influence in its widest senses. Such organizations may be found within the UN orbit, not only in economic organizations like the IMF and World Bank, but also in other equally controversial areas like the environment. Here the Intergovernmental Panel on Climate Change (IPCC), while established (in 1988) by governments who also nominate panel members, is dominated by scientists and, officially at least, by scientific discourses about the challenges of global warming. Is it not the case that debate in such circles offers a basis for more informed democratic deliberation?

Similar scientific and technical discourses are of central concern in many other global organizations from the World Health Organization and Food and Agriculture Organization, to the International Telecommunications Union and the International Atomic Energy Agency.

While not part of government processes in any formal sense, all such bodies have become central to global governance. Yet in the process any clear-cut distinction between science and objectivity and political and policy issues is impossible to make. Grundmann (2007), writing before recent revelations and allegations about manipulation of scientific data on climate change by IPCC scientists, confirms the sociological argument that 'science is not separate from society and that it does not discover uncontested truths that are then translated into policies' (ibid.: 414). This does not mean that scientists are politically biased to the extent that scientific judgement is simply arbitrary. But it does mean that the IPCC, after long years of peer-reviewed research that established near consensus on anthropogenic (or 'manmade') global warming, subsequently ignored or downplayed sceptical scientific opinion. This, together with the prescriptive policy advice on lowering emissions that ensued, helped to politicize debates by giving strong support to European governments convinced by the science, while decrying periodic US government opposition. In other words the IPCC is a hybrid organization combining science and politics rather than a purely detached scientific one.

The global polity is not totally swamped by uncontrolled information flows. Much information is translated into knowledge through scientific processes and what Haas (1992) calls 'epistemic communities'. Yet it is not clear that science is ever in a position to adjudicate on 'truth' as it enters into political discourse. While there is near-consensus on climate change science, governments vary on the policy stance they take, with the USA, as Grundmann shows, citing sceptical scientists (2007.: 421–2), while European governments in Germany and the UK remain with the dominant opinion. Yet all governments claim respect for science. This suggests that even in a case of near-scientific agreement, politics does not fall into line. A further corollary may be that governments, in part, look for science that meets some other political objective, which in the USA may be the fossil-fuel cheap-energy lobby, linking coal and oil companies with consumers unwilling to pay higher fuel prices.

In the changing global context of political activity, many types of economic and political interdependence link the fate of all nations with one another. They include continuous cross-border processes such as the mobility of capital and information, global warming or atmospheric pollution and epidemic diseases like HIV/Aids or Swine Flu. In some cases interdependence is mediated through market processes, even if initiated by other mechanisms. Tony McGrew (1992: 1) cites the following example. When Iraq invaded Kuwait on 2 August 1990, the headline in a local newspaper in the English industrial city of Coventry read

'Iraq invades Kuwait – Bus Fares to Rise'. The interdependence here occurred through the connection between invasion, a disruption of oil supplies, a rise in world oil prices, the increased cost of oil-powered transport and a rise in bus fares. In other cases, interdependence depends on outward-looking Kantian fellow-feeling for those on whom harm has been inflicted, whether by war, pestilence, or natural disasters, such as the South East Asian tsunami or the Haiti earthquake. This sympathy in turn is, as we have seen above, partly stimulated or at least amplified by mass media.

Rosenau (1980) has attempted a more systematic approach to the nature of contemporary interdependency. This focuses on the relative shift over time from issues to do with military control, territoriality and national legitimacy, to a range of social, economic and environmental issues in which nations share concerns and must cooperate to find solutions. Such problems include pollution of the natural environment, population pressure on resources and economic inequalities, such as those between North and South. These cannot be resolved by military means, and hence reliance comes to be placed on technical and scientific solutions embodied in political decisions at global and regional as much as national 'levels'.

The interdependent actions of many players is involved in the search for solutions. They extend well beyond governments, elite governance networks and globally organized forms of civil society. Thus

> the actions of innumerable farmers … are central to the problem of increased food production, just as many pollution issues depend on choices made by vast numbers of producers, energy conservation on millions of consumers, and population growth on tens of millions of parents. (Ibid.: 44)

In addition, actions in one area, such as food production, affect those in another, such as birth rate.

The processes of interdependence are typically decentralized through the actions of large numbers of people and involve non-governmental as well as governmental organizations. They are, therefore, less amenable to governmental action and redress alone, however crucial that involvement may be in terms of the mobilization of resources. This reinforces the general theme of this chapter, namely that global politics is a multi-actor system or field (see also Rosenau, 1990). involving not only inter-governmental cooperation, but also a range of other parties, from which Rosenau singles out professional experts for further attention.

This category may be drawn widely embracing technology, natural and social science, law and ethics. It embraces fundamental research into matter, energy and genetics, which link in with climate change debates, nanotechnology and bio-engineering affecting a range of industries including energy production, pharmaceuticals and agriculture, respectively. Meanwhile, social science and law contribute to areas such as international security, economic and social development and human rights.

In the next sections of this chapter, we shall explore the nature of contemporary global interdependence, as posited by Rosenau. We shall proceed first to look at institutional developments such as the UN and EC, and thence to INGOs. The underlying issue to be examined here is the nature of these trans-national political institutions. If they are not simply to be seen as creatures of nation states, how far do they represent a new form of global politics, different from that which went before?

The Internationalization of the State and the UN

The contemporary nation state is relatively resilient as an institution, even if undergoing transformation in its roles, power and authority. A central part of this transformation is that nation states are increasingly involved in a range of 'multilateral forms of international governance' (Held and McGrew, 1993: 271). Some of these, like the UN General Assembly, are multipurpose bodies, while others have a more specific remit. This ranges from trade in the case of the WTO (formerly GATT), through health under the auspices of the WHO, to the weather, as with the World Meteorological Organization, and designated species regulators such as the International Whaling Commission (IWC).

The UN was established in 1945, in the aftermath of the Second World War and upon the ruins of the League of Nations, founded in 1919. Both initiatives were responses to the globalization of war, meaning the transformation of warfare from limited regional conflicts between small sets of nations to intercontinental struggles involving far larger numbers of states, the political and economic consequences of which affect all states and regions. Such developments reflect *both* the spatial expansion of nineteenth-century Western capitalism and colonialization that intensified the global interdependence of states and regions, whether in Europe, the Americas, Africa, or Asia *and* changes in military technology that assisted the more powerful nations to wage war on a trans-continental scale.

The two world wars demonstrated that questions of security and peace were a concern of all states, since the existing machinery of inter-governmental relations, bilateral treaties and multilateral security pacts had proved inadequate. The UN was, in large measure, a response to this failure of international security. Its Charter began with the words: 'We the peoples of the United Nations are determined to save succeeding generations from the scourge of war.' Yet the UN was conceived in an even wider sense, inasmuch as wider social and political issues such as human rights were included within the new organization's Charter and foundational declarations. Alongside the UN Security Council, charged with preservation of security through peace, stood the General Assembly, part of whose powers included not only the discussion of questions of human rights, but also the capacity to develop international conventions on such matters (Cassese, 1992). These law-making powers have subsequently been extended to cover a vast range of human rights areas and have in their turn spawned a complex set of UN programmes and agencies.

There are three formal distinctions to be made in mapping the complex set of institutions of global governance involved (Koenig-Archibugi, 2002). At the centre lie the UN organs, such as the General Assembly, Security Council and International Court of Justice. Next come UN agencies, which directly execute and administer UN policies. These include the United Nations Environmental Programme (UNEP), the World Food Programme (WFP), geared very much to disaster relief, and the United Nations High Commission for Refugees (UNHCR). Beyond this lie general and more autonomous agencies, such as the World Bank, World Intellectual Property Organization (WIPO) and the International Labour Organization (ILO).

UN policies are often expressed through Conventions on matters such as human rights or on the rights of particular groups such as women, children, or refugees. These do not represent trans-national legal initiatives that are binding on all nations. Rather they can only ultimately be implemented by judicially sovereign nations if they so wish. Influence and pressure may be placed on members who refuse or whose support is not translated into action, but this is as far as it goes. Such methods of achieving compliance may often fail, but they are not necessarily without effect.

The post-1945 phase of international political and social reconstruction that resulted in the foundation of the UN was also the same period that saw the establishment of global regulatory organizations such as the IMF and World Bank (see Chapter 3). Both of these processes may be regarded as aspects of globalization, but neither represents, nor was intended to function in a manner that fundamentally usurped, the sovereignty of nation states in the name of a new global order. The same applies throughout the UN and the world of agencies around it.

The system that has emerged has made sovereignty less absolute and more conditional on trans-national regulation, but the system remains founded, from a legal point of view, on nation states as the major players in the new global polity. This is not, however, the same thing as saying that all power and influence within the system resides with nations.

Nation States and Beyond

The political and normative agenda involved in the establishment and subsequent functioning of the UN and its agencies is proof of the influence of particular nation states or sets of nation states at many moments in time. Not surprisingly, the nations that emerged victorious from the Second World War, namely the US, USSR and UK, played the most significant role in the negotiations that led to the establishment of the UN (Russell and Muther, 1958; Cassese, 1992). The primary concern here was international peace, irrespective of issues of social justice, and the UN Security Council's mandate and veto privileges for the victorious wartime nations has preserved this focus ever since.

While Western interests dominated deliberations in the early years – excluding Communist China as a 'non peace-loving nation', for example – the steady expansion of new members as a result of decolonization reduced this influence over time, especially in those bodies such as the General Assembly, based on majoritarian voting procedures. The inclusion of increasing numbers of former colonial nations in UN membership has meant a shift in the UN agenda from initial Western concerns for peace and stability, to a greater emphasis on global social justice and human rights (Mazrui, 1990; Cassese, 1992). This agenda is evident both in the largely rhetorical theatre of the General Assembly, and in the social and cultural committees of the UN.

Conflicts over access to and political participation within trans-national institutions have been redefined by many in socio-economic rather than geopolitical terms. The vocabulary is one of North–South conflicts based on inequalities of wealth and power rather than conflicts between Western and non-Western polities. Within the UN, such conflicts are reflected in conflicts over human rights.

In response to the human rights violations of the Second World War, the UN Charter of 1945 spoke of 'faith in fundamental human rights, in the dignity of the human person, [and] … in the equal rights of men and women and of nations large and small' (cited in Weissbrodt, 1988: 7). These commitments were reaffirmed in the Universal Declaration of Human Rights in 1948. Over subsequent years, what has come to be known as the UN 'human rights regime' has been established (Alston, 1992). The provisions of the Declaration have been refined in covenants and codified in multilateral treaties, while procedures for implementing and monitoring human rights have been institutionalized within a complex set of committees, centring on the Human Rights Committee, set up in 1976 under the International Covenant on Human Rights (Opsahl, 1992).

Within these complex structures, conflicts between the developed North and most other states have occurred over the meaning and insti-tutionalization of human rights. For the first 20 or so years of the UN human rights regime, the emphasis was more on the civil and political rights of individuals, reflecting Western liberal-democratic traditions. With growing post-colonial participation in the past 50 years, the shift has, in contrast, been towards a greater emphasis on the social and economic rights of groups or nations, regarded in an important General Assembly vote of 1977 as the precondition for effective political rights.

Conflicts over human rights violations and abuses cannot, however, be interpreted merely as rhetorical battles between Western and non-Western groups of nation states, asserting different political interests. There are several reasons for this. First the War on Terror by the US and its allies has served to globalize human rights abuses on both sides. Abuse is evident both in the 9/11 bombing of civilian populations and in the US Guantanamo torture camp and various secret locations outside the West, where suspects or internees were sent after extra-ordinary rendition. A second reason why human rights abuses transcend West/non-West distinctions is because human rights NGOs are active in all regions (see, for example, Davis, 1995, on Asia) and have radically changed the global awareness of the reality of human rights violations. No government, be it in the developed or the developing world, is immune from criticism on human rights issues, either from outside or from dissidents from within.

Conflict over the meaning of human rights throws into doubt any theory of the emergence of some kind of universalistic human rights framework within global politics, to which all parties subscribe. The reality is rather different. In the first place, countries within the devel-oped North seek to use UN bodies to encourage the emergence of liberal-democratic rights in authoritarian regimes within the developing South. In parallel with this, developing nations seek economic and social rights to freedom from poverty and economic exploitation for their nations, by calling for the North to divest itself of its unequal share of power. Meanwhile, dissidents within the South criticize their own governments over lack of liberal-democratic freedoms, and critics in the North point to their own governments' complicity in human rights abuse in supporting authoritarian regimes overseas.

If the UN is not grounded in any clear kind of agreement on universalistic normative principles about key issues such as rights, this weakens but doesn't dispose of the argument that an effectively *global* or *trans-national* polity exists.

Criticism of the UN for its lack of effectiveness as a trans-national organization, of course, extends well beyond human rights to a range of other issues, including international security and peace. The global political agenda in this sense has, however, become harder to fulfil as purely political senses of terms like 'security' have become redefined in wider terms (Brauch, 2008). The criticism of the UN's post-1945 record in delivering security with peace is twofold. First, the institutional machinery of the UN was marginalized during the period of the Cold War, effective power residing with the two superpowers and the security alliances of NATO and the Warsaw Pact. This power constellation curtailed the capacity of individual nations to pursue independent or autonomous foreign policies, either through the UN or outside it.

Second, with the end of the Cold War, the hoped-for revival of effective multilateral diplomacy permitting a revival of the UN has not occurred. Instead, it is arguable that the UN has conspicuously failed to prevent civil war and genocide in the former Yugoslavia, Rwanda and Somalia. Such failures relate both to inadequacies in delivering appropriate resources quickly enough to trouble-spots and, more fundamentally, to rivalries between nations and failures of collective will by the key nations (mostly in the West) to pre-empt war and conflict. In this sense, freedom from the constraints of the Cold War has not meant that international conflict resolution has been redirected through the UN. The more powerful nations or groupings, such as the USA or the EU, still reserve the right to mediate on an independent basis in international disputes. Meanwhile, the various national components of UN peace-keeping or crisis intervention forces remain under the ultimate control of national governments rather than the UN.

Negative evaluation of the UN is thus both a matter of inadequate normative consensus about what should be done to secure global peace and justice, and a matter of consistent failure in responding to immediate challenges and crises that require action. An example is the severe difficulties that the UN has faced in securing effective transitional administrations in countries with failed states that saw external intervention and mandates for state and society reconstruction (Chesterman, 2004). From the viewpoint of the mid-1990s and a poor record of intervention in Somalia, the Balkans and Rwanda, it appeared that a new breed of intra-state conflict and collapse of state institutions was overwhelming UN crisis responses.

The case against the UN as the centre point of an effective global polity, couched in these terms, may look overwhelming. Yet the extreme scepticism of this negative evaluation is unwarranted for a number of reasons.

The first is that the UN, for all its weaknesses, functions as a single global forum for the exchange of views and as a body that attempts to broker and implement solutions to problems as defined by member states and a wider set of NGOs. The existence of such a worldwide forum for discussion and interstate negotiation and problem-solving through the implementation of agreed policy measures, incorporating virtually all the nations of the world, on a limitless agenda of issues, is historically unprecedented. Such a forum may lack the power to coerce national governments into compliance, but it does possess influence and expertise in both political conflict resolution and wider socio-economic matters.

Within the conflict resolution and peace-keeping arena, for example, the UN has had some successes, such as the transfer to independence in Namibia and the partial success of political stabilization in Cambodia. Bercovitch (1996), in a survey of UN mediation of interstate conflicts, has calculated that, of 355 mediations studied, a successful outcome was achieved on 35 per cent of occasions. This record of successes is significant if not exactly outstanding.

However, Bercovitch goes on to make the further point that many of the mediations that failed involve intractable cases of conflicts between nations with long histories of disputation, such as Arab–Israeli or Balkan warfare. Equally, the UN also became involved in deeply divided countries with no recognized leadership or authority to secure peace, as in Somalia or Rwanda. In a sense, therefore, it is the most difficult cases that get to the UN, which is trying to mediate conflicts in which the parties themselves are poles apart. Here, the UN acts as mediator 'of last resort' and, in this sense, is unlikely to achieve a spectacular success rate. A final point worth making is that UN mediations are typically more successful than alternative mediations based on 'neutral' nation states such as the USA, UK or the former Soviet Union (Savun, 2009: 108–9).

The UN performance of mediation functions scarcely lives up to the utopian dreams of world peace held by some of the UN's founders. It is more akin to the conception of world order described by Roland Robertson (1992) in Table 2.2 as a global *Gesellschaft*, based on the 'weak' ties of interstate dependency rather than on any 'stronger' sense of world government. In this context, it should be remembered that at least part of the disillusionment with the UN is precisely related to the failure of utopian hopes that a world government, able to rise above nation states, would materialize (Righter, 1995). In this sense, a good deal of criticism of the UN takes the form of a failure of expectations as much as of a failure of effective political intervention.

The problem with using a 'world government' yardstick to judge UN performance, whether in conflict mediation or any other area, is that it treats the achievement of a global polity as mutually incompatible with the continuing autonomy of nation states. This broad-brush approach gives insufficient attention to the complex and more fine-grained relations between the UN and its member-states or to subtle shifts in the practice of national sovereignty that have occurred as the UN has itself evolved.

Within a global *Gesellschaft* we may expect states to maximize their self-interest and to enter into collective arrangements with other states where it is optimal to do so. Yet further subtle changes in the direction of more conditional forms of national sovereignty have emerged, as we have already seen in Chapter 4. Rosenau conceives of these in terms of a normative shift from UN action taking place 'at-the-convenience-of-states', to the more muted principle whereby 'states-are-sometimes-obliged-to-go-along' (1996: 237). Two examples of this shift are cited. The first is the decreasing use of the veto in the Security Council, signifying less readiness to push sovereign national interests to the limit. The second is the widespread appeal of nations for the UN to monitor domestic elections. This has occurred in South Africa, Mexico and Latin America, and widely in the countries of the former Soviet Union.

The conception of a global polity based on nation states exercising conditional sovereignty, insofar as they accept the procedural rules of UN mediation and conflict resolution, provides one dimension of the contemporary global order. Yet the UN, in line with the broad aspirations of its Charter, has extended its scope well beyond issues of peace, security and mediation, to include matters of economic development, social justice and human rights, including the rights of women and children, and the issue of the natural environment. These topics involve governmental and inter-governmental debate within the central forums of the UN, but are mainly conducted within a complex and wide-ranging set of consultative, technical and administrative institutions. These have the capacity to set standards and to monitor the performance of individual nation states in meeting such standards.

A second major dimension to the existence of this kind of global polity is the development of a set of specialist UN agencies, such as the WHO or the UN High Commission for Refugees, with their own bureaucratic structures, accumulated bodies of expertise and, in many cases, regulatory or interventionist capacities. Surrounding these institutions are thematic conferences, sponsored by the UN and its agencies, on issues such as population, women, social development and the environment, which are intended to assist in defining political strategies for change.

How and why has this extension of global political organization emerged? Part of the answer has already been suggested, in terms of the extension of UN membership to newly independent post-colonial nations with their own agendas of development and justice. But this is not the whole answer. Also requiring explanation are the reasons why sufficient numbers of the nation states that are members of the UN have been prepared to countenance an extension of the UN's scope.

Contemporary nation states typically find themselves faced with increasing numbers of problems that cannot be resolved on a national basis (Keohane, 1984; McGrew, 1992; Held, 1995). The difficulty here may either be that individual nations lack the technical or financial resources to address problems such as poverty or economic moderni- zation, or that nations face common cross-border problems, such as security or environmental protection, that require joint cross-border action to produce effective results. All this encourages a willingness to operate, if at all possible within international forms of cooperation.

International organizations can never operate independently of nation states, either in terms of powerful national interests such as those of the USA and other G8 nations, or in terms of national sources of funding. But they have over the years developed signifi- cant elements of autonomy. Neither US refusal to pay UN dues in the 1990s nor hostility to particular organizations like UNESCO were able to frustrate their operation, while the impact of 9/11, a gruesome reminder of global interdependence, meant an immediate US reversal of previous funding suspension to the UN.

The autonomy of international organizations is evident not only in information-gathering capacity and global agenda-setting, but also in the establishment and implementation of a range of interventionist and regulatory competencies. Autonomy is also heightened by the access to and close working relationships of such bodies to a range of non-government organizations. In the case of the human rights area, these include both professionally based organizations such as the International Commission of Jurists and broad-based social move- ments such as the Anti-Slavery Society and Amnesty International. This returns us to the theme of global civil society as an increasingly central part of the global polity alongside nation states and international organizations.

Close working relationships between national UN delegations, UN agency officials and NGOs have grown up since the UN's inception. These linkages build on even older precedents such as the humanitarian campaigns of the International Committee of the Red Cross, founded in 1863, or the peace and social reform work of the Women's International League for Peace and Freedom, begun in 1916. Such activities were designed to pressure nations into greater cooperation to achieve peace and humanitarian standard-setting in the international arena. They contributed to the earlier set of instruments such as the Geneva Conventions of 1864 for the Amelioration of the Condition of the Wounded and Sick in Armies in the Field, and the Hague Conventions of 1899 and 1907, limiting methods of warfare, and to further supplements to the Geneva Convention in 1949 and 1977 (Weissbrodt, 1988).

NGOs were present at the San Francisco Conference in 1945 that drafted the UN Charter and were envisaged under Article 71 of that document as playing an important consultative role in the deliberations of the UN's Economic and Social Council (ECOSOCC) (Suter, 1996: 258). This consultative role has been played out over the years in bodies such as the Commission on Human Rights and the Commission on the Status of Women.

It has also expanded as the number of NGOs has grown and as the UN's agenda has widened, in part at least due to NGO pressure. NGO prominence in processes of agenda-widening has been evident at the Beijing UN Women's Conference in September 1995, protests around the WTO meeting in Seattle in 1998, and most recently in the climate change summit in Copenhagen late in 2009. In 1909, according to Held and McGrew (1993), there were 176 NGOs operating in the international arena. By 1989, this figure had risen to 4,624 (ibid.: 271), while in 2001 the number had grown again to nearly 50,000 (Held and McGrew, 2002: 18–19). Although NGOs now have a presence in all continents, their activities and inter-continental networks are still skewed, in a quantitative sense, to Europe and North America (Katz and Anheier, 2006: 249ff).

Yet NGOs are not a uniform or homogeneous set of institutions. In some contexts, their principal role has been to provide political pressure to stimulate greater concern, as in a variety of environmentalist campaigns on issues such as acid rain or whaling, or in the coalition of groups behind the Make Poverty History campaign against global economic deprivation. In other contexts, they may offer expert opinion geared to international standard-setting or the monitoring of compliance with UN conventions. The latter activity is especially important in the human rights area, where expert NGOs such as the International

Commission of Jurists and Amnesty International have provided advice and information relating both to human rights standard-setting and to the monitoring of countries' compliance with treaties they have signed (Weissbrodt, 1988; Opsahl, 1992).

The emerging picture of the global polity presented here is a rather complex one, for several reasons. First, there are multiple actors, and not only nation states, involved. Second, national sovereignty remains intact in an ultimate juridical sense but is increasingly conditional upon compliance with a range of trans-national regulatory regimes. This reflects increased international interdependency and the growth of problems that nation states believe (or are pressured to believe) can only be effectively addressed through international cooperation and trans-national agreement. Yet, even when all this wider complexity is taken into account, it may still be that nation states – or at least the more powerful nation states – may be the most central players. To explore and elaborate this argument in a more concrete way, we will now look at an important case study – that of environmental protection.

Environmental Protection: A Case Study in the Operation of the Emerging Global Polity

Concern for the adverse, and possibly disastrous, impact of human activity on the natural environment has grown to become one of the leading issues in national and international politics. Ulrich Beck (1992) has argued that the character of risks facing humankind has shifted with the advent of industrial society from naturally induced disasters to risks and hazards generated by human society. In addition to the ultimate threat of annihilation by nuclear weapons, there is a long list of other socially generated environmental problems such as ozone depletion in the atmosphere, industrial pollution and acid rain, chemical pesticides, the depletion of natural resources through defor-estation, intensive agriculture and overfishing and loss of bio-diversity (Chasek *et al.*, 2006). Many of these problems compromise or threaten to compromise the food chain, as dramatized in the 'mad cow disease' crisis in the 1990s, apparently originating from inadequate management practices in the animal feed industry. Such risks are also typically cross-border problems that implicate all nation states.

The trans-border character of environmental problems means that they transcend the regulatory outreach of individual nation states. This is disturbing since so much environmental hazard is tied up with processes organizationally concentrated in the hands of multinationals. Problems arise not simply from the intensive use of hazardous industrial technologies, but more fundamentally from economic transactions that put profit and immediate economic cost minimization above broader social objectives and wider kinds of social cost. For example, multinationals have, in certain cases, located environmentally hazardous production processes in countries or regimes with lower regulatory standards, such as Mexico, rather than the USA, or operated to lower standards in developing countries than in developed ones. The 1984 environmental health disaster at the Union Carbide pesticide plant in Bhopal, India, which killed at least 2,500 people, is one of the most tragic instances of the multinational exploitation of low regulatory standards. Longer-term cumulative hazards apply to practices such as climate-damaging deforestation in Latin America and South East Asia, in which local capital and developing government support and complicity compounds the impact of multinational operations.

Many environmentalists go on to argue that the failure to address environmental problems prejudices the long-term survival of the human race. Whether or not such Doomsday predictions are valid, it is clear that environmental thinking has a strong and intrinsic tendency to think globally. However localized particular instances of environmental damage may be, they are typically subsumed within a broader global framework of thought. This is largely because of environmental interdependency, whereby damage or problems created in one area have a wider effect elsewhere, unimpeded by territorial boundaries. Thus greenhouse gas emissions primarily from the northern hemisphere have contributed to, among other things, the depletion of the ozone layer over the South Pole, which has in turn contributed to increased levels of skin cancer in Australia. Again, the fall-out from the Chernobyl nuclear disaster created adverse effects on the health of people and animals in many other parts of Northern and Western Europe as well as the Ukraine.

Awareness of adverse environmental affects of human activity goes back several millennia (Braithwaite and Drahos, 2000: 256). Yet it was only in the 1980s that environmental issues became a major policy focus for governments. This was very much a response to growing awareness and politicization of environmental issues. Major influences included books like Rachel Carson's *Silent Spring* (1962), which dealt with the effects of agro-chemicals, growing awareness of industrial pollution as manifest in acid rain, the Bhopal chemical plant explosion and disastrous oil spills resulting from the grounding of the *Torrey Canyon* in 1967 and *Amoco Cadiz* in 1978, the last of which became broadcast by television around the world.

International involvement in environmental protection dates mainly from the period since 1972 when the United Nations Conference on the Human Environment (UNHCE) was held, leading to the establishment of the United Nations Environment Programme (UNEP). Over half of the 140 multilateral environmental treaties signed since 1921 date from the period since 1973. Further intensification of UN involvement took place in the early 1990s with the United Nations Conference on Environment and Development (UNCED), or Rio Earth Summit, held in 1992. This not only laid down conventions on biodiversity and greenhouse gas emissions, but also adopted a programme of action to achieve the principles of appropriate environmental behaviour laid down in the Earth Charter. This agenda looks impressive but was criticized from the outset as a document without the teeth to secure change. It nonetheless remains important to establish exactly how such a global environmental standard-setting agenda came about and how far national governments and other powerful interests are really prepared to comply with environmental protection regimes. What, in other words, does a case study of environmental protection tell us about the emergent features of the global polity?

One of the most valuable research-based studies of such questions is *Institutions for the Earth*, a collaborative project headed by Haas, Keohane and Levy (1993). This deals almost entirely with the period before the Rio Earth Summit. The environmental challenge is disaggregated into seven particular subfields, namely oil pollution from tankers, acid rain, stratospheric ozone depletion, pollution of the North and Baltic Seas, mismanagement of fisheries, overpopulation and the misuse of farm chemicals. This choice of seven problem areas is deliberately skewed to matters that have received significant levels of institutional involvement. There are clearly other environmental areas, such as deforestation or species extinction, in which international institutional involvement has been less significant and in which environmental outcomes may therefore be expected to be worse than in the seven chosen cases.

The impact of international institutions in these areas is investigated through a three-phase model. This focuses first on agenda-setting, whereby environmental concerns are identified. Next comes international policy formulation, which turns concern into policies for collective application. Here particular emphasis is placed on the 'contracting environment' – that is, on the structure of incentives and sanctions affecting individual governments' willingness to agree to policy change. The third phase is one of implementation primarily through national policy development usually involving cross-border cooperation. This in turn centres on the capacity, both scientific and financial, of governments to take action.

One of the main findings is a lack of uniformity in responses to the various environmental problems. In some cases, such as oil pollution and fishery mismanagement, it has been very hard to raise government concern through international negotiations. In others, such as ozone depletion, concern has been successfully mobilized and policies formulated, leading to implementation strategies in the form of reduced chlorofluorocarbon (CFC) emission levels. What is not clear is how well nations are actually complying. In other environmental areas, such as acid rain and maritime pollution, the position is more ambiguous, with plenty of rhetorical concern and new policy regimes, but still uncertainty about whether the effects of such actions will actually remedy the underlying problems.

Blanket diagnoses of inexorable environmental doom or institutional success may be premature and ill-founded, but what exactly is it that explains the variations in response identified here? As far as governmental responses are concerned, it is coalitions of national governments that are in the main ultimately responsible for implementing change. Whether individual governments do respond is partly a question of whether they perceive environmental problems to be worthy of action, how they understand the connection between such problems and national interests, how far they are pressured by powerful domestic interests, whether the international institutional setting offers incentives to cooperate with other governments in global regulation, and whether governments have the capacity to act.

Another major finding is that campaigns by NGOs and/or scientists may play a major role in raising the concern of governments. In the 1970s, for example, scientists were the first to raise the problem of ozone depletion, while NGOs took the lead in publicizing the problem of chemical pesticides. Individual governments may also quickly take up issues and become leaders for change, as in the key roles of Norway and Sweden in developing recognition and more effective regulation of the problem of acid rain. More typically within Western democracies, it is only when domestic political pressure mounts (sometimes in conjunction with the added commitment of individual lead nations) that most governments take action. However, as Levy *et al.* (1993) point out, the salience to domestic publics in the West of issues of ozone and acid rain has been much greater than that of international oil pollution and the pesticide trade (408). Where public pressure is not forthcoming, environmental action is far harder to achieve.

International institutions may also amplify public pressure on laggard governments. This may take the form of public exposure before international meetings at which representatives of other nations are present. In the 1980s, for example, public exposure of the UK government's lack of action on issues of North Sea pollution and acid rain succeeded in stimulating political responses and policy developments. The presence of NGOs prepared to speak out on controversial issues at meetings of bodies such as the Long Range Trans-Boundary Air Pollution (LRTAP) has made it increasingly difficult for recalcitrant governments to simply ignore problems.

Why, then, do governments obstruct certain kinds of environmental protection regime but not others? Rowlands (1995) has compared environmental regulation in two major areas: ozone layer depletion caused by the production of chemicals such as CFC gases and the climate change resulting from greenhouse gas emissions. He argues that there has been greater success in regulating types of chemical production such as the use of CFC gases in aerosols than in regulating greenhouse gas emissions. The explanation of this contrast is complex. One reason for greater success in the ozone depletion regulatory area was the greater degree of scientific consensus compared with the greenhouse gas area. In this latter case, it was only when scientists became less divided about global warming in the 1990s that many nation states began to become more involved.

Yet scientific learning and the degree of scientific consensus are not the only relevant variables here. According to Rowlands, another reason for greater progress in the ozone depletion area is that the vested economic interests of private corporations were, in significant respects, less hostile to regulation in the ozone depletion area than in the greenhouse gas area. In the case of CFC production, for example, American chemical producers certainly resisted regulatory measures, such as the banning of CFCs in aerosols. Yet over time, US corporations, led by Du Pont, were more easily able to shift production to non-CFC alternatives compared with European producers, led by ICI, who had a greater proportion of their investment within the chemical industry tied up in CFC production. Once profit opportunities were identified in alternative technologies, the interests of American producers shifted to support the regulation of aerosol CFCs in order to achieve a competitive edge over European producers still committed to the older technology. This shift in corporate strategy helps to explain why the US government was more supportive of CFC aerosol bans than were European governments and the EU.

In the climate change/greenhouse gas debate over the last 20 years, by contrast, the USA not only has a huge investment in fossil fuels through a reliance on coal, electricity and gas, but also has a higher-cost and less efficient energy industry compared with that of Europe. The resistance to greenhouse gas regulation on the part of the private economic interests involved has been far more significant, and the US government position accordingly more hostile. This meant rejection of any kind of binding agreement on greenhouse gas emission, such as the 1997 Kyoto Protocol on climate change. Similar resistance is to be found on the part of other economic interests and governments implicated in fossil fuel burning, including rapidly industrializing nations such as China and India, the OPEC oil cartel and leading coal exporters such as Australia. This resistance remained a key obstacle to recent attempts in Copenhagen to negotiate a post-Kyoto climate change regime involving binding cuts to greenhouse gas emissions.

Obstacles to government involvement in improved environmental regulation may also emerge from difficulties in the contracting environment, and/or a lack of capacity to implement change. In the former case, the contracting environment that governments and inter-governmental agencies face may not be suited to the enforcement of regulation. If individual states cannot be assured that other states will collaborate in regulation, as has occurred in the climate change area, then they may not be prepared to take action to protect the environment, even though they recognize that a problem exists. This applies especially in cases where nations share the use of common resources, such as the atmosphere or geosphere. Another example is international fisheries management. Here the scientific evidence on overfishing did not lead to effective management owing to difficulties in preventing cheating by some countries on quotas imposed by international agreement. It was only when the more effective device of exclusive economic zones was agreed, allowing more effective policing, that the climate of distrust was partially overcome and more effective steps were taken to manage stocks.

While international bodies may increase governmental concern by providing and disseminating scientific information, their role in enhancing the contractual environment may be crucial to achieving policy development. Inter-governmental bodies serve here as bargaining forums that may remove obstacles to compliance with environmental regulation. This may happen through improved iterated bargaining procedures in which nations build up trust in each other or through the sharing of the costs of monitoring agreements once they are made. This seems to have been the assumption behind the climate change process leading from Kyoto to Copenhagen, but, as it turned out, the assumption was derailed for two reasons. One was scepticism around the scientific accuracy of the IPCC projections, which interests favourable to fossil-fuel burning could use as a legitimate 'reason' for resistance to greater regulation. The other was the inter-governmental trust built up through iterative bargaining was not sufficient to offset North/South divisions between wealthier and poorer nations over who would pay the costs of greater regulation.

A final set of issues affecting the translation of policies into practice centres on the technical, organizational and financial capacity of governments to effect reform. Such issues are especially important for developing countries or post-communist countries in Eastern Europe whose abilities to implement much-needed environmental policies are restricted by lack of resources. Here, international institutions have often provided both expert and financial advice to governments and other bodies.

Expertise has been brought to bear on issues such as agricultural pesticides through the Food and Agriculture Organization (FAO), while the International Maritime Organization's World Maritime University offers training to ship captains in the application of environmental regulations. An area in which financial assistance has been forthcoming is that of ozone depletion. Here a fund exists to help less developed countries find alternatives to CFCs. There are, however, significant general problems with arrangements of this type. First, the financial support is often very limited. Second, in a number of areas such as maritime oil pollution, there has been little upgrading of the responsive capacity of developing countries.

Environmental protection is both intrinsically important to the social ecology of globalization and as a case study in the operation of global politics. What is striking about this case is the simultaneous involvement of nation states as key players, with a wider multi-actor system of environmental regulation. The point here is neither that all environmental problems are now being addressed through effective compliance with regulation, nor that such regulations as exist are optimal for the environment. It is rather that, in the space of less than a century, from a time when the League of Nations was reluctant to get involved at all in environmental issues, there now exists a significant if incomplete global institutionalization of environmental protection.

Among the actors in this arena, the larger and/or wealthier states are a major force. For Chasek, Downie and Brown (2006: 41) they are the most important actors, especially in the formation of environmental governance regimes, although non-state actors are seen as growing in significance. This judgement is similar to that of Braithwaite and Drahos (2000: 270ff), who argue that nation states are 'often' the key actors, but are wary of turning this into a general theory. This is partly because nation states rarely instigate an environmental policy, but rather respond to external interests, whether corporate or based on public opinion. Policy change, as Levy, Keohane and Haas (1993) point out, typically arises from domestic environmental opinion at least in democratic societies. However, Braithwaite and Drahos go on to add that this opinion often crosses borders and is frequently taken up by international organizations before nations do so. It also often takes public pressure around a disaster (as in the oil spill regulatory regime) before nations acts. Knowledge and science matter too, though, as the recent climate change case makes clear, the conflation of science with politics tends to undermine appeals to science as a neutral technical arbiter of policy debate.

The particular case study of environmental protection shows that even in a world where nation states continue to be robust and resilient, they cannot be said to dominate global politics. Behind decisions taken by states, including those to cooperate or resist environmental protection, lay a range of other influences. Discussion now takes this case study as an exemplification of a wider model of global politics.

Conceptualizing Global Politics

A key question that has both engaged and perplexed commentators is whether or not a world order exists and, if so, what form it takes. One conceptual difficulty here is that the term 'order' has both sociological and normative connotations, and the two are often hard to separate. Order in the former sense might mean absence of conflict, yet this might be based on thorough-going coercion rather than consensus and thus not qualify as normative order of a desirable kind. Many commentators are, for example, loathe to describe what they see as an unjust global system, built on massive North–South inequalities, as orderly in any normative sense.

A number of attempts have, nonetheless, been made to identify the major social regularities and patterns of the global political order. McGrew (1992: 22) has very usefully identified three major paradigms, namely realism and neo-realism, liberal-pluralism and neo-Marxism, relevant to this exercise. These are differentiated according to types of dominant actors, political processes and forms of order involved.

Realist approaches, for example, take nation states and inter-governmental organizations to be the dominant actors in a world which is largely anarchic. Bargaining and conflict between states are the principal political processes at work within a global polity. This essentially interstate system is regulated primarily through the balance of power. The emphasis that this approach gives to the robustness of the nation state and interstate bargaining is important, especially in the light of premature declarations of the death of the nation. At the same time, global politics is clearly not composed simply of nation states. Other types of actor are involved, ranging from the MNEs and economic regulatory bodies that McGrew associates with neo-Marxist thinking to the wider range of UN social agencies and non-governmental bodies dealing with human rights and social justice, included in the longer list of dominant actors developed in liberal-pluralism thought.

If realism has the demerit of too narrow a view of the dominant players, its state-centred view of the political processes of the global polity is also vulnerable to criticism by the neo-Marxist emphasis on the political economy of the global division of labour constituted through MNEs as well as nation states. Neo-Marxist global political economy, with its emphasis on capital accumulation and class in the analysis of global investment and the operations of the IMF and World Bank, is an important corrective to narrowly realist depictions of global politics in terms of international security issues.

Liberal-pluralism sees multiple interests and actors involved in global politics, not simply nation states or organizations representing capital and labour. It encourages a more multidimensional account of political processes than either neo-Marxism or realism. Global political issues such as human rights and environmentalism are thereby recognized in their own terms rather than as moments in the global conflict between capital and labour, or issues solely pursued and resolved through the interaction of states.

What liberal-pluralism also adds to both realism and neo-Marxism is an alternative to solely interest-based, conflict-centred models of global order, be these between nations classes or civilizations. While liberal-pluralism may in turn be criticized for being insufficiently conflict-centred, it has merit in exploring the shift to consensual processes of global politics, especially where normative influences are evident. Norms, in the form of shared values, are seen by 'world society' theorists like John Meyer (Meyer *et al.*, 1997) as indicators of convergence between nation states around the desirability of economic development, improved education, human rights and environmental responsibility.

A final set of issues concerns differing conceptions of global order. Here, the realist conception of the interstate system is a necessary but insufficient model of global politics. It is hard to see how global socio-economic inequalities can be accounted for without greater emphasis on neo-Marxist political economy, especially as it affects the terms upon which nations are involved in trade, investment and technology transfer. The alternative and wider liberal-pluralist case in favour of global management or regulation as an increasingly overarching political framework depends on the argument that the neo-Marxist critique of realism is still too narrow, one-dimensional and reductionist. In other words, not all global political decisions are to be explained in terms of the operation of a single capitalist logic. Whether and how nuclear weapons proliferation, human rights, or environmental protection is regulated depends on more complex processes in which a range of political as well as economic interests are at stake, in which global capital does not have unilateral sway, and in which a range of governmental and non-governmental actors are involved.

The comparison of these three paradigms yields a number of general insights. These encourage us to picture global politics in terms of a multiplicity of linkages that operate across political and cultural boundaries. These are not simply inter-governmental processes, but are also the multiplicity of interconnections linking NGOs (both commercial and non-profit-making), social movements and individuals. These link producers with consumers, scientists and professionals in various countries with each other, extended families spread across diasporic migrant chains, members of worldwide churches, sporting groups preparing for the Olympic Games and the treasuries and education departments of different nations and regions, as well as bodies such as the WHO and Amnesty International.

In *Making Globalization* (Holton, 2005), the idea of webs is explored as one of a number of ways of thinking about global patterning, connectivity and interdependence. The array of conceptual types ranged from highly organized patterns, such as systems and structures, at one end of the spectrum through more loosely coupled arrangements, such as webs and networks in the middle, to the theoretical possibility of fundamental disorder even randomness, at the other end. The point of such an array, following Weber's work on concept formation, is not to torture the evidence to fit one of other conceptual type, since multiple types may co-exist, but rather to assist in clarifying the various logics of social relationships. As applied to the global polity, it may be said that the notion of webs is better able to make sense of global political complexity, and especially complexity derived from the multiple actors and interests involved, than highly structured theories based around states or corporations alone, or in conjunction. Webs, or indeed networks, are not, however, alternatives to state-centric realism or a political economy founded on corporations, but rather a way of conceiving of interactions, conflicts and cooperation between states, corporations, international organizations and the multiple elements of global civil society.

Braithwaite and Drahos (2000: 550–9), in their analysis of global business regulation, provide a more generally applicable typology of webs, including 'webs of control', 'webs of dialogue', 'webs of influence' and 'webs of reward and coercion'. Among the 500 global regulators they interviewed for this research, in areas ranging from trade and finance to labour standards and the environment, most had a strong preference for dialogue with other parties rather than coercion. This seems partly a matter of normative preference and partly because dialogue, if successful, is less costly than coercion.

Yet dialogue is not exactly the same thing as democracy, inasmuch as many voices and interests are missing or under-represented in global political dialogue. Most if not all regulators are part of a global governance elite whose existence, dynamics and preoccupations are scarcely visible to the world's poor, hungry and sick. Access to global political dialogues and the possibility of influencing them has certainly widened in the post-colonial period, both in terms of the participation of post-colonial states and civil society activists. Yet access to dialogue remains skewed to the powerful, who are simultaneously capable of using coercion – whether military or economic – as well as influence achieved through dialogue.

Braithwaite and Drahos make the obvious point that coercion in business regulation is very much the prerogative of strong nation states, mainly the USA but also China, and the interstate European Union, as well as international organizations like the IMF and World Bank. Within the global polity it may be seen at work in examples such as the use of bilateral trade sanctions by the US government to globalize the intellectual property rights of US corporations, or through the conditionality rules applied by the IMF to their provision of financial assistance to countries in financial crisis. Even so, Braithwaite and Drahos also claim that influence is a more widely used strategy (ibid.: 557–9), even by the powerful, in that it may be a better way of achieving compliance. Influence achieved through dialogue and negotiation also leaves resource-poor actors less disadvantaged than they might otherwise be, especially where NGOs and social movements put moral and political pressure on rich country governments. One example is the largely successful Jubilee 2000 campaign for debt cancellation for the poorest nations. Yet, for all this, the global polity remains profoundly unequal and global governance elites vulnerable to charges of mismanagement, especially, as the global financial crisis revealed, in terms of the mismanagement of global risk.

Conclusion

This chapter asked whether there exists a global polity. The argument is that there does. This does not mean the end of the nation state, still less the advent of world government. But it does mean that nation states are now only one element in a more complex global political arena. The institutions of global governance also include international organizations, private corporations and the range of movements and activities, captured under the notion of global civil society. This range of actors, interact, conflict and sometimes cooperate with each other, often through webs or networks within which dialogues and influence as well as power are evident. This world is not easy to capture if attention is given solely to national governments and the parliamentary arena alone.

The global polity is characterized not only by complexity, but also by inequality. There exists a huge global democracy deficit, which colonial independence and the growth of civil society activism in Asia and Africa has been unable to fundamentally correct. However size also matters, in the sense that smaller and poorer nation states and national societies are disadvantaged in comparison with larger nation states like China, Brazil and India. Focusing on state power and the political autonomy of states alone does not, however, fully explain which issues come to dominate the global political agenda, nor how cross-border issues like environmental protection or human rights play out in the wider dynamics of world opinion and popular political mobilization. States respond to events and opinion changes, as well as to each other, as much as following predetermined and proactive global political strategies.

In the previous three chapters most of the focus has been on economic and political aspects of globalization and their relationship with nation states. In the next two chapters, attention shifts to culture and its relationship with the polity and economy. This brings into focus the themes of nationalism and of cultural identities in an epoch of globalization.

6

Nationalism and Ethnicity in a Globalizing World

The social dynamics of the late twentieth and early twenty-first century have confounded social scientists and political actors alike. Conventional certainties and widely held predictions about the future have been undermined. This is partly the result of specific events like 9/11, which destroyed any sense that powerful Western countries were secure against global terrorism, or the global financial crisis, which has revealed that self-regulating financial markets are no protection against market risks and severe economic instability.

Contemporary unease has also been heightened where social change takes on seemingly new characteristics or seems to return to features of an older world thought to be obsolete. The revival of nationalism and resilience of ethnicity are often taken to be a reassertion of past allegiances. Meanwhile, the emergence of multiculturalism, a new development connected with global migration and settlement, is suggestive of post-national identities which sit uneasily with older conceptions of national citizenship.

In this chapter attention will be given to the recent resurgence of nationalism and ethnicity, and the extent to which they set limits to globalization. In the first section, three possible relationships between nationalism and globalization are outlined. Some initial comments are also made about conceptual and historical myths and misconceptions in understandings of nations, ethnicity and multiculturalism. The analysis in the second part of the chapter involves a more elaborated discussion of theories of the nation state, nationalism and ethnicity. In the final part of the chapter, discussion returns to a more explicit focus on globalization and ways in which the national and the global intersect, conflict and sometimes combine.

Some Initial Conceptual and Historical Guidelines

There are, broadly speaking, three ways of looking at the relationship between globalization and nationalism (see Table 6.1).

The first is to see globalization as a process whose radical cross-border character transforms and transcends both national institutions and national identities. Such assumptions are to be found in certain versions of modernization theory (Hobsbawm, 1990). They are also evident in many 'first wave' or 'hyper-globalist' theories of globalization. Just as globalization is seen as supplanting the nation as the centre-point of markets (elaborated in Chapter 3), the fount of sovereignty and focus of governance (elaborated in Chapters 4 and 5), so similar processes are said to be at work in relation to allegiance and identity. Here nationalism gives way to a range of possible alternatives. These include individualism, global consumer culture and cosmopolitanism, the latter founded on citizenship of the world not the nation.

Table 6.1 Simple theories of globalization and nationalism

---
1. Globalization triumphs over nationalism
2. Nationalism remains resilient in the face of globalization
3. Globalization and nationalism are mutually supportive

Such theories have come under increasing challenge, not so much because the reality of globalization is denied as from the persistence, robustness and resilience of nationalism. Just as nation states do not disappear, as we saw in earlier chapters, so nationalism itself remains intact as a major popular resistance to globalization. At face value, this is reflected in developments such as the Balkan wars of the 1990s, part of a longer history of ethnic cleansing (Mann, 2005), in responses to 9/11 involving national political mobilization against external threats and in high levels of popular anxiety to continuing culturally diverse immigration. Borders still matter, not simply to nation states and political institutions, but also to the ways in which national communities are imagined. Bans in countries like Belgium of Islamic forms of dress like the burka reflect this.

How far then does the contemporary eruption of apparently primordial loyalties and hatreds around nationhood represent a major limit to the process and scope of globalization? Many certainly see the revival of nationalism and ethnicity as resistance to a global world where boundaries are permeable, power inequalities massive and all is in flux (Kellner, 1998; Falk, 2000). National identity, especially where it is over-laid with a sense of ethnic solidarity, is seen as offering some kind of stable anchor for identity and political security in an age where imper-sonal global capital predominates. This argument has been connected with another which assumes that the primary allegiances of most populations are with particular national or local political and cultural traditions, allegiances and institutions. These, so it is supposed, have endured from the past, but have now been rekindled by resistance to globalization, seen as a universal but rootless process unable to secure popular attachment. Such assumptions are not, however, securely grounded and require further critical examination.

One of the major difficulties here is that nationalism and ethnicity are presumed to be old, while globalization is usually seen as new. The former may then be presented as a 'natural' feature of life, contrasted with the artificial or shallow nature of global ties and connections. This in turn may suggest our allegiances start out from people and things close to us, radiating outward to nation, and only then, if at all, beyond that to global allegiances that are inevitably more remote. This progres-sion from the local to the national and possibly global is sometimes taken as a critical argument against the feasibility of cosmopolitanism or global multiculturalism.

Hutchinson (2005) is one of the few to develop the argument that nationalism and globalization have long intersecting histories, and this leads him and some other scholars (Robertson, 1992; Holton, 2009) to a third theoretical position. Here, the two seemingly opposing phenomena of globalization and nationalism may, under certain conditions, co-exist and even sometimes support or encourage each other. Globalization does not lead inexorably to the death of nationalism. Equally, while resilient nationalism sometimes resists globalization, at other times the two are linked. The task, then, is to tease out the forms of interaction involved.

Just as ethnicity and senses of peoplehood may be traced back over many centuries, even millennia (Smith, 1986, 1995), so too can the history of globalization. And this applies not simply to long-distance trade or technology transfer, but to the functioning of empires and to allegiance, especially to forms of religious globalization associated with Christianity and Islam. Both these world-religions consider the world as a single space encouraging trans-local commitment. This long-run history may also be connected with relatively stable forms of multi-ethnicity and multiculturalism, which are also very far from being recent developments engendered by contemporary globalization. Both Sen (2005) and Appiah (2006) provide examples ranging from medieval Andalucia to the sixteenth-century India of Emperor Akbar, seventeenth-century Holland and the Ottoman Middle East. Such practical instances of multi-ethnicity are older than the classic phases of nationalism beginning in the late eighteenth and nineteenth centuries.

Multi-ethnicity, then, involves members of different peoples living in mixed communities, cities and empires, whether brought together by trade, migration or enslavement. Demographic multiculturalism is therefore evident, whether in the first-century Roman Empire, tenth-century Byzantium, or contemporary London. Multi-ethnic or multicultural spaces are not something new and challenging to older ideas of ethnic separation or nationhood, simply the product of recent global migration. They are themselves arrangements with a long history which preceded the modern world of nation states. Individual nation states have then often been carved out of multi-ethnic spaces, by external powers and through warfare. This is evident, for example, in the recent history of the Middle East and the creation of Israel, Palestine, Lebanon and Iraq, out of a complex geography, where individual peoples lived among each other, often in relative peace, as well as stretching across previous as much as recent political boundaries.

If humanity has been a travelling species from the outset, then there has never been an original long-standing world of primordial difference located in separate territories, which only later became disturbed by globalization in the form of Empire, migration, religious expansion, technology transfer and new forms of communication. Later disturbances may have intensified change, but they did not instigate an entirely new process that challenged an essentially older one. In this sense nationhood is no more or less natural than multi-ethnicity, nor is ethnicity any more primordial than the searches for multicultural or cosmopolitan harmony detectable throughout history (for a review of the historical evidence in support of this argument, see Holton, 2009).

One specific way that globalization may further nationalism is by diffusing nationalism as a form of political mobilization and institution-building from one context to another, as ideas and influences cross borders. This happened in the nineteenth and twentieth centuries in post-colonial settings from North and South America, through central Europe to Ireland, India, China, Africa and the Caribbean. For Hutchinson (2005), ethnic groups may also be the agents of cross-border processes; for example, as harbingers of world-religions or through business networks. He also suggests that the experience of participating in global processes may serve to consolidate ethnicity as a cohesive social force within a wider, more diffuse and unstable environment. In this sense ethnicity may serve as a social core, acting as the forerunner of nation state construction.

Even stronger positive connections between globalization and nationalism may exist where movements and institutions seek to combine global and national elements, elaborating norms developed in sets of particular nations or regions, such as social justice or human rights, as a basis for global order. Nationalisms with a more civil rather than primordial character may feed into cosmopolitanism, rather than being fundamentally at odds with it (Appiah, 1996; Kleingeld, 1999; Malachuk, 2007). This in turn raises issues about the possibility of a post-national world in which new forms of multiculturalism are emerging, which are somehow 'glocal' in form, combining global and local/national elements.

A final conceptual issue worthy of mention in these introductory comments is the coherence of the idea of multiculturalism. This is clearly a particularly confusing term with multiple meanings (Rex, 1995) that stretch through social theory and political philosophy to the sociology of culture and public policy discourses. It may, as Appiah (2006: xiii) suggests, be too inconsistent for any useful purpose, serving as a 'shape shifter', sometimes designating unconditional support for any and all cultural differences, while at other times coming closer to an updated form of liberal-democratic inclusion, claimed as suitable for a global world of culturally diverse cross-border migration, minority politics and multi-ethnic religious mobilization.

Confusions over the meaning of multiculturalism derive in part from tendencies to oversimplify the issues and processes at stake, as if there were only one form of multiculturalism, which one can then move on swiftly to denounce or applaud. One instance of this has been a tendency to assume forms of multiculturalism developed in the USA around cultural separatism apply across the board in all other contexts, including settings like Australia and Canada. Here contrasting emphases placing multiculturalism within liberal-democratic citizenship were significant in the 1970s and 1980s (Hawkins, 1989; Richmond, 1991; Kymlicka, 1995). Joppke and Lukes (1999a: 1), in their otherwise thoughtful survey of multicultural questions, assume quite arbitrarily that 'multiculturalism has mostly appeared as a polemical attack on key tenets of liberal societies and states' including universalism, nationhood, citizenship and individual rights. This is to oversimplify a far more complex set of variations and cross-currents.

Since the language of multiculturalism persists in political practice and policy discourse as much as social theory (Rex and Singh 2003), it remains important to clarify the different senses in which it appears in discourse, as well the problems and insights that may flow from them. Following Pieterse (2007), multiculturalism may signify both the demography of different cultures living in the same space, or may represent institutional changes, linked with policies of citizenship rights, cultural recognition and equal opportunity. It may also function as an ideology of sectional group advantage, rather than as a unifying form of social inclusion. And where it does have more inclusive and solidaristic elements, these may attach to national or wider cross-national entities, which, at their widest, embrace forms of vernacular cosmopolitanism (Werbner, 1999; Holton, 2009).

The historical and conceptual guidelines sketched here, serve as a way of conducting arguments about globalization and the nation state, ethnicity and multiculturalism, that avoids historical myth and simplistic conceptual dichotomies. Within this context, discussion now proceeds to a more detailed analysis of theories of nationalism and the relationship between varieties of nationalism, ethnicity and multiculturalism. We shall then revisit the broad question of relationships between nationalism and globalization.

Nationalism and the Nation State

Contemporary nationalism, in one shape or form, is evident on almost every continent, defying the projections of both Marxism and modernization theory. Whether in Western Europe, the Balkans, central Asia, Africa, or Latin America, the appeal to nation as a source of cultural identity and political security has, on most occasions, proved more powerful than the claims of social class. In addition, nationalism, in certain of its manifestations, also threatens the liberal-democratic model of a secular society of freestanding individuals able to secure their interests through the market and citizenship rights. A tragic aspect of this is the links between nationalism and racism or extremist forms of ethnicity.

These have been seen throughout the twentieth century in episodes of genocide designed to wipe out whole peoples, such as the Nazi genocide of European Jews in the 1930s and 1940s, in the name of the German fatherland and Aryan 'racial purity'. They have also been seen more recently in episodes of 'ethnic cleansing', where populations of a particular ethnicity or national identity have been forcibly moved out of territory they may have occupied for centuries, as in Balkan conflicts of the 1990s involving Serbs, Croats and Bosnian Muslims. Further examples linking nation with an exclusive sense of peoplehood are evident in Israeli–Palestinian conflict, with Israeli Jewish displacement of Palestinians from their historic territories, and conversely radical Palestinian threats to destroy Israel. Such developments have shaken the complacency of Western commentators who thought that the end of the Cold War automatically meant the triumph of liberal-democratic politics.

The wide range of contexts in which nationalism has arisen and the different forms it has taken are evident from even a cursory inspection of the history of the past 250 years and academic commentaries on the topic. Nationalism has been conceived, for example, as political or cultural, unificatory or fragmentating, ethnocentric or polycentric, and progressive or reactionary. Leaving these binary conceptual distinctions aside for the moment, it is instructive to note the distinction between three contemporary types. The first involves the association of nationalism with *democratic struggles* against autocracy and monarchical dynasticism, often with a strong internationalist tone, as in the American and French revolutions of the late eighteenth century. The second is connected with *anti-colonial struggles* against European powers by political movements in Africa and Asia, seeking to project a sense of the national community beyond tribalism. Post-colonial nationalism has sometimes projected wider trans-national aspirations, as in pan-Arabism and pan-Africanism. The third comprises *anti-liberal and chauvinistic* forms of nationalism. In this, nationalism is linked not with claims about the common aspirations of some wider entity, such as humanity or the African peoples, but with the exclusive and often racist claims of a particular people, defined as culturally distinct from and often superior to others. It is this version of nationalism that may, in extreme forms, be used to license genocide and 'ethnic cleansing'. Well-known examples include the Nazi Holocaust against the Jews and the more recent inter-ethnic conflicts in the Balkans.

Each of these examples has a complex history of its own, and the place of nationalism and ethnicity in each also varies. Yet the underlying logic to all such cases is that identity, political loyalty and political action are based on membership of a national community or people. Where analytical differences arise is, first, in how a nation is conceived and, second, in how a nation is seen to articulate with both transnational and sub-national social groups.

As indicated in earlier chapters, the institution of the nation state represents an amalgam of two entities: the state as a set of political institutions and the nation, conceived of as the political and cultural community of a people. These distinct entities have often been confused and conflated, leading to notorious difficulties in defining exactly what a nation actually is. Walker Connor regards the shorthand use of the term nation to refer to either or both of the following:

- a sense of peoplehood
- a political institution.

This has contributed to a 'terminological chaos' in discourses on nation and nationalism (Connor, 1987). One example of this is the failure to distinguish between nationalism as loyalty to the state (something Connor prefers to label patriotism) and nationalism as loyalty to a nation or people.

Failure to distinguish the two for purposes of analysis has created several problems. One is that many people are able to identify with the nation as a cultural and historical identity without necessarily identifying with the current political institutions embodied in the national state. One could be a staunch Greek nationalist under the dictatorship of the colonels without supporting the Greek state of that era, just as liberal-democratic German nationalists under the Kaiser could support and identify with the nation while criticizing the monarchist form of state. A second problem is that states can be established without necessarily being attached to strong bodies of nationalist feeling. This often occurred in the post-war process of decolonization, when the same arbitrary borders that colonial powers imposed on the territories they annexed were subsequently used as the boundaries for new post-colonial states even though they typically encompassed a range of tribal and ethnic groups. In Europe, too, it is clear that nations such as the UK are not composed of a single people or ethnicity. The UK contains the Scots, Welsh and Irish as well as the English, while Spain contains Basques and Catalans. For Connor, only a minority of nation states, such as Iceland, Japan, or Norway, are sufficiently homogeneous to be described as nation states.

Connor uses evidence of this kind to dispute as facile the proposition that the world is composed of nation states. The world may well be divided into states based upon claims of exclusive juridical sovereignty within a given territory. However, such entities are more typically multi-ethnic or multinational, in the sense of being composed of a range of peoples. The typology of relations between states and peoples given in Table 6.2 is therefore proposed. Here, states vary according to the number of peoples within them, the number of peoples whose homeland is within some part of the state, and the particular impact of immigration on patterns of state-building. Mestizo states, for example, are a category limited to Latin America based on a population of those with joint European-Amerindian ancestry, contrasted with multi-homeland multinational states, such as Nigeria and the former Soviet Union, containing the homelands of many peoples.

Another set of definitional and conceptual problems stems from the emotionality and normativity of terms such as 'national' and 'nationalism'. This normativity is reflected in Ernest Gellner's minimal definition of nationalism as a 'principle which holds that the political

Table 6.2 A typology of relations between state and nation

Type	Characteristic	Examples
Nation states	Extremely homogeneous	Iceland, Japan
Multination states	Ethnic diversity	
1. Unihomeland	Ethnic mix due to immigration, but claimed as home by only one group	Sri Lankan Sinhalese Malaysian Malays
2. Multihomeland	Ethnic mix, but claimed as home by more than one group	Former Soviet Union Nigeria
3. Non-homeland	Ethnic mix due to immigration, but no group sees the territory as the homeland	Caribbean states such as Guyana or Trinidad-Tobago
Immigrant states	Integration of ethnic mix into a single nation, without that being a historic homeland	USA
Mestizo states	European-Amer-indian mix	Latin America

Source: Adapted from Connor (1994: 77–84).

and national unit *should* be congruent' (1983: 1) (emphasis added). The proposition that polity and nation should coincide is deep-seated but also profoundly contested. For some, nation is a sublime and sacred entity; for others, it is one fundamental root cause of violence, suffering and illusion. We are dealing here not simply with ostensibly neutral social science concepts, but with matters that are charged with high levels of emotional force and embedded in often deeply held values. Nations in this sense typically have moral and aesthetic personalities, both to adherents who identify nations with positive values and all that is beautiful, and to opponents who associate nationalism with all that is bad, evil, irrational and ugly.

These simple dichotomies born of political commitment and intense social psychological engagement do, however, skew the analysis of nationalism to only some of its more powerful exemplifications. Michael Billig (1995) has cautioned against stereotyping nationalism as extremism, gripped by intense emotion and embroiled in violent pathological modes of political action. To think solely in these terms, he claims, is to neglect more mundane or banal forms of nationalism, embedded in the everyday life of nations that are more politically settled and peaceful, such as the USA or many parts of Western Europe. The national flags that hang almost unnoticed on public buildings symbolize this latter form of nationalism and stand in contrast to 'hot' activist forms of nationalism, in which flags are waved in the course of conflict and political mobilization. While the Irish tricolour is waved as a gesture of nationalist defiance of British sovereignty by many Catholics in Northern Ireland, the same flag hangs on public buildings in the Irish Republic as a more mundane symbol of nation-hood. Yet such mundane or banal phenomena are neglected by liberal theorists of nationalism, who see only irrational pathology and atavistic social aspirations.

Notwithstanding this array of difficulties, analysts of nationalism have taken a range of positions on the relationship between the two parts of the amalgam of nation state.

Theories of Nationalism and the Nation State

Hutchinson (1994) has distinguished between primordialist, modernist and ethnicist interpretations of nationalism. The primordial position argues that nations represent ancient 'natural' loyalties that originated in the mists of time but which have nonetheless driven the recent historical emergence of the nation state. Herder, the eighteenth-century German theorist of nationhood, and Bagehot, the nineteenth-century English political commentator, both, in their different ways, saw the nation state arising from the aspirations of a people (or Volk). This implied that peoples create and have a right to create political institutions. Nations come first, states come next, albeit in organic union with each other.

The appeal to historical roots is exactly how nationalist movements understand and present themselves to the world. The problem with this view is, however, that national consciousness appears to be a comparatively recent phenomenon, one which in many, although not all, respects post-dates the formation of nation states. Both Mann (1986) writing of England and Braudel (1988) of France make the point that, in late medieval and early modern times, most inhabitants of these two countries did not conceive of themselves as English or French, nor did they speak a standard language. Until the French Revolution of 1789, there was no national French flag, while the language of the Declaration of the Rights of Man was spoken by only a minority of the population (Billig, 1995: 25).

The further back in history one goes, the greater the degree of inter-group mixture cultural complexity is evident in the make-up of groups that today regard themselves as a distinct people with a continuous historical integrity. This is reflected in an ironic remark attributed to Israel Zangwill that if we 'turn time's cinematograph back far enough ... the Germans are found to be French and the French Germans'. By this, he means that the French nation was constructed on lands settled by the Germanic Franks, Burgundians, Visigoths and Normans, while modern Germany comprises lands in which Celts as well as Germanic tribes settled. Even in the mid- to late nineteenth century, there is evidence to suggest that many Europeans, especially those from rural and less educated backgrounds, identified primarily with local or regional entities rather than with the nation (Weber, 1976). Most late nineteenth-century migrants to the USA identified themselves in the official migration documents, 'as Neapolitan, Calabrian and the like, but not Italian ... Gorali, Kashubi, Silesian and so on, but not Polish' (Thernstrom, 1980, cited in Connor, 1994: 221).

Such criticisms have given credibility to an alternative approach to the analysis of nations and nationalism that may be termed 'modernist'. For analysts such as Gellner and Hobsbawm, nationalism is a modern phenomenon linked with processes such as the rise of the nation state, industrialization and the development of modern capitalism. In spite of its apparent appeal to the past, nationalism is seen as an invented tradition, fostered more by intellectuals and manipulated by political elites and special interest groups. These are the key mechanisms behind groundswells of spontaneous popular enthusiasm rather than the reawakening of ancient traditions. Hobsbawm cites the following comment by the nineteenth-century Italian nationalist Massimo d'Azeglio on the achievement of Italian unification: 'We have made Italy, now we have to make Italians' (Hobsbawm 1990: 44). The implication is that national feeling has now to be created by those political actors and nationalist intellectuals who had driven forward the unification process to military and *realpolitik* success. What pre-existed this process, as far as the populace was concerned, was regional and/or local affiliation embedded in regional languages and dialects.

Gellner (1983) sees nationalism emerging when the institution of the state has already emerged in stable form. This is connected with the transition from what he calls agro-literate to industrial societies. In the former, there was no tendency to connect political power with cultural boundaries. Privileged elites typically accentuated their distinction from the remainder of society without recourse to cultural imperialism or the cultural homogeneity of the political unit. There was no need for such congruence where hierarchy prevailed, and most of the population was 'laterally insulated' from each other in agricultural communities (ibid.: 9).

Industrial societies, in contrast, depend on much higher levels of standardization in technological competence and communication. One response to this is the drive to create a standardized national language.

At the same time, the commitment of industrial societies to perpetual growth within a specialized division of labour requires high levels of literacy, which can only be delivered by centralized systems of education. Socialization takes place outside local intimate social relations. This creates problems in finding some new principle of social integration that can tie together the new industrial state with the cultural order in a way that is suitably standardized. For Gellner, nationalism is such a principle. It is not to be seen primordially as 'the awakening of an old, latent, dormant force, though that is how it does indeed present itself. [Rather] it is ... the consequence of a new form of social organization, based on deeply internalized, education-dependent high cultures' (ibid.: 48). In the longer term, however, once industrialization is achieved, the intensity of nationalism declines.

One problem here is that the argument works better for Western than for Eastern Europe or the post-colonial states. As Hutchinson (1994: 21) points out, nationalism pre-dates industrialization. Gellner had himself considered this kind of objection in attempting a typology of nationalisms (1983: 88–109). This investigated the effect of variations in the structure of power, access to education and literacy, and levels of cultural unity on varieties of nationalist experience. One distinction drawn was between the conditions under which nationalism emerged in Western and Eastern Europe. In the latter, where industrialism was less well developed and access to high culture limited, as in the Hapsburg lands of Central and Eastern Europe, nationalism tended towards ethnically driven fragmentation and Balkanization. In the West, in contrast, where industrialization developed more rapidly and literacy was more advanced, unifying forms of liberal nationalism were more evident.

Whether this analysis of diverse forms of nationalism leaves Gellner's general theory intact is, however, debatable. This is partly because he has to dilute the bold proposition that the state precedes nationalism in order to deal with cases where the reverse is true. However, it is also because of underlying difficulties in holding to an entirely endogenous approach to nationalism, in which the conditions for its emergence in any particular location are related solely to the modernizing characteristics of the territory within which it emerges. Gellner recognizes that a broader cross-national focus is required in certain residual cases, as in the diasporic nationalism of groups such as Zionist Jews, but fails to develop the point very far to look at nationalism as a paradoxical force that both moves across borders to animate new groups and creates or reinforces other boundaries.

An alternative argument linking nationalism and modernity is offered by Eric Hobsbawm. He sees the nation state as the most suitable political framework for the development and reproduction of modern capitalism rather than industrialization *per se.* Hobsbawm is also critical of Gellner's excessively top-down approach to nationalism, preferring to see it as a 'dual phenomenon'; that is, the product of both popular aspirations 'from below' as well as capitalist development and state-building 'from above' (Hobsbawm, 1990: 10). Such developments do not, however, return us to an emphasis on the primordial, but lead into ideas of the invention of tradition and the recasting of older traditions into nationalist form.

The Invention of Tradition

The idea of the invention of tradition, historically elaborated in Hobsbawm and Ranger (1983), proposes that the seeming age-old myths and rituals of nationhood are comparatively recent inventions rather than primordial sentiments existing in some kind of unbroken line of *succession* from the dim and distant past. Hobsbawm notes, for example, national anthems, national flags and the personification of nations in symbols such as Marianne (France) or the Yankee Uncle Sam have been invented as 'entirely new symbols and devices' in the period since the 1740s (1990: 7).

Some traditions, of course, depend on older materials, although even here the extent of accretion and discontinuity is significant. In Britain, for example, myths of King Alfred or King Arthur and the Knights of the Round Table, as episodes in the history of the English or British race, represent retrospective reconstructions of a speculative history that is very much mythical. Whether or not such figures existed – the evidence for figures such as Arthur being very slender (Williams, 1994) – and whether they perceived themselves as English or British is beside the point. What is more salient is the way in which mythical stories about their deeds and exploits have been reinvented and recast in broader stories about the ancient character of nationhood. These seek out an intimate connection with institutions like monarchy and Christendom, or values such as courage and honour. Myths of Arthur and knights such as Lancelot were appropriated by late medieval Cistercian monks as spiritual figures, by the English Tudor kings to assist in legitimizing a secular claim to the throne and by nineteenth-century poets such as Tennyson to celebrate a more recognizably British nationalist past (ibid.). Aspects of nineteenth-century stories such as the Holy Grail, the Round Table or the magician Merlin are not there, so to speak, in the earliest original, but over time become accretions tying in with aspects of the reinvented story that suit a succession of religious, secular and nationalist purposes.

Nations, as Benedict Anderson (1983) has pointed out, function as 'imagined communities'. By this, he means that those who identify with a particular nation will never meet in a face-to-face way with all those others who are attached to the nation. Rather, they rely on images of the nation as a people, such that 'in the minds of each lives the image of their communion' (6). For Anderson, this process of imagining was historically dependent on the invention of mechanical printing and the mass production of the printed word in vernacular rather than arcane priestly languages (for example, Latin). This renders nationalism a relatively modern development of the past 350 years. The common features of the imagined nation are its bounded nature, its sovereign freedom within a bounded territory and, finally, its constitution as a community, regardless of other marks of difference, such as wealth or status, that may differentiate its members.

Unlike Gellner, Anderson sees nationalism as a more gradual product of social change. His analysis is also less trapped within a primarily endogenous framework. More note is taken of cross-border flows of nationalist feeling and political mobilization, as in the idea of long-distance nationalism' (Anderson, 1994). This refers to the operation of diasporic nationalist sentiments carried across borders through the global mobility of people, technology and cultural representations. This approach has been very ably developed by Skrbis (1999), in relation to the cross-border character of much recent Balkan nationalism, linking Australia and South America with Europe.

This move beyond an endogenous framework has been taken furthest in Robertson's concept of the global field (1992, 1995). This draws attention to the processes whereby, once some peoples have achieved the status of nation state, combining political institutions with a sense of national community, all those who see themselves as peoples seek the status of a nation state. In this way, national minorities within the former Spanish, Austro-Hungarian, Ottoman, French, or British Empires have sought national self-determination, with many cross-currents and linkages between them. Nationalism and a sense of peoplehood, in cases such as the peoples of nineteenth-century Latin America or twentieth-century Africa and Indo-China, have both pre-dated state formation and drawn on wider trans-national currents of thought and mobilization. In the immediate post-war period, for example, the contact of West African troops serving in Asia as part of the Allied war effort assisted in transmitting the momentum and confidence of Indian nationalism to other parts of the British Empire such as the former Gold Coast, now Ghana.

Modernist accounts of nationalism have provided a valuable and convincing critique of primordial theories. They have also offered considerable insights into certain connections between aspects of modernization, such as capitalist development or printing and literacy, and nationalism. They are nonetheless vulnerable to the criticism that they go too far in emphasizing discontinuity with the past and the novel character of nationalist feeling. This line of critique has been advanced by so-called ethnicist theorists of nationalism, foremost of whom is Anthony Smith (1971, 1986, 1990, 1995). It is also utilized in Pryke's (2009) recent critical review of theoretical debates over nationalism.

One of the most striking difficulties with the modernist position is to explain why individuals and social groups should still adhere to national feeling and national symbols in a modern, secular, and global world. How is it that individualism and self-interest, qualities associated with capitalism and liberalism, do not carry all before them? It is one thing to argue that capitalist institutions such as multinational companies need states to perform certain support functions but quite another to explain why states also become attached to a sense of nationhood based on political community. Even if it is argued that nationalism is fostered and manipulated from above by politicians, intellectuals and the media, it still remains unclear why this particular form of loyalty and identity should be chosen as a basis for adherence. Why not adherence to something smaller, like a city, region, or industry, or something larger, like the world as a whole? If capitalism operates increasingly through global investment, production and marketing strategies, why not organize ideological adherence to a global pattern?

In answering these questions, it is instructive to review the modernist argument that nationalist traditions are invented. This may well be true in the sense that there are few loyalties that can be traced in any kind of unbroken lineage in sentiment and in institutions from the distant past to the present – though senses of the Chinese as a distinct people may be one. To say this is not, however, to say that there are no long-run continuities between older forms of cultural allegiance and identity, and contemporary forms of nationalism. Ethnicity, considered as allegiance to ascriptive ties of history and place, may be one such linkage that spans either side of the supposedly 'Great Transformation' dividing the modern from the pre-modern. Processes like the Industrial Revolution or the French Revolution did not obliterate all previous allegiances and identities.

If the origins and development of nationalism pre-date the eighteenth century, how far back in history should analysis go? While modernists such as Benedict Anderson (1983) emphasize sixteenth- and seventeenth-century developments like innovation in printing and mass publication, there is a strong case for going much further back into the ancient world. Anthony Smith has argued that nationalism emerges where social groups face profound threats, whether from warfare or some other social and spiritual crisis. Warfare has been an endemic aspect of world history that clearly pre-dates the modern world. The crises created by warfare and other threatening processes do not in and of themselves create nationalism or ethnic allegiance. However, the search for a common cultural base around which to mobilize in cases of threatened invasion or colonization encourages the formation of stronger ascriptive loyalties of place and kinship. These may cohere around a range of broad loyalties, including religion, as well as ethnicity and nationhood. Smith (1971: 153–4) cites the example of the revolt of the Zealots against ancient Roman rule between AD66 and AD73, in the name of both God and the Jewish people. Hutchinson (1994: 24) cites the example of the Armenians and Georgians, living on shifting borders between warring Christian and Islamic states, who have retained a strong loyalty combining ethnic and religious components well into the modern period.

These examples indicate a historical sense of peoplehood embedded for the most part in religion and ethnic identity. For Smith they indicate that nationalism has a long history connected with religious tradition and ascriptive ties of ethnicity. It is not, in this sense, a modern invention. Culture in the modern period has not then been a *tabula rasa* on which any kind of content may be inscribed. While changes are evident in forms of nationalism between the ancient and modern worlds, and while much may be put down to modern cultural invention, this does not entirely dispose of continuity. Rather the nation has emerged, sometimes over a very long time period, out of ethno-cultural feelings and sentiments that become embodied in myths about origins and in senses of a common heritage. These components of ethno-cultural community, for example in the traditions of Jewish or Armenian people, persist over longer time-frames than modernists suppose.

This persistence may, according to Smith, be embodied in a range of aesthetic and religious cultural forms as well as military and administrative practices. These speak to the importance of ethno-symbolism in the constitution of ethnicity. Religion is especially important as a bearer of group identity, insofar as the feelings and practices of a people are expressed and codified in forms of writing such as holy books (Smith, 1986). Modern creators of the nation may seek to reinterpret or invent new senses of nation, but they do so in a context of popular attitudes and traditions that set limits to top-down manipulation by intellectuals and elites.

A case in point is the constraint that existing Muslim traditions on the Indian subcontinent had on modernizing nationalists attempting to establish a new secular nation state in the 1930s and 1940s (Ahmed, 1997).

Here the Muslim separatism that led to the establishment of Pakistan
was not simply a product of Muslim elite fears that they would be
swamped by Hindus in post-independence India. It depended also on
a persistent popular cultural tradition on the importance of living in an
Islamic society under Islamic religious law (Robinson 1979).

Modern nations, the argument continues, are often built upon pre-
modern ethnic cores, 'whose myths and memories, values and symbols
shaped the culture and boundaries of the nation that modern elites
managed to forge (Smith, 1990: 180). This has, however, been obscured
by the highly modernist bias built into definitions of nationalism,
which generalize the eighteenth-century American and French revolutions into ideal types. In this way conceptions of nation and nationalism
are associated with liberal-democratic ideals of equal citizenship rights
within the political community. Smith calls this 'polycentric nationalism',
in that it 'resembles the dialogue of many actors on a common stage'
(1971: 158).

The cost of defining nation and nationalism in this way is that
continuities with other ways of conceiving of the political community
of a people are thereby ruled out. The cases from the ancient world,
reviewed above, are regarded by Smith as an alternative type of
ethnocentric nationalism. The commonalities here are not simply
that each refers to the unifying principles that define a people, but,
further, that the ethnocentric type was the historical forerunner of the
polycentric type.

Nationalism: Making Sense of a Complex Debate

How, then, to make sense of the complexities of debates on nationalism?
One option is to take a synthetic approach, combining aspects of the
modernist and ethnicist arguments. This is more powerful than either
approach taken alone. No simple theory of nationalism is adequate.
While there are cases of inheritance of tradition (for example, the Jewish
nation), there are equally cases of invention in which, as Hutchinson
puts it, 'would-be nationalists have to concoct a common past out
of fragmentary memories or conflictual traditions' (1994: 34). French
nationalism appears to be a case of the latter process.

Synthesis between modernist and ethnicist accounts recognizes
continuities as well as contrasts in popular allegiance and cultural
identity between the modern and the pre-modern. It also recognizes
that ethnicity has played an important part in the identity of peoples,

both historically and in the contemporary world. This emphasis on ethnicity is evident, albeit in different ways, in Smith's approach to ethno-history, in Hutchinson's work on cultural nationalism and in Connor's studies of ethno-nationalism. Ethnicity is, in this sense, very far from being an obsolete relic. Yet what is it that makes the connection between ethnicity and nation so powerful and enduring?

Ethnicity and Nationhood

We return now to the question of why it is that nationhood and nationalism have been the form that much political allegiance and identity have taken in the making of the modern world. The answer is complex, relating both to the functions of nationalism as a form of cultural and political mobilization against some kind of threat, and to the attractions of the nation as a cultural symbol rooted in a sense of distinctiveness and boundedness. Ethnicity is one important way in which distinctiveness is conceived and boundedness is established.

As with other key terms, no commonly shared definition of ethnicity exists. One reason for this is that ethnicity is both a form of self-ascription (that is, a way in which people identify themselves) and a form of classification, by which groups are classified and constructed by others. In any particular case, the two may not coincide. Observers and classifiers, for example, may describe sets of people by ethnic labels or identify behaviour as being motivated by ethnicity when those concerned do not recognize or accept such forms of classification. Banton (1994), building on this point, argues that it is especially difficult for observers to distinguish between behaviour that is based on nationality and that based on ethnicity. Actors' definitions of the situation are therefore a necessary component of any analysis of the perceived operation of ethnicity. Such accounts do not, however, make sense by themselves, but also require attention to the economic and political context in which social action takes place.

One way of distinguishing ethnicity from nationality is by contrasting two contexts in which ethnicity operates. The first is endogenous, where appeals to ethnicity rest on historical claims by a people over a territory on the basis of historical and cultural descent. This is typically connected with ethno-nationalism, in which conceptions of nationhood and membership of the political community are coterminous with membership of a bounded ethnic group. Examples include the secessionist forms of nationalism that have challenged multi-ethnic empires, such as the now defunct USSR or the former Yugoslavia, or challenges by Scots or Bretons within more stable political units such as the British or French nation states. In such cases, the appeal to ethnic identity rests largely on historical connection with a particular territory with which a cultural group claims a more or less continuous attachment over a significant period of time, often as a cultural minority within a larger political entity.

Yet the appeal to ethnic identity also arises in a second rather different context, involving cross-border and global migration. This creates countries of mass migrant settlement, such as the USA or Canada, which become more multi-ethnic as a result of the mixing of populations. International migration continues to be a major component of globalization, virtually all nations and regions being involved in complex webs and long- as well as short-distance migration. Migrant ethnicity, in this second sense, typically occurs outside the national homeland, as, for example, among Indo-Chinese in Australia or West Indians in Canada.

Ethnicity plays a different role in these two contrasting settings. In the former, it may be connected with national self-determination and nation-building, reflecting the claim that each people has a right to a national home or nation state. In the latter, ethnicity may function both as source of cultural integrity and identity for minorities in a new and often hostile environment, and as the basis for expanded citizenship rights (Soysal, 1994) within a multicultural political framework. This may be true, but it may still be insufficient as an answer to the question 'Why ethnicity as opposed to some other cultural identification?'

An alternative way of grasping the attraction of ethnicity as a cultural principle requires relaxing the initial distinction between ethno-nationalism and migrant ethnicity. The case for doing this derives in part from the ubiquity of migration across boundaries within history (McNeill, 1986) and the consequent typicality of multi-ethnic culture contact and settlement patterns throughout history. Human history over the very long term has seen massive population movements. Virtually all those who consider themselves settled in a particular place, even to the point of asserting aboriginal primacy, generally migrated, be it several centuries or several millennia ago, from somewhere else. While this sometimes meant occupancy of previously unpopulated land, it increasingly meant cultural contact, conflict, sometimes genocide or expulsion, but also often fusion with other groups, which were themselves often to split again, some time later to compete as rival ethnicities. The peoples that recently fought each other in the Balkans over issues of ethnic purity do not come from cultural stock whose history is entirely separate and distinct. The further back in time one travels, the more blurred are the cultural divides between Serbs and Croats.

Nonetheless within shorter and more immediate time-frames ethnicity, defined in terms of peoples with a bounded sense of identity and history, has often functioned as a way of differentiating social groups from others who are felt to threaten or oppress them. This applies both to settled occupiers of land threatened from invaders and competitors from outside, and to migrants threatened by majorities from within. The social psychology of threat, including death in battle, rape, enslavement, forcible removal from a territory, unemployment and poverty as the result of economic competition, or migrant assimilation to the cultural mainstream, generates an intense search for new meanings and new anchors for culture and personality. Many of these psychological challenges occur in settings of heightened globalization, associated not only with population movement and migrant settlement, but also with insecurities involving economic restructuring and global financial crisis.

Ethnicity offers higher levels of security against threat than social class because it offers group members richer forms of symbolic security than mere material well-being. These include the security of a place in history and a sense of descent through history, as well as emotionally charged symbols of contemporary identity centred on personal courage and vitality in opposition to enemies. Cultural security typically yearns for the mythical stability of a natural order free from conflict and uncertainty. This order is often overlaid with religious associations, which reinforce ethnic group membership, adding the appeal of transcendent religious principles to the other symbolic gratifications of ethnicity. Sexual representations of ethnic and ethno-national sentiment, as Mosse (1985) has noted in the case of nationalism, also play a key role here, both as metaphors for the courage and fertility of the cultural stock and in terms of the capacity of groups to reproduce themselves over time.

Alternative affiliations find it hard to compete. In the case of class, for example, it is arguable that the promise of material security has rarely been enough to undercut the wider appeal of ethnicity and ethno-nationalism, especially in a crisis. The failure of proletarian internationalism to prevent the First World War is a striking if tragic case in point. Peasant-based movements against imperial domination in recent Asian history were generally only successful where economic grievance was allied with national sentiment (Johnson, 1962).

In this general model, which draws in large measure on Smith, ethnicity, either alone or in conjunction with nationhood, acts as a means of promoting and retaining identity and security in situations of challenge, destabilization and crisis.

Ethnicity and Multiculturalism

A general argument about the enduring appeal of ethnicity has been sketched above, based largely on the symbolic functions performed in contexts of crisis and threat. One serious qualification of this argument is, however, necessary before we proceed further. This concerns the material as well as symbolic advantages that accrue to the membership of ethnic groups.

A number of US commentators have argued that there are very material as well as symbolic advantages to the possession of an ethnic identity. These draw in part on the insight that ethnicity has a dual character, functioning both as a source of identification for members of a group and as a label utilized by others to represent a group. This external labelling affect may, of course, often be negative, as in forms of stereotyping that represent ethnic or racial groups in pejorative ways. Yet it may equally be positive, where ethnic groups are perceived having political rights and entitlements, including economic or social welfare resources. Glazer (1983; 318–19), writing in the context of black–white relations in the USA, makes a point of wider significance, namely that where law 'names groups … because the groups are named, individuals inevitably become beneficiaries or non-beneficiaries of law specifically because of group membership'.

Nagel (1986) sees ethnicity not as a form of primordial expression but rather as a combination of the ascriptive labelling of a group by others and a strategic opportunity for those so identified to choose to maintain or take up a particular identity that is politically recognized. This enables those thus identified to compete for economic as well as political resources. In the US context, this may be recognition as an official minority, entitled to particular labour market, small business, or educational advantages.

Ethnicity is not then a phenomenon of exclusively symbolic significance. This is true in several contexts. The first is where the ethnicity of powerful or wealthier groups is used to secure economic and political advantage in business, the labour market and governmental positions, often through ethnic networks (Holton, 2008). The second is where ethnic differences within a population are used by third parties, be these employers or colonial administrations, to divide and rule, undercutting class unity by treating ethnic groups differently or manipulating existing tensions for advantage. A third case is the recent development of a politics of ethnic identity and recognition, associated both with ethnic lobbying and with forms of multiculturalism founded on the idea that cultural groups as such have rights.

Multiculturalism is both a concept and political practice around which controversy and confusion is rife. For Joppke and Lukes (1999b: 16), 'there is no multiculturalism *tout court*, there are only specific context-dependent problematiques; the search for a universal formula and final judgement is doomed from the start'. Certainly the meanings of this term stretch so enormously and confusingly that it can mean opposite things to different commentators. Thus for some it means cultural separatism at odds with liberal-democratic citizenship, while for others multiculturalism is precisely a way of enlarging liberal-democratic citizenship (Joppke and Lukes, 1999a; Kymlicka, 1995).

What is common to all instances of multiculturalism is the context of multi-ethnic states and wider trans-national spaces character-ized by cross-border connection and mobility. These are usually the product of processes of culturally diverse population movement, whether through enslavement and transportation, refugee settlement, or voluntary migration. Discourses of multiculturalism have, in this context, been most highly elaborated in countries of the New World, notably the USA, Canada and Australia and, more recently, Europe. A growing interest in multicultural perspectives on cultural diversity is also evident in parts of South East and East Asia (Kymlicka and He, 2005). Yet the meaning of multiculturalism within these settings varies dramatically from the post-Civil Rights emphasis on cultural separatism in the USA, to issues of social justice and cultural integration *within* the liberal-democratic polity of Australia, or social-democratic Sweden, to accommodations between cultural diversity and communitarianism in parts of Asia.

Since recent Western discussion has become dominated by contro-versies between cultural separatism and liberal-democratic criticism, it is worthwhile briefly sketching a wider historical account of multi-culturalism's complex evolution. This began in Canada and Australia from the 1970s onward, and was reflected explicitly in policy-making. Multiculturalism based on multi-ethnic population movement is a characteristic of most New World societies of mass migration and settlement. The focus of multiculturalism here lacked the particular US context of unresolved black–white relations and the political agenda of Afro-Americans developed against a history of slavery. Pressure for ethnic separatism may be found outside the USA, notably among the French-speaking Quebecois of Canada. Nonetheless, in both Canada and Australia from the 1970s onwards, proponents of multiculturalism have focused far more upon the responsibility of public policy to mediate between an overarching framework of universalistic standards common to all and recognition of the specific needs of particular groups or individuals within such groups (Australian Council on Population and Ethnic Affairs, 1982; Hawkins, 1989; Office of Multicultural Affairs, 1989; Richmond, 1991). Multiculturalism has been elaborated by many precisely as a culturally inclusive form of liberal-democratic politics that seeks to unify rather than divide. This nonetheless adds to conceptual confusion, inasmuch as liberal-democrats in different countries may find themselves either for or against multiculturalism depending on how it is conceived.

In the USA, multiculturalism has been primarily associated with the politics of ethnic and racial identity and entitlement, and with moves towards ethnic or racial separatism, with particular reference to educational curricula and affirmative action programmes. Such moves have occurred in a context of radical disillusionment with the gains from the Civil Rights movement epoch. The specific terrain of debates on multiculturalism as separatism has been the politics of educational provision and curriculum content (see the debate between Ravitch, 1990, 1991, and Asante, 1991). While some critics of separatist multiculturalism have found a liberal-democratic multiculturalism more acceptable, other critics have been more uncompromising. Educational separatism, for example, has been criticized by some liberal-conservatives as both a violation of principles of social equality and as socially divisive (Schlesinger, 1992). Such criticisms arise from the perception that special advantages are given to particular persons for particularistic rather than universalistic reasons.

This line of criticism may be countered, at a theoretical level, by the claim that liberal universalism is not socially neutral, and hence is unable to avoid privileging certain dominant groups over others. Rather, liberalism (in the European sense of the word), with its emphasis on the rights and obligations of the rational individual citizen, rests on assumptions about social life that are at once too abstract and seriously incomplete (Young, 1989). Individuals are not social atoms, and the ideal of freestanding rational individuals has been criticized as being gender-blind (Pateman, 1988) as well as indifferent to cultural difference. Such debates reflect an uneasiness with any kind of social theory or moral philosophy that is too distant from the constraints and choices faced by real-world actors. They also reflect a particular way of understanding the contemporary global context. This is based not on the global dominance of the Western liberal-democratic individualism, but on a diverse set of political models and movements. These embrace many voices, including racial and ethnic minorities, post-colonial intellectuals and feminist movements, many of them bound up in trans-border population movement linked to slavery or global migration. Liberal universalism does not give these sufficient weight.

By the last quarter of the twentieth century, multiculturalism became a more significant policy focus in Europe. This is seen in Sweden in the late 1970s, where explicitly multicultural policies were adopted (Runblom, 1994). This, as in Australia, was very much a response to issues of social cohesion and social justice raised by inflows of culturally diverse migrant populations. Elsewhere, similar integrative policy initiatives are evident, though understood in other discursive terms, such as 'minority policy' in the Netherlands, or 'racial inequality' in the UK.

Bousetta and Jacobs (2006: 25) argue that in other settings policies that are close to multiculturalism in their practical effect were developed, even though the dominant political culture saw itself as opposed to multiculturalism. In France, as dramatized by conflict over the wearing of the Islamic headscarf in schools (Kastoryano, 2006), the republican tradition is strongly secular and anti-clerical, and opposed to public recognition of cultural difference. Nevertheless in many localities this formal opposition has been muted by a greater cross-cultural openness in pursuit of local social cohesion (Bousetta, 1997; Kastoryano, 2006).

Policies and programmes towards immigrants, in the Australian, Canadian, North American and European cases, in spite of differences in historical and political context, do have some important implications for the discussion of ethnicity and nationhood. The common thread here, whether labelled as multicultural or anti-multicultural, involves ethnicity becoming a specific focus for government attention in policy (whether this involved citizenship and social cohesion, social justice or welfare redistribution). At this point, ethnicity ceases to be simply a matter of the self-ascribed identity of groups and individuals, and becomes something that is politically and administratively defined as much from above as from below.

We have already come across the idea of the invention of national and ethnic tradition from above as a means of political mobilization and state formation. The more recent case of multiculturalism and the politics of ethnic identity represents another instance of ethnicity becoming embedded in broader political processes. What is not clear is whether this is to be understood in terms of the evolution of citizenship through a variety of national context-specific multiculturalisms. Does multiculturalism, in short, help to shore up nations, by redefining their identity in an epoch of global mobility? Or does ethnicity and multiculturalism point beyond a national focus to some kind of postnational identity and allegiance beyond that of the nation? The latter possibility has been dramatized both in Europe and the USA, with the expansion of Islamic migrant populations in the context of 9/11, Middle Eastern war and cultural conflict between radical Islam and the

West. This may be seen as undermining nationalism and nation-based loyalty, but this does not apply to all – possibly not even a majority of – Islamic migrants, who are themselves often divided by religious and ethnic differences from their countries of origin. This suggests a far more complex relationship between ethnicity and nationhood than is suggested by accounts looking for a single master-trend.

Globalization, Nation State and Ethnicity

Analysis returns at this point to the three simple theories of connections between globalization and nationalism, sketched at the outset of this chapter. In Chapters 4 and 5, it was argued that the nation state cannot be regarded as being in decline or overrun by globalization. This is in large measure because global capital is mostly not of an anarchic variety and still requires state functions to be performed. Nation states, in this sense, have been restructured rather than destroyed, though conflicts remain as to just how far neo-liberalism allows a sustainable basis for global political restructuring of national governance in the light of the global financial crisis.

We may now add a second reason, to do with the nation rather than state part of the amalgam that is the nation state. This concerns the robustness and persistence of national identity and nation-focused sentiments, often, although not necessarily, in conjunction with ethnicity. The revival of nationalism augurs well for the future of the nation state as a political form with popular support, whether populist or democratic in form. Accordingly theory 1, which sees nationalism being eroded by globalization as part of the destruction of nation states, is rejected.

Theory 2, which argues for the resilience of nationalism, seems therefore, at first sight, to be far more plausible. One supporting line of argument is that the revival of nationalism and ethnicity, and, one might add, fundamentalist religion, is to be interpreted as resistance to the disruptive, impersonal impact of globalization. The logic here is that culture is far harder to globalize than is the economy. One indicator of this is the spectacular failure of Esperanto as an international language. While there has been an overall decline in the number of languages in the past century, this in no way signals a convergence towards one world language. Instead, there are a set of world languages, notably English, but also Spanish, French, German, Arabic and Chinese.

Anthony Smith (1990) has argued that culture is hard to globalize because globalization destroys the particular attachment to history and place that gives meaning to the lives of individuals. Global culture has been attempted, in the form of standardized consumer styles found in

McDonald's or Coca-Cola, but these offer few meaningful or enduring attachments. For Smith, the attraction of national cultures as forms of social solidarity is that they are 'particular, time-bound and expressive' (ibid.: 178). Their appeal is thus bounded to those who claim the reality of a common experience that others do not and cannot directly share. This may comprise shared memories of a collective history, a sense of continuity across generations, and some sense of a common destiny. The implication of this argument is not only that cultural identity is hard to globalize, but also that the very persistence of national identities and images speaks to the deficiencies of global identity as an anchor for meaning and security in the lives of individuals.

The persistence of national identity is not, however, an even and constant phenomenon. Its significance is more accurately seen as episodic, achieving its greatest significance perhaps in times of crisis, such as war, when insecurity and pressures of boundary-setting tend to be more intense. Globalization as a process of (both perceived and very real) change, taking place across political and cultural borders, is perhaps as overtly challenging as war. Threats of global economic restructuring leading to job loss, a declining sense of national economic sovereignty in an interdependent world, perceptions of declining social cohesion associated with mass culturally diverse migration and the sheer pace of unfamiliar technological change nonetheless all create an atmosphere in which security and identity are felt by many to be under threat. The case of radical Islam also suggests that it is possible to globalize religion and politics into a major cross-border phenomenon.

As with war, although for different reasons, symbols of stability and order may become attractive and may, of course, be manipulated by national power-holders, as occurs in wartime, to maintain particular kinds of political and cultural order. Nationalism, in the sense of cultural identity and association with both history and place, thus remains a fundamental means of responding to globalization in all and any of its manifestations, as it is to war. It is obviously very far from dead, and Smith clearly establishes the core of one argument for why this should be so. What is not so clear is whether contemporary nationalism is necessarily to be seen as a reaction against globalization *per se* and whether the global and the national should be seen as warring principles, locked in a conflict that one or other will win, even if only for a limited period of time. This brings us back to theory 3 in which globalization and nationalism may be seen as mutually reinforcing and in some sense furthering each other.

This, in turn, encourages arguments that see nations and nationalism as elements in a complex 'field' (Robertson, 1992). Here 'global' and 'national', 'universal' and 'particular' interact and are mutually self-constituting and interdependent. One way of describing this is in terms of 'glocalization'. This approach emphasizes paradox and inter-penetration rather than any kind of simple clash between the global and the national, or the economic and the political or cultural.

One pertinent example of this is the paradox that the institutions of the nation state and nationalist consciousness have been glocalized, in the sense of being diffused across all regions of the world. All who claim to be peoples expect rights of self-determination as a nation and recognition as a nation state, with a seat at the UN. In this way, one may speak of the globalization of particularism; that is, of the model of nationhood as the embodiment of the specific claims of particular groups with a discrete history and identity of their own. The paradox is that the institutions of the nation state and nationalism have been diffused across existing boundaries and borders, typically leading to the collapse of imperial and colonial borders while concurrently redrawing fresh boundaries as new nations are formed. At the same time, the form that nationhood and national consciousness takes in these various settings varies markedly depending on historical traditions, such that we may speak of the particularization of nation state building.

There is also a further general paradox involved in the revival of nationalism of whatever kind in the epoch of globalization. The para-dox is that globalization has assisted in constituting a world of discrete nations and nationalist politics by diffusing models of political organi-zation, even while much nationalism has arisen as a reaction against larger external political forces.

Such forces may involve aspects of globalization, as in the case of Western colonialization and global capitalist economic domination. The nationalism of the former colonial nations of Africa and Asia, for example, may be read as resistance to aspects of capitalist or Western globalization. Theory 2 seems very apposite in such cases. However, in other instances, the external force against which nationalism reacts may be better described as regional in character. This applies in the case of political empires such as the old Soviet Union, or multinational or ethnic states like Great Britain or the old Yugoslavia. The recent nationalism of Latvians, Ukrainians and Chechnyans, for example, is related to the regional political dominance of the old Soviet Union. In yet other variants, the recent nationalism of Serbs and Croats, or Scots and Welsh, is related more to grievances associated with the terms of their incorporation into wider national political entities, such as the former Yugoslavia or the United Kingdom.

Regionalism, in its trans-national rather than sub-national sense, has also prompted various kinds of national counter-reaction within the EU. Tensions over European and national sovereignty have been reflected in the troubled reaction to the terms of the Maastricht and Lisbon treaties and to a sense of the emergence of a federal European super-state. There has also been continuing opposition to the superior juridical status of the European Court of Justice and European Court of Human Rights over national legal systems. Nonetheless national reactions to European regionalism are not simply those of reactive local oppositions. It is often opinion in the largest nations, with the strongest sense of historic sovereign power, that expresses the most vocal opposition to EU centralization, while minority nationalist movements within larger nations often see the EU as a counterweight to the majorities that dominate them. This argument has been applied to cases like Scotland within the UK and Catalonia within Spain (Keating, 2001; Pryke, 2009: 105–7).

In such ways, one cannot regard nationalism as a reaction against globalization *per se*. There is a range of different external entities against which local and particular nationalist movements struggle or define themselves, and these may be national or regional rather than global in scope. In addition, the grievances at the heart of national feeling pertain as much to symbolic value-laden issues, including immediate forms of cultural domination and humiliation, as to material deprivation, and these may as easily be applied to other nations and peoples, rather than entities such as Europe or the world as a whole.

There is, however, a further major line of objection to seeing the current world in terms of fissures between the global and the national, and between global capital and national political culture. This objection might be labelled in a shorthand way as the problem of cultural pluralism. The difficulty here is that contemporary identity takes many forms, some of which differentiate different groups of people from each other, some of which are evident as multiple identities within particular individuals. Such identities may be local, national, regional or global, or a combination thereof.

The following example may help to establish the face-value nature of this problem. It concerns migrants to Australia from particular Greek Islands, who may see themselves simultaneously as Greek and Australian, may have taken out Australian citizenship, but may also see themselves as part of the Greek diaspora around the globe, with family in the USA as well as Greece and Australia. Yet they also simultaneously identify with their island of origin. Let us further disaggregate the category 'they' by generation and gender. While those who first migrated were both Greek, the children born in Australia may have intermarried, perhaps with an Anglo-Australian, perhaps with a Serbian migrant to Australia, who is also part of the Orthodox church. One member of the family may have returned permanently to Greece. Maybe an Anglo-Australian wife has returned with her Greek-Australian husband to Greece (see the testimony of Bouras, 1986). Now let us introduce the question of salience of identities. Is ethnicity and nationality the strongest identity for the group of individuals involved? Do recent generations of young people, for example, identify more with global youth or sporting culture, around secular icons rather than with symbols of Greek heritage, or are the two combined in some way And would global themes recede in importance if Greece became involved with war with Turkey, just as the Croatian heritage of second-generation Croatian-Australians became more intense with the break-up of the former Yugoslavia and the Balkan wars (Skrbis, 1999)?

The point of these speculations is to throw into doubt the simple idea of a polarization between global and national identities, and to reinforce Robertson's sense of the complex interpenetration of global, national, regional, local and individual elements within the global field. The choice here is thus nowhere near as simple as deciding how far globalization is creating global people or, as a reaction, reborn nationalists.

When Smith argues that the idea of global culture lacks the specificity and historicity that individuals require to find meaning and security in their lives, he gives insufficient attention to the ways in which the global and the national or local may co-exist in people's lives. Global culture is taken to be a singular post-national identity and caricatured as a syncretic commodity, constructed out of bits from here and there, but decontextualized so that it can be packaged and sold in a standardized form.

This way of dismissing the possible development of global culture has some force, but it neglects the possibility of particular global cultures forming, linked initially to specific origins but diffusing outward in space and time. Syncretization and hybridization may thereby create viable cultural forms to which individuals may attach meaning and value. Alternatively particular regional and cross-border movements such as radical Islam have revived their global presence with forms of allegiance as equally powerful as those that Smith associates with nationalism.

Conclusion

This chapter has covered a great deal of ground and identified some very complex issues. It is therefore worth summarizing exactly what may be concluded from the arguments and evidence under consideration.

This book is about globalization and the nation state. In previous chapters we looked more at the 'state' part of this theme, rather than the 'nation' part. This chapter extended the discussion to nations, and senses of nationhood and national allegiance among different peoples. It set out identifying three simple ways of linking nationalism and globalization. Is globalization destroying nationalism, or is the precise opposite true, in the sense that globalization cannot create a binding global culture? Or do globalization and nationalism co-exist and intermesh? And if so what form does this intermeshing take? Is it perhaps connected with multiculturalism as a form of public policy? Or is this idea too inchoate and confused for analytical purposes?

In relation to this set of questions, this chapter advances the following propositions and arguments.

First, globalization is not destroying nationalism as a form of identity and allegiance, and this applies whether we think of globalization as an economic, political, or cultural force. This finding parallels the discussion in previous chapters that challenged assumptions that the institutions of the nation state were being destroyed by globalization. Nationalism remains part of the global 'field'.

Second, globalization is not destroying nationalism, but nor is nationalism the predominant and unshakeable identity and allegiance within the world. There is a tendency to take any instance of resilient nationalism as one more instance of its overwhelming salience, producing a kind of arbitrary methodological nationalism.

Third, while nationalism has many connections with ethnicity, both historically and in the contemporary world, these are not a fundamental default setting for human identities and allegiances, against which other identities and allegiances are too weakly rooted in communal experience to have much purchase. Multi-ethnic states and regions abound in human history and have created a range of relationships from extreme conflict to co-existence to multicultural engagement to cross-cultural cooperation and solidarity. Ethnicity is also part of the 'global field'.

Fourth, there are no convincing reasons to presume that cultural life cannot be globalized, as the case of radical Islam indicates.

Fifth, multiculturalism is a very confused term analytically and in policy discourse, but not so inchoate as to prevent any useful purchase on social and political institutions and processes. Aside from its demographic meaning as cultural mixture, its policy resonance, whether explicit or implicit, is not insubstantial. The meaning of multicultural politics has been arbitrarily restricted by many to its largely US sense as cultural separatism and relativism, and placed under the shadows of polemical culture wars. This has obscured alternative perspectives which seek to develop multiculturalism as a way of extending the citizenship framework of nation states under conditions of global culturally diverse immigration and settlement.

Six, multiculturalism indicates one way in which globalization and nationalism intersect, and this may be elaborated conceptually as a form of glocalization, following Robertson. This means that the global and the local do not have to be seen as conflicting principles.

In the light of these six propositions, some more highly developed in the present chapter than others, attention turns in the following chapter to a consideration of what is happening to global culture. This deepens the analysis beyond familiar global/national dichotomies.

7

Globalization and Culture?

Those who analyze globalization in terms of the capitalist world-system and the activities of powerful multinational companies generally assume that economic globalization creates a dominant version of cultural globalization in its own image. In contrast, for those who emphasize the resilience of national identity or who see nationalism and ethnicity (in part at least) as resistance to globalization, contemporary culture is far from dominated by the logic of the dominant economic system.

Neither of these two interpretations is, however, acceptable to a third school of thought, which sees global cultural forms emerging that are trans-national in form yet far from dominated either by global capitalism or by the nation state. Beyond this, many other observers point to the ways in which trans-national developments are linked with local and sub-national cultural processes and identities. So what is really happening to culture, and how are cultural identities and practices articulated with other aspects of globalization?

Defining Culture

Such questions are rendered harder to answer by notorious difficulties in defining what is meant by culture (for a further elaboration, see Holton, 1992: 182–5). One very simple definition involves 'ways of life' which provide meaning, identity and appropriate ways of acting in the world. These are defined by their social function, and spread across politics and economic activity, as well as activities such as religion or art, that are conventionally seen as cultural. From this viewpoint culture is not separate from politics and the exercise of power, nor from the material world of economic production, distribution and exchange. Accordingly there may be particular cultures of class, nation and community, as well as a cultural economy (Appadurai, 1990, 1996) and a cultural politics of globalization.

A more difficult problem has been created by the tendency to define culture in terms of ideas as distinct from actions. This opposition is arbitrary because it severs the recurring feedback loop between thought and action that constitutes human experience. The intimate connection that exists between practical and contemplative or imaginative activities has been denied for a number of complex historical reasons. Not least of these has been a considerable weight of philosophical and religious backing for the proposition that thought represents higher, more worthy human functions than practical activity in the material world.

In what follows, 'culture' refers both to ideas and practices that have in common the function of providing meaning and identity for social actors, and which combine cognitive, expressive, evaluative and practical elements. Culture, then, may be thought of as both a *tool box of practices* (Swidler, 1986), which help us to understand (for example, science and religion) and act upon the world (for example, technology and prayer), deploying power and influence in pursuit of a variety of interests, and as a source of *emotional symbols* (for example, national identity) *and values* (for example, freedom and justice) by which we orientate and justify our actions.

Considered in this way, culture may be both a cause of change and be profoundly affected by change. Here, we strike against a third problem in the analysis of culture, often found among economists, whereby culture is seen as the conservative limit on economic change. On this assumption, economies change and cultures adapt. The argument in this chapter, by contrast, takes up Eisenstadt's (1992) point that culture may be either order-maintaining or order-transforming. In this sense cultural globalization may be both cause and consequence of other forms of globalization.

Having clarified what is meant by culture, we now turn to the more substantive analysis of the relations between culture and globalization, and what this means for the nation state.

Globalization, Cultural Dominance and Cultural Homogenization

Arguments connecting globalization with cultural dominance may take a number of forms. These have often emphasized cultural homogenization of various kinds. Claude Lévi-Strauss, for example, in lamenting the global challenge to local cultural variation, argued that 'humanity is installing itself in monoculture; it is preparing to mass-produce culture as if it were beetroot' (1955: 37). From this perspective individual national cultures are losing their distinctiveness and becoming the same.

A very popular version of the homogenization argument contends that globalization means Westernization, and that global processes function to impose Western cultural imperialism on the non-Western world. Such Western traits are taken to include capitalism and the profit-centred market economy, democratic politics, secular thought embodied in scientific reason, individualism and human rights. These ostensibly Western developments have a strong normative and value-laden significance, many Western commentators approving homogenization of this kind, while critics both outside and inside 'the West' regard such developments as either flawed or, at best, inadequate as a basis for the good society. The alternative value positions against which 'the West', and by implication globalization, are found wanting include the often interrelated values of community, religion and spirituality.

Mernissi (1993), the Moroccan sociologist, recounts popular criticism of Western cultural dominance within the Arab world around standardized world-time and the standardized calendar. This critique was prompted, in part, by the organization of the Western allies' Gulf War attack on Baghdad in relation to timetables derived from prime-time television opportunities. Mernissi develops this argument in a wider frame, seeing Coordinated Universal Time and the Western calendar as creating a 'horrible colonization' that is an affront to Arab and Islamic dignity. This is symbolized in the marketing of a Japanese-produced Kabir watch that chimes five times a day at the hour of prayer and a more expensive version that recites different Koranic verses:

> The tiny silicon chip, on which a holy calendar, cyclical by definition is inscribed, is a technological device that denies the sacred vision of the cosmos and declaims the triumph of the electronic age, where profit is the be-all-and-end-all – the age of scientific man, who no longer fears death and draws power from his very mortality, for he has buried his gods long ago, and reduced the earth and the stars to numbers processed by satellite. (Ibid.: 141)

There is no doubt that globalization has assumed a negative, and at times almost demonic, significance in many quarters as Western imperialism – cultural as well as economic. The voices of critics who originate from, live in, or identify with the non-Western world are significant evidence of this, whether or not they are represented in Western scholarly literature. The voices of those who are well represented include the Palestinian intellectual Edward Said. He argues that Western cultural imperialism operates, in part, through discourses of power, whereby the non-Western world is constructed as 'different' in nature, as the 'other' against which the West is defined. For Said, such discourses suffuse literary as well as political and scientific cultures.

A major example is the construction of the Middle Eastern Islamic world as 'Oriental' in contrast to 'Western Occidentalism' (Said, 1978; Hussain, 1990). Whereas the Orient is seen as stagnant and unchanging, or aggressive and fundamentalist, the West is constructed as dynamic and innovatory, tolerant and democratic. Western scholars can, in this sense, only get to know the Orient through an exploitative and demeaning form of discourse. In a later study (Said, 1993) this analysis was extended to a more general argument about empire and culture, applicable to Western thinking on Africa, the Caribbean, India and the so-called Far East.

Others have applied Said's analysis very productively across a range of cultural spheres. In the case of world football, for example, Giulianotti and Robertson (2009), detect an Orientalizing of differences in playing styles with Europeans characterizing Latin American and African playing styles as flamboyant, irrational, magical and unpredictable, compared with European reliability, rationalism and dependability (50). Media also portray footballing regions in different ways, speaking, for example, of European coaches squeezing the 'natural juice' out of African players.

Said's main point is that 'difference' serves discursively as a basis for cultural domination. Put another way, the drive to power overrides the search for truth, while caricature replaces subtleties of conceptualization. As a result, populations and voices that link Westerners with *their* 'others' are ignored or marginalized, overlaps in their experience are discounted, and 'the interdependence of cultural terrains in which colonizer and colonized co-existed and battled against each other through rival geographies, narratives, and histories' (Said, 1993: xxii) is missed. One strength of Said's argument is thus that both Westerners and *their* 'others' have been drawn into and implicated in globalization in recent centuries, through exploitative colonizing processes. While this broad discursive sense of colonization is co-terminous at many historical moments with political empire and territorial annexation, it extends far wider in a cultural sense to all 'West/East' encounters.

One general difficulty with arguments of this kind is that they present Orientalism in a unitary or homogeneous manner, creating a rather gross caricature of Western opinion and thought. Critics of Said, including some like Amartya Sen (2005), from the post-colonial world, claim that Western Orientalist scholarship was more varied than he suggests and that much of it has been positive towards non-Western cultural phenomena such as Islam. Recent scholars have increasingly moved away from the discredited Orientalist assumption that Said and others rightly challenge (for an elaboration, see Hourani, 1991: 55ff.).

A second, potentially more damaging, problem with Said's argument is that it rebounds on his own intellectual procedures. That is to say, the charge of Orientalism levelled against Western scholars can be met with the counter-charge of Occidentalism as a practice of non-Western critics (Ahmed, 1992). Just as certain Western scholars may have constructed the Orient as the 'other', so certain non-Western scholars have constructed the Occident as the 'other', regarded in a similarly pejorative manner. These similarities should not conceal differences in the political and cultural power accorded to Orientalism and Occidentalism, yet they are indicative of similarly problematic intellectual procedures and hence equally worthy of criticism. In this sense, we are left with a titanic battle between two politically expedient caricatures and the sense that such an encounter may be intellectually barren. This line of criticism rebounds, of course, not only on Occidentalists, but also on Western scholars such as Samuel Huntington (1993, 1996), who portray the world order as riven by a cultural fault-line separating Western civilization from an Islamic–Confucian civilizational axis.

Said himself is critical of Afrocentric and Islamocentric as much as Eurocentric approaches (Said, 1993: xxiii). His alternative reaches for a broader historical approach, which somehow transcends the immediate political context in which there is temptation to rest content with 'the radical purity or priority of one's own voice' (Said, 1993), and the voices of one's own 'side' or 'culture'. This alternative to polarized caricatures is consistent with the long-run historical approach to globalization suggested in Chapter 2. From this viewpoint, the West and the world beyond are not two separate and discrete regions, one of which is the source of globalization and the other the victim of global processes developed by others. The West and the world beyond have long been engaged in interchange and interaction as well as exploitation and conflict, including cultural as well as economic and political institutions and technologies. Global interchange was already well advanced before the religious wars (or Crusades) between Christendom and Islam, which led to the cultural representation of West and East, Europe and Asia, as sharply distinct social regions or civilizations (Delanty, 1995). The terms 'west'/'occident' and 'east'/'orient', or 'Europe' and 'Asia', are indeed cultural constructions, as Said suggests, that have been imposed on the fluidity and complex interchanges of the global field.

While acknowledging this, a possibly unintended consequence of Said's work is an effective undermining of the search for agency among colonized peoples, arising from the very emphasis given to a discursive obsession with Western views, eyes and discourses (Pratt, 1992). This provides very little incentive to look for alternatives to Orientalist engagements between Westerners and their 'others' (Holton, 2008: 142–3) Part of this difficulty may be associated with an ambiguity in Said's argument that 'from the beginning of Western speculation about the Orient, the one thing the Orient could not do was represent itself' (1978: 283). While this might mean that the West claimed for itself a monopoly of wisdom – successfully or otherwise – it might equally mean that Western Orientalism did succeed, leaving little point in looking for critical anti-Orientalist responses – at least until late twentieth-century processes of decolonization.

To think in the latter way, is both methodologically dubious and historically problematic. To brand the discourses of Western anthropologists and colonial administrators simply as Orientalist undervalues the agency of native informants (Bayly, 1996). For Lewis (1973), the diagnosis of Orientalist discourse, on the part of its critics, ends up creating the same ethnocentric bias against the agency of the 'other', that such critics seek to undermine. Fisher (2000) seeks a finely balanced position, which neither underestimates the distorting effect of Westernized lenses, nor underestimates the agency of the informant. Holton (2008), meanwhile, drawing both on his empirical analyses of East/West networks in the nineteenth and early twentieth centuries, and on other rich bodies of historical work (Hopkins, 2002a); Raychauduri, 1988, 1994), maintains that political empire, for all its conflicts and colonizing discourses, cannot simply be assimilated into the Saidian Orientalist framework.

From an early twenty-first-century perspective, it is quite clear that cross-border cultural encounters, conflicts and exchanges are very widespread, involving technology and the professions, religion and sport, music and forms of personal consumption. A range of processes such as global migration, travel and enhanced communications, as well as global trade, marketing and mass media representation, have encouraged such encounters, but the net effect is multi-centred global complexity rather than a straightforward domination by the West of the rest. Thus, the West diffused nineteenth-century industrial technology to the East, but has famously also imported earlier printing and explosives technology from the East. Religious flows also go in both directions, while musical and artistic fusions in jazz and popular music do the same. Much of this is represented within cross-regional circuits rather than more macroscopic intra-civilizational terms – that is, in cultural linkages between different parts of Asia in the case of Islam or Buddhism, or between Western and Eastern, Northern and Southern Europe, or around the Mediterranean or the Caribbean regions.

One reason why this sense of multi-centred flows has not been fully appreciated is the widespread currency of a number of theories stressing centralized power operating across economic, political and cultural domains. Orientalism is one of these. Another involves Americanization.

Cultural Homogenization and Americanization

Ideas of the Americanization of global culture offer a less generalized and more empirically specific version of the cultural homogenization argument. Here the culture of a particular nation state – the USA – is seen as becoming the basis for global culture.

While not discounting traditions of US isolationism, there are clearly many phases of US history where outward-going engagements have been paramount, from war to trade to cultural expansion. Writing in the 1940s, Henry Luce, the editor of *Time* and *Life* magazines, predicted that the twentieth century would be the 'American century', not simply in its role as economic powerhouse, but more broadly as a source of inspiring cultural and political ideas such as personal freedom and justice (cited in Reynolds, 2002: 243). Many would see this prediction as having come true, especially with the collapse of the Soviet Union and the end of the Cold War. Yet has the US cultural role been more a case of global cultural domination?

The American domination thesis builds on a number of key elements. One is the theme of predominant American ownership of key resources for the manufacture and transmission of culture, including satellite systems, information technology manufacture, news agencies, the advertising industry, television programme production and export, and the film industry. Cultural homogenization, in this sense, is linked with the predominant role of the USA in the multi-media ownership and the global export of television, film, computer hardware and software applications, including social networking sites, and information provision including global news (McChesney, 1999). Prominent examples include the worldwide diffusion of television programmes such as *The Simpsons*, *Friends* and *Sex and the City*, and TV genres such as docu-soaps featuring the life of celebrities. CNN, the pioneering global news channel, has helped to spawn a wide range of global TV news shows across Europe and Asia. Further aspects of the Americanization thesis embraced film and the historic dominance of Hollywood. From the early 1990s, when films like *Terminator 2* and *Dances with Wolves* dominated box offices worldwide, to 2010 when *Avatar* and the animated *Toy Story 3* did the same, the argument has been that Hollywood has dominated box office and film genre, making it hard for local content to get a foot in the global mass market.

A second theme in the Americanization literature focuses on the USA's role in constructing a regulatory framework within culture and information industries that favours US interests. Schiller (1976), in particular, draws attention to the consistent post-war policy of US governments and businesses to challenge other countries' use of governmental control or regulation as a means of protecting aspects of national cultures against US domination. 'Freedom of information' was thus used to break the immediate post-war grip of British news-gathering cartels, to disseminate Cold War propaganda through UN agencies in the 1950s and 1960s, and, more recently, to undermine attempts by UNESCO to establish a regulatory framework for global communications with priorities other than private profit-making for business, such as increased worldwide literacy or global professional education. The bogey of state censorship was used to challenge almost any kind of regulatory arrangement that did not provide free trade in information and cultural products as an open door to the US culture industries (Wete, 1988).

A third approach to issues of globalization, cultural homogenization and Americanization looks at the diffusion of cultural practices beyond the information and culture industries to the very characteristics of modern social organization. A prime example is George Ritzer's (1993) theory of the 'McDonaldization of Society'. This refers not merely to the spectacular worldwide rise of the American fast-food industry, but more generally to certain broader cultural traits in the economy, organization and personal life, of which McDonald's is a manifestation.

McDonald's fast foods, which began in the USA in 1955, opened its 12,000th franchise operation in 1991. In that year, more new restaurants were opened abroad (427) than in the USA itself (ibid.: 2–3). By 1994 McDonald's had 5,000 restaurants abroad (Fantasia, 1995: 204), including Moscow and Beijing. By 1995, around 20 million customers were served daily around the world, and 45 per cent of company profits derived from international operations. By 2010 the number of daily customers has more than doubled, with over 30,000 restaurants operating in 119 countries, employing 1.5 million people, mainly part-time (Hoovers, 2010).

Ritzer's argument is that McDonald's corporate strategy, based on efficiency, calculability, predictability and control over both products and the labour force, represents a leading example of the process of global rationalization. This perspective draws on Max Weber's argument that the modern world would see the driving out of personalized value-centred relationships in favour of impersonal technocratic modes of organization, symbolized as an Iron Cage. Exemplified previously in Henry Ford's assembly line and in mass-produced and standardized suburban housing, this is now reflected in the rationalization and standardization of personal consumption. Cultural homogenization, with the US playing a leading role, is thus embodied in a wide range of social processes.

Ritzer (2004) goes on to link these Iron Cage characteristics with globalization. Thus, the globalization of rationalized products consumed in rationalized fast-food restaurants amounts to 'the globalization of nothing'. This is not simply an expression of moral dislike of such cultural products, but an argument about the divorce of such products from any kind of particular 'social substance'. This is linked with the idea of globalization as 'growbalization'; that is, the mere pursuit of growth – having more of something – as distinct to forms of globalization which engage with the local context, termed 'glocalization'. Examples include artisanal production of food linked with particular locations and histories, but becoming available in multiple locations.

Yet do the American origins and Americanized business methods of McDonald's necessarily mean the Americanization of consumers? It is important here to avoid the trap of assuming that any message sent is necessarily received in the manner intended. How far, for example, do McDonald's customers patronize the chain simply because it is cheap and convenient? There are a number of aspects to any answer.

First, the idea of McDonald's as a cheap option may be culturally specific to Western countries. Dash (2005), writing of India, notes that such products are beyond the reach of the poor and have become a more middle-class form of consumption. Second, it is not entirely clear what kind of symbolic cultural messages are involved. The evidence is mixed. There is certainly some evidence that the experience of McDonald's in countries other than the USA is perceived very much in American cultural terms. Stephenson (1989), in a study of Dutch patrons of McDonald's, for example, found that Dutch patterns of sociability, including presentation of self and queuing behaviour, became altered to fit Americanized informality. For Fantasia (1995), writing on France, it was precisely the informality and lack of status hierarchy associated with self-service that appealed to the primarily young clientele. More recent evidence from India indicates the reverse, that it was only when McDonald's showed the capacity to adapt products to Indian tastes that it became popular, suggesting significant limits to Americanization (Dash, 2005)

Another criticism that may be levelled at the Americanization thesis is that it is capitalism rather than Americanization that is becoming globalized. Many aspects of capitalism, such as mass production, the Taylorist scientific management, or McDonald's-style consumerism may be seen as originating largely in the USA. Yet management techniques and mass marketing are not an American invention (Pollard, 1965), nor have practices such as Taylorism remained unaffected by modifications and innovation elsewhere. In Japan, for example, Taylorism imported form the USA (Warner, 1994) has subsequently been modified and reformulated from a market-based to an organizationally based practice. The Toyota 'just-in-time' system of work organization, total quality management and quality control circles, while drawing in some respects on the American legacy, have emerged under Japanese modes of innovation to be exported back to the USA (Lillrank, 1995). Another example of modification and re-export in the fast-food business involved French-inspired innovations such as the 'croissanterie' (Fantasia, 1995: 202).

The net effect, then, is global interchange and partial convergence towards similar types of business organization and economic culture, rather than Americanization *per se*. This in turn suggests that the mechanisms behind convergence are not solely the product of a single national source, even allowing for disproportionate US power and influence over much of the post-war period. Rather, cross-cultural interchange similar to that found in previous epochs of world history has continued, even if in a more intensified form. The sources of cultural influence with respect to the economy and to other aspects of social life are, in other words, diverse rather than unitary with respect to national or regional origins.

One reason for this is that standardized global supply cannot necessarily dominate or manipulate world markets. As we have already seen in Chapter 3, multinational companies have encountered limits to mass marketing. These are not necessarily insurmountable, but they have led to a greater emphasis on niche marketing and an acceptance of variation. One example of this is variations made to the marketing and content of Music Television, generally known as MTV, to different youth markets in the USA, Europe and Asia. MTV, which features as one element in Barber's spectre of McWorld, has found it necessary to vary the mix of musical styles and programme format to satisfy different tastes (Sturmer, 1993). Similarly, McDonald's, another component of

McWorld, developed the *shudh shakari* pure vegetarian veggie burger
to cater for specific segments of the Indian market (Dash, 2005).
A third example is the deliberate use of the marketing of cultural
diversity in campaigns of the clothing manufacturer Benetton (Giroux,
1994), which research suggests connects with the values of consumers
(Polegato and Bjerke, 2006).

A general proposition worth restating at this point is that the global
field is multi-centred rather than dominated by a single centre. This
applies in the cultural domain as elsewhere. There is no single dominant centre, in spite of the dominance of the USA or certain American
symbols in particular markets and sectors, such as information technology, fast food and many aspects of youth culture. In arenas like film,
the rise and global impact of Bollywood, based in Bombay, alongside
other European and Asian film industries, indicates that Hollywood
does not have everything its own way. In popular music too, the USA
is influential without being dominant. And where culture intersects
with the public policies of nation states, as noted above in the case
of US policies on global communication and free trade in cultural
production, other models of state support for culture industries is
evident in countries like France and Australia.

Another aspect of this multi-centredness is that, for many locations, it
is not Americanization but some other cultural force that is perceived as
threatening. As Appadurai (1990: 295) points out, 'for the people of Irian
Jaya, Indonesianism may be more worrisome than Americanization,
as Japanization may be for Koreans, Indianization for Sri Lankans,
Vietnamization for the Cambodians, Russianization for the peoples of
Soviet Armenia', and so forth.

Such fears, especially for small nations with large neighbours, are
clearly linked to political as well economic and cultural imperialism.
In this respect, the thesis that the nation state is far from dead, advanced
in previous chapters, is reinforced. Fear of invasion across borders is, in
some of the areas listed by Appadurai, as powerful if not more powerful than anxiety about economic penetration or cultural concern about
Coca-Colonization.

Another more positive aspect of multi-centredness within the global
field emphasizes that which attracts rather than that which generates fear. If we ask what people in different locations identify with,
the answer is not necessarily Coca-Cola and McDonald's. One reason
for this is that much of the influence of the cultural centres of former
imperial nations remains intact in spite of political independence for
former colonies. Significant elements in the populations of France's
former African or Caribbean colonies, for example, still look to Paris,
be it for cultural style, intellectual sustenance, or both. However, they

do so largely on their own terms rather than in a slavish imitation of French models.

This is evident in Jonathan Friedman's (1994) study of the *sapeurs* (literally, those who dress elegantly) of the former French Congo. To be a *sapeur* in Brazzaville is to seek prestige, beginning with the importation of European goods and then going to live in France itself. The subsequent return should be with Parisian *haute couture*, whose labels are sewn on the outside of clothing as a badge of status. Meanwhile, the Coca-Cola that is consumed is not the bottles locally produced under US franchise but the Dutch-made imported cans. What is going on here, according to Friedman, is neither American Coca-Colonization, nor Francophilia *per se*, but the channelling of pre-existing traditions of prestige accumulation in new and exaggerated directions (ibid.: 107). For those who make it to Paris, the typical squalor of eking out a living there, the fate of so many post-colonial migrants in First World cities, possesses few intrinsic satisfactions, for it is the Brazzaville audience that is more salient.

Emphasis on the multi-centredness and complex flows of cultural interaction and challenge within the global field has not gone unnoticed among those who think of the global order as a world-system or global-system. The challenge facing system theorists is, however, to determine what implication multi-centredness has for the system as a whole. Put simply, is it indicative of system instability and disorder, or is it quite consistent with continuing system resilience and orderliness?

For Friedman, mounting evidence of cultural challenge to modern Western cultural identity is indicative of the end of the cultural hegemony of modern identity based solely on the familiar characteristics of individualism, secularism, an orientation towards achievement and democracy. Like all previous dominant cultures, Western modernity is subject to a cycle of rise and fall. Multi-centredness reflects the incapacity of modern Western institutions to provide adequate cultural supports for social identity in a post-colonial setting. This encourages a more eclectic cultural pluralism. This does not turn its back on all that is modern or Western, but nor does it reject tradition, or a range of ethnic, nationalist, religious and indigenous identities, that may combine new features with old. Just as the world-economy has become multi-centred, creating increased competition and instability, so now is culture subject to high levels of decentralization.

The emphasis on disorderliness is, however, challenged by Wallerstein's world-system approach to culture. He sees culture as 'the idea system of the capitalist world economy' (1990: 38). This system is expressed spatially in terms of a dominating 'core' of leading nation states like the USA, Germany and the UK, a marginalized 'periphery' of poor Third World countries and a 'semi-periphery' of those in between, such as Australia. Interestingly, the functions and substance of culture are to be understood not as expressions of a unitary homogeneous capitalist culture (as in some versions of the homogenization thesis), but rather as varied ways of coming to terms with the conflicts and tensions of that system, and of giving legitimacy to that system. For Wallerstein, an array of cultural ideologies has arisen, ranging from racism and sexism to the idea of universalism. All are regarded as conservative ideologies that serve to perpetuate a world order characterized by systemic inequality and exploitation. However, the hierarchical notions of racism and sexism differ significantly from the more inclusive notion of universalism. While the former, in his view, justify hierarchy and inequality, the latter appeals to the idea of a single world and the dream of a global humanism wedded to progress. Hierarchy helps capitalism to divide and rule, and to use patriotism and patriarchy to undermine anti-systemic resistance to capitalism. Meanwhile, universalism offers the promise, but not the reality, of a better, harmonious future.

Such arguments are liable to the criticism of reductionism, reducing all cultural forms to a top-down form of dominance in which challenge to the system is impossible (Boyne, 1990; Holton, 2005). However, they are equally problematic in view of their highly generalized and speculative character, standing somehow above the day-to-day interaction of human actors and the operation of concrete institutions. Others working within 'world-system' theory have sought to apply this approach to institutions and practices such as racism and sexism (Smith, 1988), identity (King, 1991) and ecology (Goldfrank *et al.*, 1999), though much of this still applies macro structural theory in a rather top-down way to micro-level social interactions.

An alternative way of thinking about world-system theory is to see it as one potential resource in capturing those aspects of global culture which are susceptible to top-down core–periphery cultural flows, but not as the sole or even major theoretical resource. Giulianotti and Robertson (2009), in their recent study of globalization and football, provide a good example of this approach. They recognize 'core' cultural flows organized by corporate television and other media and by powerful European football leagues, beaming matches and commentaries 'remorselessly into developing societies' in Africa, East Asia and elsewhere (ibid.: 39–40). But not all economic 'cores' (the USA is an obvious case) are sources for these flows, while so-called 'peripheries' or 'semi-peripheries', such as South America, contain footballing 'cores', in terms of national teams and leading clubs. Theories suggesting multi-centredness and complexity do far better in explaining the latter examples.

While recognizing the continuing salience of capitalist power and social inequality, they equally suggest that power is far from unitary and that economic power does not necessarily dominate all aspects of politics and culture. Reverse flows from so-called cultural peripheries back to supposed cores are possible, while core messages may be vernacularized rather than taken as given. Cultural pluralization, in particular, reveals that human agency and resistance remains a significant element in social life that cannot be subsumed into the singular logic of capitalism.

For all these reasons, Wallerstein's response to the cultural challenges facing the world order is rejected as one-dimensional and inadequate. Yet, having said this, there still remains considerable scope for establishing what additional forces lie behind the dynamics of social change. If resistance to economic globalization is one of these, it is clearly not the only one. While some are busy re-erecting political and cultural barriers, others are clearly selecting aspects of globalization that suit their purposes, even if this also means a considerable element of indigenization or fusion of global and national or local elements.

One response to this complexity is to think of the world order in terms of polarization rather than homogenization.

Polarization, not Homogenization

The 9/11 attack on the USA by Al-Qaeda brought polarization theory very much to the fore in debates over global culture. Such theories had been advanced in the 1990s by writers like Barber (1991, 1995) and Huntington (1993, 1996). Their work represents a major challenge to the proposition that global culture is dominated by global capitalism. With the end of the Cold War and the collapse of the Soviet Union, Fukuyama (1989) had famously announced the 'end of history', in the sense that Western capitalism and democracy had been victorious and no other contender for global cultural-political dominance was evident. 9/11, more than any other event, and the processes of Islamic radicalism that lay behind it, now suggested quite the opposite. History would continue to be marked by fundamental clashes of values, but these required close attention to the multiple dynamics of globalization and their historical trajectories, to fully comprehend the contemporary world. Global culture, in short, is not dominated by a single logic.

For Barber, global polarization centres on a conflict between McWorld and Jihad. The former involves the forces of global consumer capitalism, while the latter Arabic word *'jihad'* means holy struggle or war, which for Barber also signifies retribalization. The idea of polarization here may be extended through further dichotomies between Disney and Babel, between commercial artifice, technology and pop culture on the one hand, and self-righteous faiths that generate war and bloodshed on the other. For Huntington, by contrast, the polarization is between civilizations in general, and between the West and an emergent Islamic–Confucian axis in particular. Civilizations are culture-based rather than centred on markets. The spectre that emerges is not wars between nation states, but one of 'global civilizational war'.

Behind these two passionate studies there clearly lies a strong normative and value-laden agenda. For Barber, the problem of polarization between McWorld and Jihad is that both options are hostile to democracy, the former by virtue of unaccountable global economic power, the latter through violent fundamentalist disregard for difference and dissent. In Huntington's case, in contrast, there is no room for moral equivalence between different civilizations and clear-cut support for the moral superiority of the Western way.

Notwithstanding the broad canvas and bright colours with which polarization theory operates, there is at least some awareness of what Roland Robertson would see as interpenetration between the two separate logics. In Huntington's case, this is rather fleeting, as in the comment that even extreme anti-Westernizers do not hesitate to use global technologies such as e-mail, cassettes and television, a list to which might be added both Western military technology and Western medical technology. Barber is, in contrast, far more open to the extent of interpenetration and interchange. Thus:

> Iranian zealots keep one ear tuned to the mullahs urging holy war and the other cocked to Rupert Murdoch's Star TV beaming in *Dynasty*, *Donohue*, and *The Simpsons* ... Chinese entrepreneurs vie for the attention of party cadres in Beijing and simultaneously pursue KFC franchises ... the Russian Orthodox church, even as it struggles to renew the ancient faith, has entered a joint venture with Californian businessmen to bottle and sell natural waters ... Orthodox Hasids and brooding neo-Nazis have both turned to rock music to get their traditional messages out to the new generation. (Barber, 1995: 5)

Barber identifies Jihad with McWorld in a number of senses. These include both the provincial and separatist movements of Europe and also the American Jihad of the Radical Right linked with radical Christianity (ibid.: 9). This diagnosis has found considerable support in the 15 or so years since it was written, with the election of George W. Bush and the pursuit of a National Security Strategy involving regime change in Iraq and pre-emptive war to spread 'liberty' across the

Middle East. This harnessed Christian religious fundamentalism and evangelicalism to the outward-projection of US military political and cultural power (Phillips, 2006). Fundamentalism, if this pejorative term has any clear analytical meaning, is to be found within Christianity (and ethnic nationalism), not in Islam alone.

Taken overall, polarization theory has a number of strengths. First, it draws attention to key elements of cleavage in the contemporary post-Cold War world that are not associated with socio-economic divisions between capitalism and socialism, and are thus not of class warfare. The lack of connection between political economy and global cleavage is greatest in Huntington's vision, where culture and civilization loom largest. Examples of the civilization fault-line between the West and the Islamic–Confucian axis include conflict over human rights and the Olympic Games. At the Vienna Conference on Human Rights in 1993, according to Huntington, China and her non-Western allies outsmarted the West by diluting the Vienna statement on Human Rights principles to allow their effective short-circuiting by individual nation states. Later that year, in contrast, Sydney rather than Beijing won the International Olympic Committee's approval to hold the year 2000 Olympic Games, voting being 'almost entirely along civilizational lines'.

A second strength of polarization theory is that it draws attention to an irreducible divergence of cultural and to a lesser extent political practice within the world order. All is clearly not converging to a specific Western model as homogenization theory has supposed. As was argued in Chapter 6, the argument that ethnicity, nationalism, or religion are somehow withering away in the face of economic development and secularization, is no longer tenable, nor is the proposition that such phenomena are of merely transitional significance in preparing the way for a modern social order.

The resurgence of Islam is the most visible manifestation of the contemporary challenges to global homogenization centred on the secularization of life and on the dominance of individualism. Islam takes many forms, and should not be conflated with fundamentalism (Arjomand, 2003). What many strands of Islam hold in common is more a profound objection to the spiritual emptiness of both global capitalism and secular individualism (Wickham, 2005). These sentiments are also to be found among many Christians and Buddhists. Pope John Paul II's much-quoted homily in Havana in 1998 was directed precisely at the deleterious effects of 'capitalist neo-liberalism' on social justice for human beings (cited in Lechner, 2005: 122).

Evidence of global cultural polarization associated with 9/11 and the destruction of the World Trade Center is thus only one of a number of connections that might be drawn between religion and globalization. Some trends within global religion do indeed point to polarization, whether this is between globalization and anti-globalization, or between different types of globalization (such as the economic and the religious, or the Christian and the Islamic). However, there is a good deal of difficulty here in distinguishing the global from the anti-global. Thus, it is not clear whether groups like Al-Qaeda or those American Evangelicals imbued with a sense of national moral superiority should always be labelled as 'anti-global' (Robertson, 2003). In the case of radical Islam, much of the objection is to global capitalism and materialism, with Islam being projected as an alternative global force with political as well as religious objectives. Meanwhile, in other parts of the religious cosmos, there is counter-evidence of ecumenism and inter-faith dialogue (Smart, 2003; Rudolph, 2005), rather than unequivocal polarization and schism. Two points emerge. The first is that trends in religion do not necessarily lead in one single direction towards religious and cultural polarization. The second is that trends in religion indicate pro-global as much as anti-global features. And hanging over all discussions of globalization and religion are difficulties in moving beyond nineteenth-century Western Christian notions of what a religion should look like – in terms of characteristics like central texts and official organization – in a manner that is sensitive to diversities of religious experience in Africa and Asia (Beyer, 2007).

Doubts about an all-encompassing polarization also apply to notions of separate and discrete civilizations facing global cultural war. Such arguments vastly exaggerate and over-inflate cultural and other differences within the global field. Cultural differences and schisms exist, but they are often local, national, or regional in form. And whatever differences are evident, they are not distributed between autonomous freestanding territorially separate civilizations or cultures. Rather there is, as we saw in Chapter 2, a long and complex history of interaction and interchange, stimulated by trade, war, population mobility, religious expansion and communications technology.

Key social institutions through human history, such as markets and trading networks, technological innovation, or religious communities, span the so-called civilizational divide. Capitalism is as alive in the East as the West, and the interaction between the two has a long although recently intensified history. Christianity, which originated as an Oriental religion, and which has many non-Western adherents, largely through colonization processes, cannot claim to be a primordially Western religion. The varieties of Christianity lead in many different social and political directions, from fundamentalism to global community-building. Islam is similarly varied, with adherents in

Europe and many Western cities, arising from colonization or migration, as much as outside the West. Islam has many voices, including those of peace and community as much as global Jihad.

The same kinds of criticism that apply to primordial theories of ethnicity and ethno-nationalism apply equally to primordial theories about distinct civilizations. Just as nation states and national cultures borrow and indigenize elements from the external world, so too do civilizations learn and borrow from each other. Taking the argument one step further, Wilkinson (1987), as we saw in Chapter 2, speaks of the emergence of a singular central civilization. In the contemporary epoch this is not based on cultural homogeneity nor agreed social cohesion. It is centred rather on ties of global cultural inter-connection and convergence in economic institutions, the use of similar technologies, engagement with a common agenda of problems such as social development and environmental sustainability, and an awareness of the world as a single inter-connected space. This civilization may be fractured by regional and local conflicts, as well as gross inequalities of power and life-chances, but its reality may be said to be present where what unites us is greater than what separates. On this basis the limits of such a global civilization would be set by phenomena such as genocide, ethnic cleansing and fundamentalist intolerance and division.

The controversial issue of human rights is perhaps an acid test both for Huntington's theory of civilizational cleavage and for ideas of a single global civilization. Donnelly (1998) lends weight to this view by declaring that the norm of human rights is operating increasingly as a new 'standard for civilization'. Such standards have varied historically according to whether they are exclusive or inclusive in scope. Exclusive standards are associated either with classical notions of civilization as a characteristic of particular societies (such as those of Western Europe) seen as superior to others, or with fundamentalist conceptions linked with a singular religious affiliation. Inclusive standards, by contrast, may either take a 'minimal' form based on the juridical equality of individual sovereign nation states, or a 'stronger' form, based on some kind of trans-contextual norm, such as human rights. While the minimal standard, based on political self-determination, is perfectly compatible with internal authoritarianism and denial of rights, the latter requires positive adherence to norms and expression in law. In the post-1945 world, as was argued in Chapter 5, human rights took on this positive role, generating a global political culture where civilized states were supposed to adhere to international human rights law.

Donnelly, it should be noted, is very far from regarding what has been achieved as a conflict-free political utopia. Nor does he deny the particularistic origins of human rights thinking in Western thought and politics. His point is rather the emergence of a new inclusive normative climate which seeks to limit the polarizations of political culture.

An important global moment, relevant to the assessment of such claims, was the 1993 Vienna UN conference on Human Rights. Here, the argument that China and many Islamic states watered down the conference commitment to human rights looms large. This particular confrontation was, of course, part of a more consistent opposition to the implementation of human rights by non-Western or post-colonial coalitions within the UN Commission for Human Rights. Such defensive actions may, in turn, be seen as reflecting a far worse contemporary human rights record in the non-Western than the Western world.

There is no doubt that Chinese and most Islamic governments reject the view that universal human rights should override national political and religious traditions. There is equally no doubt over the strength of popular religious or anti-Western fundamentalism in many such countries. On the other hand, there are voices in both China and the Islamic world that take a different view. These may be politically repressed, as in Tiananmen Square, or may find it difficult to organize in nations without rights of free assembly, but they are present.

Tibi (1994), in his account of the 1993 Vienna Conference, emphasizes the tension within the Muslim world. While diplomats from Muslim countries were arguing on the conference floor in favour of the specific character of their culture and against the universality of human rights, 'human rights activists from Muslim countries – like Iran and the Sudan – were drawing attention to the severe violations of human rights in their own countries, acting in the basement of the Vienna Centre' (ibid.: 277–8). This resistance may well be in the minority, in part for fear of persecution. However, it is clear that considerable internal debate exists in both Islamic and Chinese circles about human rights.

Such debates focus, in part, on the compatibility of Islamic or Confucian thinking with European-derived notions of individual human rights. Tibi notes the views of the Sudanese legal scholar Abdullah An-Na'im, student of the executed reformer Mahmoud M. Taha, and the Egyptian judge Muhammed S. al-Ashmawi that the Islamic *Shari'a* or holy law is not adequate to prevent totalitarianism. Such arguments draw on the liberal Islamic proposition that the *Shari'a* is a construction of Muslim jurists and hence not a divine text of the standing of the Koran. For Na'im, this requires a fundamental reform of Islamic law so that human rights can be established in the Islamic world. In this process of reform, the interests of humanity in the fate of all human beings are more important than the fact that human rights are of Western origin or that Western countries may not always practise what they preach in human rights areas. This argument depends, as Tibi points out, on the drawing of a distinction between Western hegemony in international affairs and the normative force of universalistic human rights standards.

Tibi argues that most existing attempts at Islamic reform do not accept that Western individual human rights are compatible with Islam. Instead, an attempt is made to 'Islamicize' the notion of rights. This, however, fails to problematize the relationship between the individual and the state, and is highly evasive on issues such as freedom of religious expression (see, in particular, Mayer, 1990). This diagnosis flows from a more general argument in which Tibi (1988) posits a fundamental antagonism between the dominant theocentric cosmology of Islam and the cultural modernity of the global order based on reason and individual rights. This antagonism is not, in his view, quite the same thing as a clash of civilizations. Rather, it represents a clash between a global civilization that recognizes individual subjectivity and a fragmented set of local cultures, trapped in versions of pre-modernism.

A similar, perhaps even more prominent, debate over human rights is evident within China, as evidenced in episodes of official and unofficial pressure for political reform, including some designed to coincide with the Beijing Olympics in 2008. Some of the intellectual underpinnings and challenges posed by such moves are reviewed in the collection of essays brought together in Davis (1995). In a manner similar to that of internal debate within Islam, a distinction may be made between those who seek purely Confucian sources of human rights and those more open to the reception of Western versions of liberal democratic universalism. Du Gangjian and Song Gang (1995) argue that aspects of classical Confucianism, such as justification of resistance to authority or of individual moral (as distinct from legal) challenges to government, are compatible with human rights notions, although the Confucian legacy itself is largely undemocratic and elitist. As with Islam, the key problem seems to be the difficulty of making any notion of individual rights compatible with cultural traditions that subsume the individual within collectivities such as the state or the family. To this extent, the human rights challenge appears consistent with Huntington's civilizational schism.

Such ostensibly cultural differences over human rights may, however, be exaggerated and misconceived. For one thing, much official Chinese resistance to human rights draws on Western Marxist hostility to what is called bourgeois individualism. If, as Du Gangjian and Gang argue,

'Confucian theory finds resonance in modern Marxism' (1995: 50), is that because Marxism, like Confucianism, is un-Western, or is it because official Chinese resistance to human rights draws on both Confucian and Marxist traditions? In the latter case, we are clearly dealing with the interpenetration of political as well as cultural practices between West and East, rather than purely culturally centred civilizational conflict.

Christine Loh (1995) adds to the complexity of the issue by challenging the notion that specific cultures have a discrete and more or less unchanging position on human rights. While many Asian governments at the Vienna Conference used cultural difference as a justification for resisting the application of universalistic human rights principles to their own country, dissidents within the same countries have often been killed or jailed for supporting human rights. In the cases of Wei Jingsheng, jailed in China for 15 years for the crime of publishing a pro-democracy newsletter, or Aung San Suu Kyi, held under house arrest for many years in Burma, how are we to interpret their actions? Are they simply pro-Western, often Western-educated dissidents fruitlessly trying to effect political reform in an inhospitable civilizational environment, or are they also members of the same society and heirs to the same cultural traditions as the rulers who jail them? Or are these alternatives too stark?

Western education and exposure to Western culture may indeed assist in securing adherence to particular kinds of support for human rights. Yet this is clearly not the only stimulus for resistance to torture, arbitrary arrest and imprisonment without trial, nor the only basis for a sense of social injustice and a commitment to political reform. To suppose otherwise would be to assume that non-Western cultures are essentially incapable of generating dissent or pressure towards greater democracy. The dilemma here is that if any support for human rights is identified with Western influence, the link between the West and human rights cannot then in principle be falsified and is hence a philosophical assertion rather than an empirically secure proposition.

To sum up, polarization theory is an attractive alternative to homogenization theory in a world where cultural difference rather than conformity is widespread. Yet polarization theory comes in a number of varieties, not all of which are equally persuasive. Barber's scenario of Jihad versus McWorld has the advantage of integrating economic and political as well as cultural elements into processes of polarization, keeping open a multidimensional approach to global social change. Unlike Huntington, he does not see polarization as primarily driven by culture or by civilizational characteristics. This leaves space for an awareness of the importance of global capitalism, with its technological dynamism, brash consumerism and unequal power relationships within the new world order and the consequent resistances that emerge around retribalized culture and politics. The West, in other words, is not treated as a beneficient civilization bringing democracy, wealth and human rights to other less fortunate civilizations. More than that, Jihad and McWorld interpenetrate, at least up to a point.

A bigger problem with both Barber's and Huntington's versions of polarization theory is nonetheless to determine whether there is a more adequate paradigm, which would make better sense of the complexities of global cultural development than polarization, without falling back into the problems of homogenization theory. One obvious candidate here is what might be called hybridization theory.

Hybridization

> Each year ... the countries of Europe meet in a televised song contest ... watched by hundreds of millions of people. There is first a national contest in each country to choose its own entry for the international competition. A few years ago, a controversy erupted in Sweden after this national contest. It was quite acceptable that the ... first runner up had been performed by a lady from Finland, and the second runner up by an Afro-American lady ... Both were thought of as representing the new heterogeneity of Swedish society ... What was controversial was the winning tune, the refrain of which was 'Four Buggs and a Coca-Cola': Bugg, like the name of the soft drink, was a brand name for chewing gum ... Of the two, Coca-Cola was much the more controversial, as it was widely understood as a central symbol of 'cultural imperialism' ... what drew far less attention was that the winning tune was a Calypso. (Hannerz, 1992: 217)

This anecdote reflects the development of a body of theory that emphasizes cultural hybridity, creolization, or syncretism within global culture (Hannerz, 1992; Pieterse, 1995, 2007). This current of thought emphasizes cross-cultural borrowings and inter-cultural fusion and blending to create hybridized or mixed cultural forms. All this occurs in a world where Coca-Colonization or global capitalism is an ever-present but not all-determining force, and where nationalism, ethnicity, or some other kind of quasi-tribal affiliation is not the exclusive source of cultural identity.

This situation has been constituted through flows of people, ideas and cultural styles across political and cultural boundaries. These, it may be added, are sometimes violently forced, as in slavery, which brought black African musical traditions to the Americas, and sometimes market driven, as in voluntary migration in search of work, which has vastly extended the cultural diversity of many European, North and South American, Middle Eastern and Australian nations and cities. Hannerz's examples include the migration of people and musical styles to Sweden.

Hannerz posits a global cultural ecumene defined as a 'region of persistent cultural interaction and exchange' (1992: 218). Instead of thinking in terms of distinct cultures within the global field, this ecumene includes subcultures of the whole; that is, entities with only 'fuzzy boundaries' separating them from each other. Another word for this process is creolization, defined by Hannerz as 'a process where meanings and meaningful forms form different historical sources, originally separated from one another in space, come to mingle extensively' (ibid.: 96).

Against those world-system approaches, which think in terms of cultural diffusion outward from a metropolitan political economic core to the Third World periphery, Hannerz sees a far more complex intersection of inter-cultural relations, in which religious connections do not necessarily follow economic connections, and in which different cultural influences such as film, or music, or literature do not follow each other. US influence may be strong in personal computer software, fast food and types of popular music, involving cores such as Silicon Valley, New York corporations, or the grunge music of Seattle. However, as Hannerz points out, places such as the Vatican or the Shia holy city of Qom also organize different aspects of culture within core/periphery relations. In addition, some countries may have a disproportionate regional cultural influence, such as Mexico in Latin America, or Egypt in the Arab world, without exerting a trans-regional global influence.

Much of the contemporary evidence in favour of creolization or hybridization is drawn from the sphere of music. The most overt example here is the development of self-styled world music, a dynamic amalgam and blending of various styles. One way of describing the process of inter-cultural syncretization is to speak of the indigenization of Western styles in non-Western settings and the fusion of non-Western influences into Western music (Roberts, 1992). In the former category is the *bhangra* music of Britain's Asian youth, which combines Indian music with Western dance-beats, or Algerian *rai* music based on Arabic chants mediated by the technologies of Western pop. In the latter category might be included the blending of Western classical music with Afro-American jazz or the Indian *raga*.

One difficulty that soon emerges in describing the inputs into hybridized music in this way is that as soon as inter-cultural contact takes place, the notion of separate Western and non-Western musical or cultural sources becomes blurred. Jazz, for example, draws on African and African-American as well as European sources, including military marches and religious music. The impact of the Brazilian *bossa nova* in the USA, as Roberts points out, also creates conceptual difficulties, already being built on fusions of Portuguese, African and indigenous cultural elements (ibid.: 230). In order to avoid this problem, Simon Frith argues that 'there is no such thing as a culturally pure sound' (1989: 3). The implication here is that music has become thoroughly glocalized.

World music is, in a sense, self-consciously unbounded, and is thus a particular subset of hybridized cultural practices. Other hybrid forms set boundaries, but these may be far from co-terminous with the nation state or nationally bounded ethnicities. A striking example is what Paul Gilroy refers to as the 'black Atlantic'; that is, an 'intercultural and trans-national formation' linking blacks in Britain and France as well as the USA and Caribbean. This is a formation that is intermediate between the global and the local, and which has a dynamic history in which slavery, colonization and migration, including the migration of intellectuals and artists, play a part. So too does the crossing of national cultural boundaries by ideas and cultural practices, including music. Mechanisms and symbols of transmission have included the ship and the long-playing record.

A similar analysis has been provided by Waxer's (2001) study of the spread of salsa music. This looks not at the black Atlantic but to the similar cross-regional cultural world of Latin American worlds linking both North and South America with the Caribbean. Salsa originated in Cuba and Puerto Rico in the mid–twentieth century, but was spread through the Cuban and Puerto Rican diaspora in New York City to global cities such as Caracas in Venezuela and Cali in Columbia. Salsa came to these new settings initially through Caribbean seamen, but then took off in a bigger way to become 'a sort of musical lingua franca' (ibid.: 223) for Latin working-class communities, linked with dress, talk and street style.

While both the black Atlantic and Latin diaspora are trans-national and trans-cultural, they generate local manifestations that are not identical with each other. Gilroy argues that black British cultures, for example, 'have been produced in a syncretic pattern in which the styles and forms of the Caribbean, the United States, and Africa have been reworked and reinscribed in the novel context of modern Britain's own untidy ensemble of regional and class-oriented conflicts' (Gilroy, 1993: 3). When north London's Funki Dreds (itself a hybridized name) made their record 'Keep on Moving', for example, this was initially produced in England by English-born children of Caribbean migrants and then remixed in a Jamaican dub format in the USA by an African-American, including segments of records made in the USA and Jamaica.

Music plays a key role in accounts of global hybridization, but how important are musical practices as indicators of trends in global culture? Gilroy argues that music has particular resonance for groups that do not privilege rational cognition above aesthetics, nor separate social and political commentary from cultural performance. In addition, the very fluidity of syncretic cultural forms may be very important to sustaining identity in an epoch of globalization. Thus 'music and its rituals can be used to create a model whereby identity can be understood neither as a fixed essence nor as a vague and utterly contingent construction to be re-invented by the will' (ibid.: 102). From this viewpoint, black music is not to be read as the authentic product of some fixed and essential black identity but is instead a dynamic cultural resource for a group whose fate and future has been profoundly affected by globalization. If it is bounded, it is not so by nation or black culture but by the experience of slavery, racism and migration.

If, as Frith believes, there are no culturally pure sounds, we may question, by extension, whether there are any culturally pure institutions, nations and communities. Are not all social arrangements – from languages such as English or Arabic to cultural practices such as the contemporary English Christmas or Ramadan – constructed out of a variety of elements with complex origins across time and space. The sociological answer may broadly be 'yes' for most of human history, yet we are left with the difficulty that many wish to re-erect boundaries that others find it advantageous to ignore, permeate, or burst through. While Gilroy's Black Atlantic is trans-national, in other parts of the global field, national, ethnic and other kinds of cultural boundary are being re-erected to the point of promoting or enforcing purity by various means. Western publishers, as Griswold (1992) has shown, prefer Nigerian novels to focus on village and rural themes, thereby contributing to the representation of Africa as tradition-bound and satisfying the African roots market. Meanwhile, there remains support for bounded primordial constructions of cultural identity, as we saw in Chapter 6, both among white and black, Western and non-Western. The difficulty, then, is in deciding how far cultural syncretization and hybridity extend *as a form of cultural identity* and what their limits are.

The debate over deterritorialization and cosmopolitanism offers some answers to this question. Here, global mechanisms of colonization, transportation, migration and cultural interaction across political boundaries are seen as leading to a loss of singular territorially based cultural identities and a shift towards new forms of trans-national social interaction (Appadurai, 1996; Papastergiadis, 2000). The nature of this supposed shift is, however, controversial for two main reasons. First, it is very unlikely that deterritorialization is taking place in any strict sense. Second, while there is some evidence of a shift towards cosmopolitanism, the term itself is often very vague and ambiguous, and it remains unclear whether cosmopolitanism means an abandonment of all territorial identities.

Deterritorialization, to take up the first of these issues, is a very problematic idea (for a trenchant critique, see Elden, 2005). First it operates with a very undeveloped notion of exactly what territory is. Second, and at its most extreme it tends to assume the cultural capacity to abstract oneself from any particular context or viewpoint. There is very little evidence that this is happening, even for people who are physically mobile, living and/or working in more than one location. Similarly, even for people who identify with the world as a whole, or planet Earth, this is usually combined with attention to particular territorial locations, as in the environmentalist slogan 'Think globally, act locally'. Some care is then needed in depicting the complex fate of territory.

The following three propositions seem supported by argument and evidence. First, as we saw in Chapter 6, national identity and nationalism is not dead, and in some contexts it is very much alive, whether for peoples who lack a functioning nation state, or those who feel insecure in a world of real or perceived cross-border threats from bigger powers, economic globalization and terrorism. Second, there are many others who feel that national forms of peoplehood are not sufficient or not relevant as a basis for identity and cultural expression. Third, even those who find themselves detached from an exclusive national allegiance typically become reterritorialized rather than deterritorialized.

These three propositions may be applied to diasporic communities of migrants or peoples forcibly removed from homelands by enslavement. In some cases, migrants dispersed to other continents remain long-distance nationalists (Anderson, 1994; Skrbis, 1999), not only keeping their sense of traditional culture alive, but sometimes returning home to fight in wars, whether Jews or Arabs from the Middle East, or Serbs and Croats from the Balkans. In other cases, senses of dual or multiple identities become more evident. These may combine older allegiances, with those of new countries of settlement, especially among the second generation. Joseph O'Neill's novel *Netherland* (2008) depicts these processes well for migrants from both post-colonial and

European backgrounds in New York City. Here, migrant identity and activities are refracted through past memories of the homeland, as well as through the evolving challenges and initiatives of the new environment including the establishment of a cricket team on Staten Island.

Finally, in relation to the third proposition, the diaspora of the Black Atlantic, discussed by Gilroy, develop a 'new topography of loyalty and identity in which the structures and presuppositions of the nation state have been left behind' (1993: 16), and newly imagined affiliations emerge as in the Afro-centrism of black Rastafarians in London. Such new topographies, for writers like Gupta and Ferguson (1992), represent processes of reterritorialization, arising from the uprooting that occurs with mobility. The global city is often the locale for this. Thus:

> India and Pakistan apparently reappear in postcolonial simulation in London, prerevolutionary Tehran rises from the ashes in Los Angeles, and a thousand similar cultural dreams are played out in urban and rural settings all across the globe … While actual places and localities blur, ideas of culturally distinct places become more salient as displaced peoples cluster around remembered and imagined homelands, places or communities, in a world that seems increasingly to deny such firm territorialised anchors in their actuality. (Ibid.: 10–11)

The idea of reterritorialization is a useful corrective to the idea that globalization will create a context-free global culture that is thoroughly post-national. This should not, however, obscure the profound ambiguity that the experience of inter-cultural mixing may create for individual identity. Whether reterritorialization takes place and what direction it assumes may both be highly contingent on personal autobiography. This is made very clear in the following account of an 'English' white reggae fan from the culturally diverse area of Balsall Heath in the city of Birmingham:

> There's no such thing as 'England' any more … welcome to India, brothers! This is the Caribbean! … Nigeria! … There is no England, man. This is what is coming. Balsall Heath is the centre of the melting-pot, 'cos all I ever see when I go out is half-Arab, half-Pakistani, half-Jamaican, half-Scottish, half-Irish. I know 'cos I am [half-Scottish/half-Irish] … who am I? … Tell me who I belong to? They criticise me, the good old England. Alright, where do I belong? You know, I was brought up with Blacks, Pakistanis, Africans, Asians, everything, you name it … who do I belong to? I'm just a broad person. The earth is mine … you know we was not born in Jamaica … we was not born in England. We were born here, man. It's our right. That's the way I see it. (Hebdige, 1987: 158–9)

Is Global Culture becoming Cosmopolitan?

This question is difficult to answer in part because 'cosmopolitanism' is a rather loosely defined term that stretches from a moral philosophical world-view, at one end of the spectrum, to a form of worldly cultural experience at the other (this discussion draws on the critical re-evaluation of cosmopolitanism in Holton, 2009). For the former, cosmopolitanism is associated with ideas of being a world citizen seeking peace and human rights. For the latter it is cross-cultural experience and expression that counts most, without any necessarily moral component. Many discount the former approach in view of the persistence of nationalism, but this rules out the possibility that both nationalism and cosmopolitanism are co-present within the global arena, and may even in some cases be compatible with each other (Appiah, 2006; Malachuk, 2007; Holton, 2009: 75–82, 115–19). Meanwhile, the latter approach is discounted by many because cosmopolitan culture is seen as a privileged middle-class preserve, a position which neglects the possibility of working-class cosmopolitanism (Werbner, 1999). A more serious problem is that there may be no single or unitary phenomenon able to serve as the core to the many varieties of cosmopolitanism, rendering the term inchoate.

For both Hannerz (1990, 2004) and Szerzynski and Urry (2002) cosmopolitanism, in its many modalities, may be defined as *openness* towards different and divergent cultural experiences, practices and institutions. Cosmopolitanism may then be a characteristic, not simply of individuals and their attitudes, but also of ways of life, forms of government and law. Evidence about the scope and limits of cosmopolitanism within global culture must, therefore, look across a wide range of settings.

The balance sheet that may be drawn up is a complex one. In terms of attitudes dealing with identity, nation shows up as the primary identity, but the world as a whole is significant for many, whether in combination with nation or with locality. There can, in other words, be cosmopolitan patriots who see their best national or local traditions as a valuable resource to contribute to a more global world, as well as local (or perhaps glocal) cosmopolitans, able to locate their particular setting in a wider frame, perhaps through civil society organizations discussed in previous chapters. Cosmopolitan attitudes also correlate with greater education and with youth (Norris, 2000, 2006). What is not evident though is an unambiguous global groundswell towards cosmopolitan attitudes, as might be expected if simple theories linking globalization with cosmopolitanism were accurate.

The major institutional evidence in favour of cosmopolitanism is not so much the existence of the United Nations, which is scarcely an effective form of world government able to secure peace, but rather the existence of human rights. The norm of human rights cannot be regarded as a universal bundle of rights agreed across all the world peoples, since it is rejected by some and defined differently by others. But it is a norm of trans-national significance supported by many as the basis for cultural as much as political freedom.

Within global culture, the significance of religion remains central, including a revival of both Christianity and Islam. Their relationship with cosmopolitanism is, however, complicated due to the diversity of global religious expression, from fundamentalist closure, the apotheosis of cosmopolitanism, to more open ecumenical multi-faith encounters and initiatives. As with political identity or migration then, the evidence is ambivalent concerning connections with cosmopolitanism, with some positive and some negative evidence.

From this, it is impossible to conclude that cosmopolitanism is either fading or becoming dominant in the arena of global culture (for further elaboration, see Holton, 2009).

Conclusion

There are no simple answers to the question 'What is happening to culture in the epoch of globalization?' None of the three approaches to contemporary culture and the global order reviewed here stands up to critical scrutiny in every respect.

Most problematic perhaps is the homogenization theory of global culture, which the events of 9/11 have rendered outmoded. Theories of homogenization certainly draw attention to power inequalities in cultural production and representation, linked both with economic globalization and the liberalizing policies of the USA as the dominant global nation state. Yet such theories do not provide a convincing account of the multi-centred nature of power, let alone of bottom-up processes of cultural development and identity formation. They also operate from assumptions of a singular logic to the contemporary world, flying in the face of evidence about counter-trends that identify competing logics, which generate cultural conflict rather than conformity. Resistance to Americanization in the guise of cultural globalization remains widespread.

Polarization theory is more alert to divergent trends, in particular the co-presence of global and particularistic, national, tribal and ethnic cultural affiliations. It tolerates a greater level of complexity and successfully recognizes competing logics. Yet the notion of a clash of civilizations remains at best unproven and at worst subject to the criticism that it oversimplifies and over-generalizes the nature of contemporary cultural schisms. It also tends to operate with insufficient regard for interpenetration and areas of common ground between the large-scale entities with which it operates. This leaves out higher levels of complexity and a more fine-grained approach. This theory does, however, add to understandings of connections between cultural globalization and the nation state in the sense that particularly powerful nation states – notably the USA – have acted as leaders and promoters of civilizational warfare.

The hybridization approach avoids the pitfalls of homogenization and polarization theory. It does this by drawing attention both to the significance of inter-culturalism for cultural identity, and fusions of global and local culture. Hybridization also connects with some versions of multi-culturalism as public policy where this focuses on culturally inclusive forms of national social integration as distinct from cultural separatism. In this regard theories of free-floating cultural deterritorialization are no more convincing than theories of the political death of the nation state considered in previous chapters. Territory still matters, though often as a complex symbolic domain, such as the Black Atlantic, rather than in any strict geographical sense. Cosmopolitanism is far from vanquished, with variants of this very complex set of phenomena evident at both a personal and institutional level. Yet this does not presage a global culture free from particular national or regional loyalties, but rather a glocal set of global and local fusions. Hybridization theory, meanwhile, offers insights into the subcultural life of global cities, but is rather unclear about the limits of hybridity as a chosen cultural form. The difficulty, then, is how to balance evidence of polarization with other evidence of inter-culturalism and, in a deeper sense, of how to balance a sense of globalization as opportunity with globalization as constraint.

While many of the nationalist and ethno-nationalist currents reviewed in Chapter 6 respond to globalization by re-erecting defensive cultural barriers, inter-cultural connections – often the product of migration – are in many other respects explicitly welcomed and built into cultural practices. Globalization, in this sense, functions as it has always done as a repertoire of cultural practices, albeit one to which access is mediated though available resources, such as wealth, state policies such as human rights and personal mobility, and from which selections and choices may be made under various kinds of constraint. Such constraints include the relative bargaining position of nations, groups and individuals *vis-à-vis* the suppliers of resources available within the global field. This in turn includes the framework of economic and political regulation, prescribes rules of world trade, intellectual property, or movement of persons, processes in which nation states, or at least those that are wealthier, play a continuing role.

The global repertoire is not, then, to be seen as a consumer paradise or a life-enhancing inter-cultural smorgasbord, but neither is it a demonic system of top-down system domination. We know this not because optimistic and privileged Western or Northern voices say so but because it is also expressed through a competing range of global voices. Many of these are located in the South and East, but may often be better thought of as spanning the conventional divide between West and the rest, perhaps as post-Western cultural expressions.

8

Conclusion

The study of globalization and the nation state poses major challenges, of both an analytical and normative kind. In terms of analysis the aim here has to produce an explanation of globalizing trends and the changing role of nation states, based on logic, evidence and theoretical reasoning. Meanwhile, questions about whether globalization is good or bad, and what should therefore be done about it, are the stuff of normative debate and moral concern.

The analytical challenges outlined throughout this book centre on the range of misconceptions that have become associated with globalization and their replacement with more plausible alternatives. Thus the globalization process is not a single, all-conquering and homogenizing force, driven by the systemic logic of capitalism or Western cultural imperialism. Globalization does not totally overwhelm nation states and destroy cultural differences based on ethnicity or some kind of local cultural affiliation. Nor is it a recent phenomenon. In rejecting these propositions, the aim is not, of course, to deny that globalization has profoundly influenced patterns of social change, the capacity of nations of various kinds to determine their own future, or the global distribution of power and inequality. Nor is it to neglect the rapid intensification of globalization over the last century. The underlying analytical challenge, then, is to balance a sense of the dynamic significance, historical periodization and enduring effects of globalization with a sense of its limits, set by counter-trends.

The normative issues posed by globalization are equally challenging, although they have not so far been discussed in any explicit or sustained manner in this study. If we ask, 'Is globalization a good or a bad thing?' the responses that might be made will clearly be influenced both by the evaluative yardstick that is utilized and by how the globalization process is understood. As we saw in Chapter 2, within the discussion of images of world order, the range of evaluative standpoints from which globalization might be assessed is enormous. They range from the commitment to cosmopolitan ideals of world harmony and community

220

free from conflict, to values of national autonomy and localism. The same values can also lead in different directions. Values of community or democracy, for example, are, for some, entirely compatible with globalization, or at least with particular forms that it can take, while the same values can lead others to a strongly anti-global position.

To be committed to 'green' values of environmental protection and harmony between humankind and the environment leads some to champion localism, reflected in campaigns such as the reduction of the air miles involved in cross-border transport of foodstuffs, and the support for local producers' markets. Yet others promote environmental values by participating in global social movements such as Greenpeace International, and trans-national organizations such as the UNEP or the EU. The slogan 'Think Globally, Act Locally' adds further complexity to this picture. For a global response on one level (for example, knowledge of the cumulative planetary effects of pollution and environmental degradation) may be compatible with a local response (for example, campaigns against a local polluter) on the other. In the normative *arena*, as in the analytical one, it seems that the global and the local or national not only co-exist but also interpenetrate.

In this concluding section, we return to a powerful way of reconciling the global and the local, suggested at various points in this book, and associated with Roland Robertson. Attention then shifts to the question 'Is globalization reversible?'. The book concludes with further comments on normative issues arising from the challenge of globalization to democracy.

Analytical Challenges

One of the greatest analytical challenges is to make sense of the way in which political and cultural boundaries are being simultaneously permeated and re-established, transcended and reinvented by complex processes of global change. Rather than globalization destroying the nation state, the two sets of forces, institutions and processes labelled 'global' and 'national' interpenetrate. If this is the case, what alternative forms of analysis and explanation are available?

Robertson's culture-inclusive, cognitively centred approach is intended to challenge both the economic determinism of Wallerstein's world-system theory and its undervaluation of cultural agency. Robertson pursues this objective by rejecting the idea of globalization as a system. His alternative is to reconceptualize globalization as a *field* (see Figure 8.1). This field includes *within it* the challenges and

Figure 8.1 Roland Robertson's global field

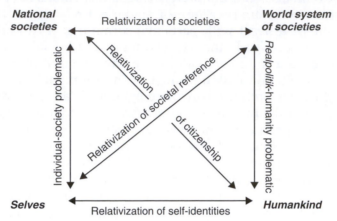

Source: Robertson (1992: 27).

contradictions that make the modern world such a paradoxical place. This field is constituted by the complex interpenetration of 'global', 'national' and 'local' or 'individual' aspects of social life analyzed in previous chapters.

Robertson sees globalization as the 'interaction of different forms of life' (1992) rather than as the dominance of trans-national forces over the national, or the triumph of modernity over tradition. The 'global' field comprises, four major 'reference points' (one at each corner of the square), between which global interactions take place. Two of these, namely 'national societies' and individual 'selves', are familiar elements in modern social theory. What Robertson adds to this picture is first of all the 'world system of societies' and second 'humankind'. By the former, he means the system of interaction between national societies, while the latter evidently refers to conceptions of humankind as a single entity. These four reference points serve to emphasize the simultaneous importance of large institutions and the life-world of individuals within the global field. In this sense, Robertson rejects those who see the 'global' purely as a macro-level process that dominates the lives of individuals, who in turn may only organize micro-level or local resistance to global trends. His global field is, from the outset, an attempt to bridge the macro–micro divide in understandings of globalization.

Having defined the four key reference points, the interactions between them are represented in Figure 8.1 in terms of six bilateral relationships (depicted by the four interactions along the perimeter and two along the diagonals). The nature of the interaction involved is cognitive as well as normative, in that the parties involved are faced both with tensions between conflicting principles and with opportunities to reconcile such tensions through mutual recognition. These abstract deliberations are made more concrete in Tables 8.1 and 8.2.

If, for example we start from the position of an individual national society, the ensuing challenges involve interaction with the world-system of societies, with humankind in general, as well as with individual selves. In Table 8.1, the general patterns of interaction involving the nation state are outlined, and illustrations are provided of the interactive challenges involved in terms of particular features of contemporary globalism. It should be emphasized that the interactions are two-way processes rather than one-sided challenges of adaptation to global developments.

A similar exercise may be conducted starting with the position of individual selves. This is outlined in Table 8.2. Here the global field embodies new challenges in the relations between individual selves, on the one hand, and the world-system of societies and humankind,

Table 8.1 The interactions of national societies within the global field

Aspect of the global field	Process involved	Examples of interactive challenge
World system of societies	Relativization of societies	Problem of the relative sovereignty of individual nations in relation to that of other national societies as reflected in trans-national regulatory bodies and international law. Problem of the capacity of trans-national bodies such as the United Nations to gain the adherence of nations to stable patterns of regulation
Humankind	Relativization of citizenship	Problem of the relative nature of national citizenship in relation to global ideas of human rights and environmentalism. Problem of applying general notions such as human rights to the specific needs of particular groups
Selves	Individual-society problematic	Problem of the adherence of autonomous individuals to nations. Problem of the integrity of the self in relation to the surveillance capacities of the nation state

Table 8.2   The interactions of particular selves within the global field

Aspect of the global field	Process involved	Examples of interactive challenge
World system of societies	Relativization of societal reference	Problem of the place of individual selves within large-scale interstate and trans-national structure. This problem is symbolized by the remoteness of inter-governmental structures such as the United Nations from individuals, and the highly abstract nature of ideas of global citizenship
Humankind	Relativization of self-identities	Problem of how or whether individuals with local or national identities can relate to notions of humankind as a whole. Problem of whether global consciousness can mobilize particular selves located in a diverse range of social settings
Selves	Individual-society problematic	Problem of the adherence of autonomous individuals to the social collectivity. Problem of the integrity of the self in relation to the surveillance capacities of the nation state

on the other, as well as in the more familiar relationship between individuals and the nation state.

Tables 8.1 and 8.2 are designed to clarify how the general and schematic nature of the global field may be applied to more concrete issues in the contemporary world. This in turn offers a major resource for making sense of the co-presence and interaction of the global and the national, the central analytical challenge identified in this book.

This inter-relationship may be further elaborated through the paradoxical development of both universalism and particularism. 'We are in the late 20th century,' says Robertson, 'witnesses to – and participants in – a massive, twofold process involving the interpenetration of the universalisation of particularism and the particularisation of universalism' (1992: 100). This Delphic observation requires some unravelling before its meaning becomes clear and in recent work on globalization and football Giulianotti and Robertson (2009: 32–3) provide some helpful and more concrete ways of doing this.

The 'universalization of particularism' is taken to mean the explosion of social difference, as in the revival of ethnicity or the contemporary proliferation of individual lifestyles. The ubiquity of cultural identification through assertions of difference reflects a situation in which claims to uniqueness and particularity have become almost limitless. In the case of global football this is manifested in the ways 'different national supporter groups' at internationals 'converge and commingle, displaying their particularistic dress, songs, and patterns of social behaviour' (ibid.: 32). At a more general level this explosion of difference has led, according to Robertson, to the widespread cultural expectation that all claims made by particular groups for particular purposes are legitimate.

The 'universalization of particularism' has a second meaning. This involves the diffusion of particularistic practices on an increasingly global scale. A leading example of this is the demand and spread of the nation state, as a political institution, across an increasing range of peoples. Here, the nation state becomes a universal model of what political arrangements should look like, while at the same time the interstate system functions to further the particularistic interests of the more powerful nation states and peoples.

Meanwhile, 'the particularization of universalism' involves the process whereby 'the idea of the universal is given global-human concreteness' (Robertson, 1992: 102). What this means is the translation of the would-be universal ideas like humanity, human rights, or a global community into particular forms of cooperation and institution-building that have a resonance in different locales. In the case of football, this is seen in the pyramidal structure of the Federation of International Football Associations (FIFA), where global standardization of rules operates through the participation of particular national and local associations (Giulianotti and Robertson, 2009: 33).

Another way of elaborating the general features of this type of analysis is through consideration of the relationship of women to the issue of universalism or particularism. A major issue for feminist movements is whether to stress equality with men or to focus on difference. One major strand in feminism has challenged the universalistic claims that modernity has triumphed over particularistic principles and traditions. What this neglects is the foundation of notions of modernity on the suppression of gender difference. Concealed behind ostensibly universalistic notions such as individual sovereignty or freedom of contract are patriarchal structures of power that have appeared to offer gender equality but actually constrain women to a private or domestic sphere that lies outside the universalized realm of public life (Pateman, 1988). Insofar as globalization reproduces the existing gender division of labour, it too may be seen as suppressing gender equality. But where does this critique lead?

In one sense, the feminist challenge to the quasi-universalistic patriarchal dominance of men might be seen as leading simply to the assertion of gender difference, an aspect of the universalization of particularism. Yet in another sense, following Robertson's argument (1992: 105–8), there is a counter-trend towards women's involvement in the particularization of universalism. This may be seen in moves to apply the universal notion of human rights to women's issues such as abortion or rape, by means of notions such as women's human rights. Women have had limited access to the public worlds of global politics and economic management, while also being victims of global processes such as people trafficking, sex tourism and the trans-national market in domestic servants (Enloe, 1990). At the same time, the resistance to such trends has depended not only on the assertion of difference, but also on the articulation and institutionalization of globally valid rights for women within trans-national organizations. These have been publicized at major world conferences such as the 1995 UN Conference on Women in Beijing, and in meetings of the World Social Forum (Vargas, 2003).

We have dwelt on the strengths of Robertson's argument, but what of its limits? One is the uncertain place of the political economy of global capitalism in the schema. Robertson certainly rejects the argument that the logic of capitalism directs culture. As an alternative, he suggests that culture and economy interpenetrate and that this is reflected in the interaction between universalistic globe-wide consumer capitalism on the one hand, and particularistic demand on the other. This refusal to privilege producers over consumers is attractive in principle since, as we saw in Chapter 3, the power of producers has been exaggerated. Yet the disproportion between multinational power and that of consumers, especially those who lack financial resources and information to make effective choices, is still a fundamental source of inequality, one that has only partly been redressed by regulatory frameworks that seek to address North–South disparities of wealth or, on an individual level, to uphold consumer rights.

This criticism connects with a second, namely that Robertson is exclusively concerned with cognitive issues to do with how the globe is understood and how that understanding reflects and embodies relations between universalization and particularism. This focus is very important but it still downplays the importance of patterns of institutional power and inequality.

For Friedman (1995: 72), Robertson's culturally centred cognitive approach leads him into the trap of suggesting that competing understandings and interpretations of 'global circumstances' actually constitute much of the global field itself. No attempt is made to confront alternative power-centred political economy models 'on their own ground'. In this way, Robertson neglects the post-war global institutionalization of political-economic structures. It is these structures which have constituted many key elements of the global field. The analytical task is thus to connect issues of global awareness, theorized by Robertson, with issues of global political economy, rather than replacing Robertson's cognitively centred global field with an exclusively political-economic focus. Reductionist general theories that seek a political-economic or cultural explanation of any global phenomenon only take analysis so far. This is because the culture of a particular epoch, group, or nation cannot necessarily be read off from a purely political-economic understanding any more than cultural analysis can explain all patterns of political-economic activity.

The revival of nationalism and ethnicity, for example, presents powerful criticisms of a general political economy approach to globalization. Wallerstein's political economic approach (1984, 1990, 1991), for instance, maintains that nationalism, ethnicity and cultural particularism may well take on anti-global forms, yet they function to promote the dominance of the capitalist world-system by undermining class unity and resistance. This broad-brush approach has some merit, but it is insufficiently fine-grained to explain cases such as the recent revival of ethno-nationalism in the Balkans. Here, nationalism and ethnicity took the form of resistance to regional integration in the former Yugoslavia rather than resistance to globalization, while the effects of civil war have obstructed capital accumulation rather than promoting it. Others, like Barber (1995), reason in a more general way, that tribalism, old and new, is alive and well, and a threat to both globalization and democracy.

So does the resilience of nation states, national identity, ethno-nationalism and cultural particularism mean that globalization is already in reverse?

Is Globalization about to be Superseded by a Resurgence of Nation States?

This book is about globalization and the nation state. The first edition was written in the late 1990s and argued that globalization was not about to destroy the nation state. Global and national trends intersect, sometimes in conflict and sometimes in harmony. Where the two fuse together or at least interpenetrate we may speak of glocalization. This analysis has been updated in the present edition to take account of recent developments, but remains persuasive.

To reiterate, while some versions of nationalism are compatible with globalization and cosmopolitanism, this is very far from ruling out anti-global, particularistic or tribal loyalties, political resistance to globalization and a continuing role for nation states (Hutchinson, 2005). For all these reasons the interstate system and national societies remain irreducible features of Robertson's global 'field'. The analytical choices are not then simply between a global or a national future, because the third possibility is a simultaneous global and national – or glocal future.

This prospect has, however, been challenged by those who feel that globalization is faltering and may indeed be reversible. This argument connects with discussions of the history of globalization (discussed in Chapter 2), and the observation that global upsurges are often followed by national or local reactions, which lead on, at some future point to renewed global upswings. Harold James (2001), for example, thinks in terms of phases of economic globalization followed by phases of deglobalization. These rhythms are linked more with political economy than with culture and ethno-nationalism.

In recent history, this pattern is linked with a global upswing measured in terms of increased world trade, capital mobility and labour migration after 1850, reaching its peak around 1900, but then prompting deglobalizing trends. These include the advent of national central banks to regulate finance and capital movements, increased restrictions on immigration and trade protectionism. Many such reactions were evident before 1914, but they only became dominant features of the protectionist inter-war period between 1918 and 1939, when the global gold standard regulating currencies, trade imbalances and interest rates was abandoned. After 1945, under the Bretton Woods system, globalization resumed, but by the early twenty-first century has generated increasing discontent (Sassen, 1998; Stiglitz, 2002), brought to a head by the liberal deregulatory policies of the Washington consensus, amplified by the resurgence of nation state dominance over market autonomy during the global financial crisis.

Underlying these patterns of advancing economic globalization and deglobalization are the rhythms of social differentiation and integration, famously analyzed by Karl Polanyi (1957). His argument was that the processes of market expansion through free trade and deregulation eventually came to sever previous ties that regulated market freedom either through state policies or community sanction, in attempts to preserve social cohesion. When markets become too 'free' in this sense, social and political crisis leads to a resumption of regulation. This was seen, according to James (2001), in pre-1914 moves to regulate financial and labour markets against destabilizing effects of economic globalization. It has been seen again with states stepping in to rescue and reregulate banks and certain industrial corporations in the name of economic stability and social cohesion.

In this kind of argument, economic globalization, while dynamic, eventually becomes dysfunctional and pathological and this leads, at least for a time, to deglobalization, in an economic sense. But deglobalization of this kind, it seems, is not likely to survive indefinitely as capitalist globalization revives. James' argument adds a further dimension to reversibility arguments beyond ethno-cultural or culturalist accounts of counter-trends to globalization. Yet despite the plausibility of the cyclic phasing of globalization and deglobalization, this still fails to displace the idea of a predominantly glocal future. Rather it demonstrates that global 'field' is not a static phenomenon, but is rather one riven by internal conflicts and accommodations between global and national elements.

Beyond this the dynamics and sustainability of globalization are also threatened by political-economic considerations linked with land, food supply and population. Focus on finance and industry typically directs attention away from these problems, on the assumption that science and technology will necessarily continue to deliver adequate food for a rapidly growing population. Research by Alston, Bedow and Pardey (2009) disputes this assumption, claiming that there has been a recent slowing in the pace of yield-increasing technology. This is partly a product of unsustainable intensive agricultural techniques that are sapping soil fertility and vulnerable to water shortage. It is also a result of a relative decline in agricultural research, and its skewing to private corporate objectives rather than sustainability. Other destabilizing aspects of agrarian developments include increases in land used for bio-fuels at the expense of cheap food for poorer populations.

These developments are crucial, but it is difficult to assess their impact on globalization. While deglobalizing movements to achieve local food-security exist (Bello, 2009), they are unlikely to have the political impetus to succeed. What seems more likely in the medium term is that food shortage in the South will adversely effect patterns of global inequality and magnify regional disparities in welfare still further. Food shortage, like climate change, or world peace, is a problem that demands global solutions achieved through some kind of global cooperation but it remains unclear that an irreversible momentum has been created.

What Should be Done about Globalization? Is it Good or Bad?

There remain normative challenges about whether globalization is good or bad, or perhaps good in parts. It is perhaps disappointing to those who see globalization as thoroughly good or thoroughly bad to be faced with the complexities and paradoxes entailed in the analyses of globalization offered here.

The complex multidimensional approach to globalization developed in the present study rules out any notion of globalization as a unitary process with a single logic, and this in turn sensitizes us to similar complexities in normative debates. For example, many of those who reject economic globalization, in terms of the penetration of market relations and powerful MNEs into national communities, are more positive about political aspects of globalization such as the attempts to secure global human rights or environmental protection regimes. Opponents of multinationals may also sometimes join global social movements such as Greenpeace International. The obverse is also true, in that many economic liberals who welcome unfettered free markets in capital and commodities are socially conservative in rejecting many UN or European human rights initiatives or in rejecting global environmental protection initiatives (Alston, 1995). The social multi-dimensionality of globalization is thus also mirrored by a normative multidimensionality. In this sense, it may be preferable to think in terms of globalizations rather than globalization.

Further normative complexities emerge when we come to consider the voices and interests that come to evaluate global processes. Most discussion about such matters has hitherto been directed towards public political norms – that is, to the future of ideals of democracy and the autonomous nation state in an epoch of globalization. The place of individuals, families and households in normative debates over globalization has received less attention in the past, but this is now changing. The advent of the personal computer and the internet, together with the global expansion of personal consumption and tourism, all raise issues concerning the positive and negative effects of such global developments on human welfare. So too does the expansion of voluntary labour migration and the growth of refugee popula-tions. All such examples raise public policy issues, of course, ranging from consumer rights and questions of personal privacy in electronic communications, to levels of migrant intake and global humanitarian responsibilities. However, they also represent areas in which individual evaluations are made, often repeatedly but in a typically private and less vocal way.

Hirschman (1970) has pointed out that if 'voice' is the typical mode of operation in the public life of democracy, 'exit' is the typical orien-tation to the 'market'. Since economic globalization is founded on market relations, it is not perhaps surprising that much of the norma-tive orientation of individuals and households towards globalization within everyday life takes place over decisions of whether to enter or exit particular markets. For those whose choices are circumscribed by poverty, such decisions may relate to the purchase of a limited range of desired commodities, many imported or produced locally by global capital. Economic globalization may be evaluated positively insofar as such products (televisions, computers, the Big Mac) are brought within reach. Greater complexities emerge when traditional products (foodstuffs and music) are valued more highly. This may mean a rejection of imports or Westernized/Americanized goods and an exit from globalized markets, but it may equally lead to a newly globalized supply of previously local products and services, as where migrants import products from the homeland.

Meanwhile, on the labour market side, foreign capital may increase or decrease access to local employment, depending on the type of activity pursued and the impact made on the existing employment structure. This can be highly destabilizing for poor and unskilled rural workers seeking to enter industrial employment. Global migrants may seek out new employment opportunities but many of these involve low-paid manual and service work, leading to investment in the education of children as a pathway out of poverty.

Exit from one country and settlement elsewhere, perhaps organized through kin-based chain migration, represents a specific example of private choices and evaluations of global opportunities. Exit of this kind is, however, increasingly circumscribed by the toughening of immigration policies in the more prosperous countries. This trend has been described by Richmond (1993) as a 'new cultural apartheid', whereby national barriers act to segregate the relatively wealthy and powerful from the relatively poor and powerless. The trend has further tightened in the twenty-first century.

For those with greater material resources, normative evaluation of globalization depends on how far such resources are seen as threatened or enhanced by the range of global developments. Greater global access to information technology and tourism, or employment and investment opportunities in other places, all of which look positive, may be offset by greater job competition in skilled labour markets and greater instability in globalized finance markets. Tourism may narrow as well as broaden the mind. Professional and technical migrants may do well economically, but remain culturally detached from their new environment. There is thus no compelling reason why economic globalization will necessarily produce middle-class cosmopolitanism. Even though some segments of the geographically mobile may move in this direction (Hannerz, 1990), the determinants of cosmopolitanism are far more complex (Holton, 2009).

To depict a world of private choices, expressing positive and negative evaluations of such global products and opportunities, is useful in the sense that it affirms globalization as a personally and privately enabling as well as a constraining process. Given the contemporary disillusionment with politics in so many parts of the globe, there is, for the moment at least, a strong mood of privatism within the day-to-day life of individuals. This enters into the way in which globalization is approached, utilized, or rejected, quite apart from public political debate about this or that UN decision, or negotiations between governments and multinational companies, the IMF, or World Bank over economic policy and investment decisions. The private world presented is, however, an incomplete and artificial one, in that it brackets out the institutional framework within which private activity takes place. Exit is, in short, not enough. Voice exercised within the public sphere is very far from extinguished. Yet the challenges to effective democratic voice posed by globalization are especially difficult and seemingly intractable. Why is this so?

The ideal of a self-governing people presumes the capacity to exercise self-determination. The globalization process nonetheless permeates and penetrates those political boundaries that have hitherto defined the territorially based units within which democratic self-determination has been practised, notably those of the nation state. Questions then arise not only about the democratic viability of the nation state under global conditions, but also on the feasibility of institutions capable of expressing cross-border democracy, whether on a global or regional basis.

We have already noted in Chapter 4 that it is unhelpful to think of the global challenge to democracy at the national level in terms of the loss of some absolute sense of national sovereignty. This has rarely existed and is in no sense a historical or contemporary norm. The challenges that globalization pose to democracy are more to do with increased global interconnectedness and with inequalities of access to power both between nations and between different interests within them. Beyond that, the cognitive complexities of global governance also create additional difficulties for democratic ideals, not least of which are the reliance on experts and the powerful position of epistemic communities of scientists and professionals in relation to citizens.

Barber's (1995) analysis of global polarization between McWorld and Jihad is pessimistic for the future of democracy on two counts. First, McWorld, that amalgam of fast food, fast computers and fast music, corrodes democracy, in Barber's view, through the ideology of *laissez-faire* that leaves little scope for political action in the name of the public good. Public political participation is discouraged through 'a culture of advertising, software, Hollywood movies, theme parks and shopping malls hooped together by the virtual nexus of the information super-highway closes down free spaces' (ibid.: 276). Second, the opponents of McWorld, symbolized as Jihad, the holy war of tribalization and funda-mentalism, also undermine democracy in different ways. Principles of democratic process safeguarded by human rights and the rule of law are undermined by a totalitarian politics that represses dissent and open debate.

Other commentators concerned with the positive potential of cosmo-politanism are more optimistic. This wide-ranging and somewhat confusing term may, in one sense, link 'voice' and democracy, with 'loyalty' and social solidarity. Held (1995, 2004) and his associates (Held and McGrew, 2007) have fruitfully elaborated ideas of 'cosmopo-litan democracy', 'cosmopolitan social democracy' and 'cosmopolitan governance'. These are seen as alternatives to three prevailing notions of global order, namely (a) the Westphalian model of a system of national sovereignty, (b) the UN-centred global polity and (c) the Washington consensus conception of liberal global governance. While a system founded solely on national sovereignty is outmoded in an increasingly interdependent world, the UN system is so constituted as to be ineffective in achieving compliance with its policies. Both suffer from an inability to reimagine what effective democracy might look like in a global order, or to connect with 'bottom-up' initiatives around global social movements and global civil society. The same applies to the discredited Washington consensus, which has failed to secure sustained economic advance capable of fundamentally reducing global poverty.

Cosmopolitan ideals can be applied to many kinds of social practices (Vertovec and Cohen, 2002), from cultural expression to political organ-ization, and from social movement activism to new forms of regulatory governance. They also embrace forms of law that are trans-national in scope, which recognize human rights and citizens as component parts of an emergent cosmopolitan polity, but which also invoke the self-determination of all peoples collectively as well as individually.

Against the criticism that all this is simply utopian projection, Held makes two moves. First, he argues that cosmopolitan democracy builds on emergent social trends. Foremost of these, as argued above in Chapter 5, is a sense of the global order as a complex cobweb of linkages between governmental and non-governmental bodies. The argument for cosmopolitan democracy rests in part on the 'multiple and overlapping networks of power … which constitute the inter-connections of different peoples and nations' (1995, 271). Within this context, democratic rights are no longer sustainable within or limited to the territorially bounded world of nations but require a more complex globally organized polity to be effectively exercised. This not only requires a global as well as national and local level of organization, but must also recognize the diverse cross-cutting communities of which individuals may be part. Held's second normative move is to detach democratic rights from any necessary relationship with territorial entities, beyond that of the globe as whole. Cosmopolitan democracy, embodied in law, should rather be applicable to all those with an interest in that aspect of human welfare involved, be it health, world security, the economy, or whatever.

Beyond market 'exit' and the democratic institutionalization of 'voice', there remains the issue of 'loyalty'. This is the element that pertains to questions of normative commitments to community. Barber sees commitment in an era of globalization as polarized between the consumerist seductions of McWorld and the particularistic tribalism and stern moral fundamentalism of Jihad. The suggestion is that polarization of this kind is so entrenched that loyalty to a globalized democratic political or legal order will remain weak.

Are there Grounds for Global Optimism?

Held (1995, 2004) and Beck and Grande (2007) offer an optimistic alternative to Barber's pessimism. This is partly linked with contrasts in the view from Europe as against that from the USA. Held's confidence in the capacity of trans-national political and legal arrangements to constrain the actions of nation states according to a framework of norms seems to draw for many of its examples on the impact of decisions of the EU and the European Court of Justice on certain member states, notably the UK. Beyond this, Held, like a number of other observers, emphasizes the key role of global NGOs in reviving the political activism of civil society, even in the face of McWorld and Jihad. NGOs, as discussed in Chapter 5, do not have the power or the legitimacy of nation states. Yet they have helped change the agenda of global politics – for example, in relation to environmental issues – and continue to be drawn on for expert opinion in standard-setting and the monitoring of compliance.

Held is less concerned to canvass the state of contemporary loyalty in relation to globalization, but he does take up the challenge posed by cultural difference to the ideal of cosmopolitan democracy. In contrast to the argument of Anthony Smith (1990), the presumption is that a strong sense of global culture or loyalty to some overarching set of global values is not necessary for the functioning of cosmopolitan democracy. Different cultural patterns are already interlinked through globalization, such that 'sealed cultural diversity' (Held, 1995: 284) no longer exists.

Even so, the recent explosion of ethno-nationalism and the revival of ethnicity in settings of migrant settlement, together with the robustness of more ordinary or banal forms of nationalism, all suggest in their different ways that the project of mutual accommodation between contrasting loyalties is an extremely difficult one. While cosmopolitan cultures remain limited in scope, and are often expressed outside formal politics (Hannerz, 2004), there is every reason to expect territoriality, real or imagined, to continue to play a major part in social identities. The issue, then, is the extent to which territorially bound cultural identities lend themselves to mutual accommodation instead of conflict.

Here, the test case remains Europe, where closer integration in terms of markets and political decisions does not depend on any clear sense of European loyalty. The implications of this are ambivalent. In one sense, the EU shows how far trans-national relations and institutions can be created to allow mutual accommodation of parties without a strong base of popular cultural loyalty to the framework being created (Beck and Grande, 2007). On the other hand, the lack of such a base and the elitist nature of many EU processes, notably the bureaucratic regulatory institutions centred in Brussels, render the whole edifice vulnerable to national and local resistance. Even if mutual accommodation of interests and cultural orientations should prevail in one crucial region such as Europe, this is no guarantee that similar developments would arise elsewhere. Regional cooperation in North America through NAFTA or in the Asia-Pacific through APEC is still restricted to economic matters. Contrasts between European and Asian-Pacific regional trans-nationalism alert us to the great unevenness of globalization processes, especially in trans-national institution-building. The globalization of loyalty seems, for the moment, more remote in comparison with the globalization of voice or of exit.

Normative debates around globalization, democracy and cultural loyalty are clearly far from resolution. This applies both to the analysis of emergent social trends and to the coherence of norms such as that of cosmopolitan democracy. While a heavy dose of scepticism may be applied to all such utopian projections into the future, it is equally the case, as Eric Hobsbawm once remarked, that utopias may equally prove fruitful as barren.

Drawing a Moral Balance Sheet?

There is, then, no definitive or even provisional balance sheet to be drawn on where globalization is headed or whether it may be regarded as good or bad. There is, however, no reason that I regard as convincing for seeing globalization in demonic terms as an unstoppable force, a juggernaut driven by technological change, or as a process whose direction is monopolized from above in a manner that is, in principle, out of reach of the peoples of the globe. Globalization is best seen not a unitary process or system, but as a set of intersecting processes that falter as much as they advance. These often have the quality of networks (Holton, 2008) rather than structures. They also have limits set by counter-trends and movements within the global field. Globalization, in terms of any of its manifestations, is also potentially reversible, as we see from its long cycles of expansion and contraction.

The politics of the 'global field' has been and will continue to be the site of conflict as well as cooperation since major issues of global inequality and injustice remain unresolved. In this respect, global politics is no different from any other political struggle over social purposes and the allocation of resources between conflicting interests. Since it is not a system, however, I doubt whether an anti-systemic challenge to globalization *per se* makes much analytical or political sense.

Understood in this way, globalization processes are not necessarily to be feared and can even, in some contexts, be something to be enjoyed or in which to find fulfilment. It has been said of some schools of social enquiry that they function to talk people out of their happiness and into a more critical standpoint towards social life. A critical approach to global rhetoric and to pieties about globalization as an unambiguous social good is certainly highly necessary. Identifying the winners and losers from processes of globalization is a major task of social science. Yet it may equally be said that certain social enquiries into globalization stand in need of less gloom and despair. What is required instead is a greater appreciation of the ways in which social groups in all parts of the world have been influenced by and borrowed from each other, thereby meeting a wider range of human needs, including the need for enhanced cooperation.

Bibliography

Abu-Lughod, J. (1989) *Before European Hegemony, The World System, AD 1250–1350*. New York: Oxford University Press.

Abu-Lughod, J. (1993) 'Discontinuities and persistence: one world system or a succession of systems', in A. G. Frank and B. K. Gills (eds), *The World System: Five Hundred Years or Five Thousand?*. London: Routledge, 278–91.

Ahmed, A. S. (1992) *Postmodernism and Islam*. London: Routledge.

Ahmed, A. S. (1997), *Jinnah, Pakistan, and Islamic Identity*. London: Routledge.

Albrow, M. (1990) 'Introduction', in M. Albrow and E. King (eds), *Globalization, Knowledge and Society*. London: Sage, 3–13.

Albrow, M. and Glasius, M. (2008) 'Democracy and the possibility of a global public sphere', in M. Albrow, H. Anheier, M. Glasius, M. Price and M. Kaldor (eds), *Global Civil Society, 2007–8*. London: Sage, 1–18.

Alexander, J. (1982–4) *Theoretical Logic in Sociology*, 4 vols. London: Routledge.

Allen, K. (2000) *The Celtic Tiger: The Myth of Social Partnership in Ireland*. Manchester: Manchester University Press.

Alston, J., Bedow, J. and Pardey, P. (2009) 'Agricultural research, productivity, and food prices in the long-run', *Science*, 325(5945): 1209–10.

Alston, P. (1992) 'Appraising the United Nations human rights regime', in P. Alston (ed.), *The United Nations and Human Rights*. Oxford: Oxford University Press, 1–21.

Alston, P. (1995) 'Reform of treaty-making processes: form over substance', in P. Alston and M. Chiam (eds), *Treaty-Making and Australia*. Sydney: Federation Press, 1–28.

Anderson, B. (1983) *Imagined Communities*. London: Verso.

Anderson, B. (1994) 'Exodus', *Critical Inquiry*, 20, Winter: 313–27.

Anglade, C. and Fortin, C. (1990) 'Accumulation, adjustment and the autonomy of the State in Latin America', in C. Anglade and C. Fortin (eds), *The State and Capital Accumulation in Latin America*, 2 vols. Pittsburgh: University of Pittsburgh Press, 211–340.

Appadurai, A. (1990) 'Disjuncture and difference in the global cultural economy', in M. Featherstone (ed.), *Global Culture*. London: Sage, 295–310.

Appadurai, A. (1996) *Modernity at Large: Cultural Dimensions of Globalization*. Minneapolis: University of Minnesota Press.

Appelbaum, R., Felstiner, W. L., and Gessner, V. (eds) (2004) *Rules and Networks: The Legal Culture of Global Business Transactions*, Oxford/Portland Oregon: Hart Publishing.

Appiah, K. A. (1996) 'Cosmopolitan patriots', in M. Nussbaum and J. Cohen (eds), *For Love of Country*, Boston: Beacon Press, 21–9.

Appiah, K. A. (2006) *Cosmopolitanism: Ethics in a World of Strangers*. London: Penguin.

Arjomand, S. A. (2003) 'Islam', in M. Juergensmeyer (ed.), *Global Religions: An Introduction*. Oxford: Oxford University Press, 28–39.

Asante, M. K. (1991) 'Multiculturalism: an exchange', *American Scholar*, 60: 267–72.

Australian Council on Population and Ethnic Affairs (1982) *Multiculturalism for All Australians*. Canberra: AGPS.

Babb, S. (2005) 'The social consequences of structural adjustment', *Annual Review of Sociology*, 31: 199–222.

Bailey, D., Harte, G. and Sugden, R. (1994) *Transnationals and Governments: Recent Policies in Japan, France, Germany, the United States and Japan*. London: Routledge.

Banchoff, T. (ed.) (2008) *Religious Pluralism, Globalization, and World Politics*. Oxford: Oxford University Press.

Bank for International Settlements (BIS) (2007) *Triennial Central Bank Survey, 2007*, http://www.bis/org/publ/rpfx07.htm

Banton, M. (1994) 'Modelling ethnic and national relations', *Ethnic and Racial Studies*, 17(1): 1–19.

Barber, B. (1991) 'Jihad vs McWorld', *Atlantic*, 269(3): 53–63.

Barber, B. (1995) *Jihad vs McWorld*. New York: Ballantine.

Bartlett, C. A. and Ghoshal, S. (2000) *Transnational Management*. Boston: McGraw Hill.

Bayly, C. (1996) *Empire and Information: Intelligence Gathering and Social Communication in India, 1780–1870*. Cambridge: Cambridge University Press.

Bayly, C. (2002), '"Archaic" and "modern" globalization in the Eurasian and African arena', in A. G. Hopkins (ed.), *Globalization in World History*. London: Pimlico, 47–73.

Bayly, C. (2004) *The Birth of the Modern World, 1780–1914*. Oxford: Blackwell.

Bayly, S. (1999), 'The evolution of colonial cultures: nineteenth century Asia', in A. Porter, (ed.), *The Oxford History of the British Empire, volume 3: The Nineteenth Century*, Oxford: Oxford University Press, 447–69.

Beck, U. (1992) *Risk Society: Towards a New Sociology of Modernity* (London: Sage).

Beck, U. (2000) 'The cosmopolitan perspective: sociology in the second age of modernity', *British Journal of Sociology*, 15(1): 79–105.

Beck, U. (2002) *What is Globalization?*. Cambridge: Polity Press.

Beck, U. (2003) *Power in the Global Age*. Cambridge: Polity Press.

Beck, U. (2006) *The Cosmopolitan Vision*. Cambridge: Polity Press.

Beck, U. and Grande, E. (2007) *Cosmopolitan Europe*. Cambridge: Polity Press.

Beckford, J. (2004), 'New religious movements and globalization', in P. Lucas and T. Robbins (eds), *New Religious Movements in the 21st Century*. London: Routledge, 253–64.

Bello, W. (2009) *The Food Wars*. London: Verso.

Bennison, A. (2002) 'Muslim universalism and western globalization', in A. G. Hopkins (ed.), *Globalization in World History*. London: Pimlico, 74–97.

Bercovitch, J. (1996) 'The United Nations and the mediation of international disputes', in R. Thukur (ed.), *The United Nations at Fifty: Retrospect and Prospect*. Dunedin: University of Otago Press, 73–88.

Bercovitch, J. and Gartner, S. (eds) (2009) *International Conflict Mediation: New Approaches and Findings*. Abingdon: Routledge.

Berman, P. S. (2004–5) 'From international law to law and globalization', *Columbia Journal of Transnational Law*, 43: 484–556.

Bernal, M. (1987) *The Afro-Asiatic Roots of Classical Civilization*. New Brunswick: Rutgers University Press.

Beyer, P. (1994) *Religion and Globalization*. London: Sage.

Beyer, P. (2006) *Religions in Global Society*. London: Routledge.

Beyer, P. (2007) 'Globalization and the institutional modelling of religions', in P. Beyer and L. Beaman (eds), *Religion, Culture, and Globalization*. Leiden: Brill, 167–86.

Billig, M. (1995) *Banal Nationalism*. London: Sage.

Blainey, G. (1966) *The Tyranny of Distance*. Melbourne: Sun.

Blankenburg, S. and Palma, J. G. (2009) 'Introduction: the global financial crisis', *Cambridge Journal of Economics*, 531–8.

Boatca, M. and Costa, S. (2010) 'Postcolonial sociology: a research agenda', in E. Rodriguez, M. Boatca and S. Costa (eds), *Decolonising European Sociology: Different Paths Towards a Pending Project*. Aldershot: Ashgate, 13–32.

Boddewyn, J., Soehi, R. and Picard, J. (1986) 'Standardization in international marketing', *Business Horizons*, November/December, 69–75.

Bouras, G. (1986) *A Foreign Wife*. Fitzroy: McPhee, Gribble/Penguin.

Bousetta, H. (1997), 'Citizenship and political participation in France and the Netherlands: some comparative reflections', *New Commentary*, 23(2): 215–31.

Bousetta, H. and Jacobs, D. (2006) 'Multiculturalism, citizenship, and Islam in problematic encounters in Belgium', in T. Madood, A. Triandafyllidou and R. Zapata-Barrero (eds), *Multiculturalism, Muslims and Citizenship: A European Approach*. London: Routledge: 23–36.

Boyne, R. (1990) 'Culture and the world-system', in M. Featherstone (ed.), *Global Culture: Nationalism, Globalization and Modernity*. London: Sage, 57–62.

Braithwaite, J. (1993) 'Transnational regulation of the pharmaceutical industry', *Annals*, AAPSS, 525: 12–30.

Braithwaite, J. (1995) 'Sovereignty and globalisation of business regulation', in P. Alston and M. Chiam (eds), *Treaty-Making in Australia: Globalisation versus Sovereignty?* Sydney: Federation Press, 115–28.

Braithwaite, J. (2008) *Regulatory Capitalism*. Cheltenham: Elgar.

Braithwaite, J. and Drahos, P. (2000) *Global Business Regulation*. Cambridge: Cambridge University Press.

Brandt, W. (1980) *North–South: A Programme for Survival: The Report of the Independent Commission on International Development Issues*. London: Pan.

Brauch, H. G. (2008) 'Conceptualizing the environmental dimension of Human Security in the UN', in M. Goucha and J. Crowley (eds), *Rethinking Human Security*. Oxford: Blackwell, 19–48.

Braudel, F. (1982) *Civilisation and Capitalism 15th–18th Century*, vol. 2, *The Wheels of Commerce*. London: Collins.

Braudel, F. (1988) *The Identity of France*, vol. 1, *History and Environment*. London: Collins.

Brenner, N. (1998) 'Global cities, glocal states: global city formation and state territorial restructuring in contemporary Europe', Review of International Political Economy, 5(1): 1–37.

Brett, E. A. (1985) The World Economy Since the War: The Politics of Uneven Development. Basingstoke: Macmillan.

Bridge, G. (2008) 'Global production networks and the extractive sector: governing resource-based development', Journal of Economic Geography, 8(3): 389–419.

British Broadcasting Corporation (BBC) (2010a) 'Daimler agrees to pay $185 million after admitting bribery', http://www.bbc.co.uk/2/hi/business/8600241. stm (accessed 6 April 2010).

British Broadcasting Corporation (BBC) (2010b) 'Rio Tinto Executives handed out lengthy jail terms', http://www.bbc.co.uk/2/hi/business/8592226.stm (accessed 6 April 2010).

Burawoy, M. et al. (ed.) (2000) Global Ethnography. Berkeley: University of California Press.

Cameron, D. (1978) 'The expansion of the public economy: a comparative analysis', American Political Science Review, 72(4): 1243–61.

Carnoy, M. (1993) 'Multinationals in a changing world economy: wither the nation state?', in M. Carnoy, M. Castells and S. S. Cohen (eds), The Global Economy in the Information Age. University Park, PA: Pennsylvania State University Press, 45–96.

Carnoy, M., Castells, M. and Cohen, S. S. (eds) (1993) The Global Economy in the Information Age. University Park, PA: Pennsylvania State University Press.

Carroll, W. and Carson, C. (2003) 'The network of global corporations and elite policy groups', Global Networks, 3(1): 29–58.

Carson, R. (1962) Silent Spring, Boston: Houghton-Mifflin.

Cassese, A. (1988) Violence and the Law in the Modern Age. Cambridge: Polity Press.

Cassese, A. (1992) 'The General Assembly: historical perspective 1945–89', in P. Alston (ed.), The United Nations and Human Rights: A Critical Appraisal. Oxford: Oxford University Press, 25–54.

Castells, M. (1993) 'The information economy and the new international order', in M. Carnoy, M. Castells and S. S. Cohen (eds), The Global Economy in the Information Age. University Park, PA: Pennsylvania State University Press, 15–44.

Castells, M. (1996) The Rise of the Network Society. Oxford: Blackwell.

Castells, M. (2001) The Internet Galaxy: Reflections on the Internet, Business, and Society. Oxford: Oxford University Press.

Chakrabaty, D. (2000) Provincializing Europe; Postcolonial Thought and Historical Difference. Princeton, NJ: Princeton University Press.

Chase-Dunn, C. (1989) Global Formation: Structures of the World-economy. Oxford: Blackwell.

Chase-Dunn, C. and Barbones, S. (eds) (2006) Global Social Change: Historical and Comparative Perspectives. Baltimore, MD: Johns Hopkins.

Chasek, P., Downie, D. and Brown, J. (2006) Global Environmental Politics. Boulder, CO: Westview Press.

Chen, X. (2009) 'A globalizing city on the rise: Shanghai's transformation in comparative perspective', in X. Chen and Z. Zhou (eds), *Shanghai Rising: State Power and Local Transformation in a Global Megacity*, [Globalization and Community series no 15]. Minnesota: University of Minnesota Press, xv–xxxv.

Chesterman, S. (2004) *You the People: The United Nations, Transitional Administration and State-Building*. Oxford: Oxford University Press.

Cohen, R. (2006) *Migration and Its Enemies: Global Capital, Migrant Labour, and the Nation State*. Aldershot: Ashgate.

Cohen, S. S. (1993) 'Geo-economics: lessons from America's mistakes', in M. Carnoy, M. Castells and S. S. Cohen (eds), *The Global Economy in the Information Age*. University Park, PA: Pennsylvania State University Press, 97–148.

Connor, W. (1973) 'The politics of ethno-nationalism', *Journal of International Affairs*, 27, 1–21.

Connor, W. (1987) 'Ethno-nationalism', in M. Weiner and S. Huntington (eds), *Understanding Political Development*. Boston: Little, Brown, 196–220.

Connor, W. (1994) *Ethno-Nationalism: The Quest for Understanding*. Princeton, NJ: Princeton University Press.

Cooper, F. (2001), 'Networks, moral discourse, and history', in R. Kassimir and R. Latham, (eds), *Intervention and Transnationalism in Africa*, Cambridge: Cambridge University Press, 23–46.

Corley, T. A. B. (1989) 'The nature of multi-nationals', in A. Teichova *et al.* (eds), *Historical Studies in International Corporate Business*. Cambridge: Cambridge University Press, 43–56.

Crotty, J. (2009), 'Structural causes of the global financial crisis: a critical assessment of the new financial architecture', *Cambridge Journal of Economics*, 33: 563–80.

Curtin, P. D. (1984) *Cross-cultural Trade in World History*. Cambridge: Cambridge University Press.

Dash, K. (2005) 'McDonalds in India', *The Garvin School of International Management*, Thunderbird Case Series no: A07-05-00151.

Dassbach, C. A. (1989) *Global Enterprises and the World Economy: Ford, General Motors, and IBM, the Emergence of the Transnational Enterprise*. New York: Garland.

Davis, M. C. (ed.) (1995) *Human Rights and Chinese Values*. Oxford: Oxford University Press.

Delanty, G. (1995) *Inventing Europe: Idea, Identity, Reality*. Basingstoke: Macmillan.

Dicken, P. (1986) *Global Shift: Industrial Change in a Turbulent World*. London: Harper and Row.

Dicken, P. (2007, 5th edn) *Global Shift: Mapping the Changing Contours of the Global Economy*. London: Sage.

Dinopoulos, E. Krishna, P. Panagariya, A. and Wong, K.-Y. (eds) (2008) *Trade, Globalization and Poverty*. Routledge: London.

Donnelly, J. (1981) 'Recent trends in UN human rights activity: description and polemic', *International Organization*, 35(4): 33–56.

Donnelly, J. (1998) 'Human Rights: a new standard for civilization', *International Affairs*, 74(1): 1–23.

Dony, M. (2009) 'The EU's external relations and their evolving legal framework', in M. Telò (ed.), *The European Union and Global Governance*. Routledge: London, 131–55.

Dore, R. (1973) *British Factory, Japanese Factory*. London: Allen & Unwin.

Drahos, P. (1995) 'Global property in information: the story of TRIPS at the GATT', *Prometheus*, 13(1): 6–19.

Du Gangjian and Song Gang (1995) 'Relating human rights to Chinese culture: the four paths of the Confucian analects and the four principles of a new theory of benevolence', in M. C. Davis (ed.), *Human Rights and Chinese Values*. Oxford: Oxford University Press, 33–56.

Dunning, J. H. (1993) *The Globalization of Business*. London: Routledge.

Dunning, J. H. and Lundan, S. (2008) *Multinational Enterprises and the Global Economy, Second Edition*. Cheltenham: Edward Elgar.

Eisenstadt, S. N. (1992) 'The order-maintaining and order-transforming dimensions of culture', in R. Munch and N. Smelser (eds), *Theory of Culture*. Berkeley, CA: University of California Press, 64–87.

Elden, S. (2005) 'Missing the point: globalization, territorialization, and the space of the world', *Transactions of the Institute of British Geographers*, 30(1): 8–19.

Elvin, M. (1973) *The Pattern of the Chinese Past*. Stanford: Stanford University Press.

Enloe, C. (1990) *Bananas, Beaches, and Bases: Making Feminist Sense of International Politics*. Berkeley: University of California Press.

Euben, R. (2006) *Journeys to the Other Shore: Muslim and Western Travellers in Search of Knowledge*. Princeton, NJ: Princeton University Press.

Fabi, R. (2009) 'Fiscal constitutional issues delay Nigerian Oil Bill', 15 December, at http://blogs.reuters.com/randolph-fabi.

Falk, R. (2000) 'The decline of citizenship in an era of globalization', *Citizenship Studies*, 4(1): 5–17.

Fantasia, R. (1995) 'Fast food in France', *Theory and Society*, 24, 201–43.

Featherstone, M. (ed.) (1990) *Global Culture*. London: Sage.

Featherstone, M., Lash, S. and Robertson, R. (1995) *Global Modernities*. London: Sage.

Ferguson, N. (2009) *The Ascent of Money: A Financial History of the World*. London: Penguin.

Ferry, J.-M. (2009) 'European integration and the cosmopolitan way', in M. Telò (ed.), *The European Union and Global Governance*. London: Routledge, 329–45.

Finley, M. (1999) [1973] *The Ancient Economy*. Berkeley: University of California Press.

Fischer, M. M. J. (1992) 'Is Islam the odd-civilisation out?', *New Perspectives Quarterly*, Spring: 54–9.

Fisher, M. H., (2000), 'Autoethnographic representations by Asians in late 18th century British Society', in J. Malek (ed.), Perspectives on Mutual Encounters in South Asia History, 1760–1860. Leiden: Brill, 157–87.

Flora, P. (ed.) (1987) *Growth to Limits: The Western Welfare States Since World War Two*, 4 vols. Berlin: de Gruyter.

Forbes Global 2000 (2009) at www.forbes.com/lists/2009/18/global-09_ The-Global-2000_Rank.html.

Fortin, C. (1984) 'The failure of repressive monetarism: Chile 1973–83', *Third World Quarterly*, 6(2): 310–26.

Frank, A. G. (1990) 'A theoretical introduction to 5000 years of world-system history', *Review*, 13(2): 155–248.

Frank, A. G. and Gills, B. K. (eds) (1993) *The World System: Five Hundred Years or Five Thousand?* London: Routledge.

Freemantle, B. (1986) *The Fix: Inside the World Drug Trade.* New York: Tom Doherty Associates.

Friedan, J. (1991) 'Invested interests: the politics of national economic policies in a world of global finance', *International Organization*, 45(4): 425–51.

Friedman, J. (1994) *Cultural Identity and Global Process.* London: Sage.

Friedman, J. (1995) 'Global system, globalization and the parameters of modernity', in M. Featherstone, S. Lash and R. Robertson (eds), *Global Modernities.* London: Sage, 69–90.

Friedmann, J. (1986) 'The world city hypothesis', *Development and Change*, 17: 69–83.

Frith, S. (ed.) (1989) *World Music, Politics and Social Change.* Manchester: Manchester University Press.

Frobel, F. *et al.* (1980) *The New International Division of Labour.* Cambridge: Cambridge University Press.

Fukuyama, F. (1989) 'The end of history', *The National Interest*, 16(Summer): 3–18.

Fukuyama, F. (1992) 'Asia's soft-authoritarian alternative', *New Perspectives Quarterly*, Spring: 60–1.

Garrett, G. and Mitchell, D. (1996) 'Globalization and the welfare state: income transfers in the industrial democracies, 1966–90', unpublished paper presented to the 1996 Annual Meeting of the American Political Science Association, San Francisco.

Gellner, E. (1983) *Nations and Nationalism.* Oxford: Blackwell.

Gereffi, G. (1994) 'The organization of buyer-driven global commodity chains', in G. Gereffi and M. Korzeniewicz (eds), *Commodity Chains and Global Capitalism.* Westport: Praeger, 95–122.

Gereffi, G. (1996) 'Global commodity chains: new forms of coordination and control among nations and firms in international industries', *Competition and Change*, 1: 4.

Gereffi, G. and Korzeniewicz, M. (eds) (1994) *Commodity Chains and Global Capitalism.* Westport: Praeger.

Gerlach, G. (1992) *Alliance Capitalism: The Strategic Organization of Japanese Business.* Berkeley: University of California Press.

Ghils, P. (1992) 'International civil society', *Social Science Journal*, 133: 417–31.

Giddens, A. (1981) A *Contemporary Critique of Historical Materialism*, vol. 1, *Power, Property, and the State.* Berkeley, CA: University of California Press.

Giddens, A. (1990) *The Consequences of Modernity.* Cambridge: Polity Press.

Giddens, A. (1999) *Runaway World.* London: Profile.

Gilpin, R. (1975) *US Power and the Multinational Corporation*. New York: Basic.

Gilpin, R. (1984) 'The Richness of the Tradition of Political Realism', *International Organization*, 38(2): 287–304.

Gilroy, P. (1993) *The Black Atlantic: Modernity and Double Consciousness*, London: Verso.

Giroux, H. (1994) 'Consuming social change: the "United Colours of Benetton"', *Cultural Critique*, Winter: 5–32.

Giulianotti, R. and Robertson, R. (2009) *Globalization and Football*, London: Sage.

Glazer, N. (1983) *Ethnic Dilemmas 1964–1982*. Cambridge, MA: Harvard University Press.

Goldfrank, W., Goodman, D. and Szasz, A. (1999) *Ecology and the World System*. Westport: Greenwood.

Goldman Sachs (2007) 'BRICs and beyond', http://www2.goldmansachs.com/ideas/brics/BRICs-and-Beyond.html (accessed 10 November 2009).

Goldman Sachs (2009) 'BRIC's lead the global recovery' http://www2.goldmansachs.com/ideas/brics/lead-global-recovery-doc-2.pdf (accessed 10 November 2009).

Granovetter, M. (1985) 'Economic action and social structure', *American Journal of Sociology*, 91: 481–510.

Griswold, W. (1992) 'The writing on the mud wall: Nigerian novels and the imaginary village', *American Sociological Review*, 57, December: 709–24.

Grundmann, R. (2007) 'Climate Change and Knowledge Politics', *Environmental Politics*, 16(3): 414–32.

Gupta, A. and Ferguson, J. (1992) 'Beyond "culture": space, identity and the politics of difference', *Current Anthropology*, 7(1): 6–23.

Haas, P. M. (1992), 'Introduction: epistemic communities and international policy co-ordination', *International Organization* 46(1), 1–35.

Haas, P. M., Keohane, R. O. and Levy, M. A. (eds) (1993) *Institutions for the Earth: Sources of Environmental Protection*. Cambridge, MA: MIT Press.

Habermas, J. (1989) [1962] *The Structural Transformation of the Public Sphere: An Enquiry into a Category of Bourgeois Society*. Cambridge, MA: MIT Press.

Habermas, J. (1979) *Communication and the Evolution of Society*. London: Heinemann.

Hannah, L. (1999) 'Marshall's "trees" and the global "forest". Were "giant redwoods" different?', in N. Lamoreaux, D. Raff and P. Temin (eds), *Learning By Doing in Markets, Firms, and Countries*. Chicago: University of Chicago Press, 253–94.

Hannerz, U. (1990) 'Cosmopolitans and locals in world culture', in M. Featherstone (ed.), *Global Culture*. London: Sage, 237–51.

Hannerz, U. (1992) *Cultural Complexity*. New York: Columbia University Press.

Hannerz, U. (1996) *Transnational Connections*. London: Routledge.

Hannerz, U. (2004) *Foreign News: Exploring the Worlds of Foreign Correspondents*. Chicago: University of Chicago Press.

Hardt, M. and Negri, A. (2000) *Empire*. Cambridge, MA: Harvard University Press.

Harper, T. N. (2002) 'Empire, diaspora, and the languages of globalism, 1850–1914, in Hopkins, A. G. (ed.) (2002a) *Globalization in World History*. London: Pimlico, 141–66.

Harris, N. (1986) *The End of the Third World*. London: Penguin.

Harvey, D. (1989) *The Condition of Postmodernity*. Oxford: Blackwell.

Harvey, D. (2003) *The New Imperialism*. Oxford: Oxford University Press.

Harvey, D. (2006) *Spaces of Global Capitalism*. London: Verso.

Hawkins, F. (1989) *Critical Years in Immigration: Canada and Australia Compared*. Kingston: McGill-Queen's Press.

Hebdige, D. (1987) *Cut n' Mix: Culture, Identity, and Caribbean Music*. London: Methuen.

Held, D. (1991) 'Democracy, the nation state and the global system', in D. Held (ed.), *Political Theory Today*. Oxford: Polity Press, 197–235.

Held, D. (1995) *Democracy and the Global Order*. Cambridge: Polity Press.

Held, D. (2004) *Global Covenant: The Social Democratic Alternative*. Cambridge: Polity.

Held, D. and McGrew, A. G. (1993) 'Globalization and the liberal democratic state', *Government and Opposition*, 28(2): 261–8.

Held, D. and McGrew, A. G. (2002) *Globalization/Anti-Globalization*. Cambridge: Polity Press.

Held, D. and McGrew, A. G. (2007) *Globalization/Anti-Globalization*, 2nd edn. Cambridge: Polity Press.

Held, D., Goldblatt, M., McGrew, A. G. and Perraton, J. (1999) Global Transformations: Politics, Economics, and Culture. Cambridge: Polity.

Henderson, J. (1999) 'Uneven crises: Institutional Foundations of East Asian Economic Turmoil', *Economy and Society*, 28(3): 327–68.

Henderson, J., Dicken, P., Hess, M., Coe, N. and Yeung, W.-C. (2001) 'Global production networks and the analysis of economic development', *Manchester Business School: Working Paper no. 433*: 1–41.

Hirschman, A. (1970) *Exit, Voice and Loyalty*. Cambridge, MA: Harvard University Press.

Hirst, P. and Thompson, G. (1992) 'The problem of globalization: international economic relations, national economic management, and the formation of trading blocs', *Economy and Society*, 21(4): 357–96.

Hirst, P. and Thompson, G. (1996) *Globalization in Question*. Cambridge: Polity Press.

Hobsbawm, E. (1990) *Nations and Nationalism Since 1780*. London: Clarendon.

Hobsbawm, E. and Ranger, T. (eds) (1983) *The Invention of Tradition*. Cambridge: Cambridge University Press.

Hodgson, M. (1974) [1958–9] *The Venture of Islam*, 3 vols. Chicago: University of Chicago Press.

Holm, H.-H. and Sorensen, G. (1995) *Whose World Order: Uneven Globalization and the End of the Cold War*. Boulder, CO: Westview Press.

Holton, R. J. (1985) *The Transition From Feudalism to Capitalism*. Basingstoke: Macmillan.

Holton, R. J. (1992) *Economy and Society*. London: Routledge.

Holton, R. J. (1998) *Globalization and the Nation State*, 1st edn. Basingstoke: Macmillan.
Holton, R. J. (2005) *Making Globalization*. Basingstoke: Palgrave Macmillan.
Holton, R. J. (2008) *Global Networks*. Basingstoke: Palgrave Macmillan.
Holton, R. J. (2009) *Cosmopolitanisms*. Basingstoke: Palgrave Macmillan.
Hoovers (2010) 'McDonalds Corporation', at http://www.hoovers.com/company/McDonalds_Corporation/rfskci-1-1njdep.html
Hopkins, A. G. (ed.) (2002a) *Globalization in World History*. London: Pimlico.
Hopkins, A. G. (2002b), 'Introduction: globalization: an agenda for historians', in A. G. Hopkins, (ed.) (2002), *Globalization in World History*. London: Pimlico, 1–10.
Hopkins, A. G. (2000c) 'The history of globalization and the globalization of history', in Hopkins, A. G. (ed.), *Globalization in World History*. London: Pimlico, 11–46.
Hossain, M. (1988) *Credit for the Alleviation of Rural Poverty: The Grameen Bank in Bangladesh*. Washington, DC: International Food Policy Research Institute.
Hourani, A. (1991) *Islam in European Thought*. Cambridge: Cambridge University Press.
Huntington, S. (1993) 'The clash of civilizations', *Foreign Affairs*, 72(3): 22–49.
Huntington, S. (1996) *The Clash of Civilizations and the Remaking of World Order*. New York: Simon & Schuster.
Hussain, A. (1990) *Western Conflict with Islam: Survey of the Anti-Islamic Tradition*. Leicester: Volcano.
Hutchinson, J. (1994) *Modern Nationalism*. London: Fontana.
Hutchinson, J. (2005) *Nations as Zones of Conflict*. London: Sage.
Inglis, D. and Robertson, R. (2004) 'Beyond the gates of the polis: reconfiguring sociology's ancient inheritance', *Journal of Classical Sociology*, 4(2), 165–89.
Inglis, D. and Robertson, R. (2005) 'The ecumenical analytic: "globalization", reflexivity, and the revolution in Greek historiography', *European Journal of Social Theory*, 8(2), 99–122.
Inglis, T. (2008) *Global Ireland*. Abingdon: Routledge.
International Monetary Fund (IMF) (2009) *Global Financial Stability Report. Responding to the Financial Crisis and Measuring Systemic Risk*. Washington, DC: IMF.
Ionescu, G. (1993) 'The impact of the information revolution on parliamentary sovereignties', *Government and Opposition*, 28(2): 221–41.
Jackson, P. (2004) 'Local consumption cultures in a globalizing world', *Transactions of the Institute of British Geographers*, 29, 165–78.
Jackson, R. H. (1990) *Quasi-States: Sovereignty, International Relations and the Third World*. Cambridge: Cambridge University Press.
James, H. (2001) *The End of Globalization: Lessons from the Great Depression*. Cambridge, MA: Harvard University Press.
Johnson, C. (1962) *Peasant Nationalism and Communist Power*. Stanford, CA: Stanford University Press.
Johnson, C. (1982) *MITI and the Japanese Miracle*. Stanford, CA: Stanford University Press.

Joppke, C. and Lukes, S. (1999a) 'Introduction: Multicultural Questions', in C. Joppke and S. Lukes (eds), *Multicultural Questions*. Oxford: Oxford University Press, 1–24.

Joppke, C. and Lukes, S. (eds) (1999b) *Multicultural Questions*. Oxford: Oxford University Press.

Kaldor, M. (2003) *Global Civil Society: An Answer to War*. Cambridge: Cambridge University Press.

Kapstein, E. (1994) *Governing the Global Economy: International Finance and the State*. Cambridge, MA: Harvard University Press.

Kastoryano, R. (2006) 'French secularism and Islam: France's headscarf affair', in T. Madood, A. Triandafyllidou and R. Zapata-Barrero (eds), *Multiculturalism, Muslims and Citizenship: A European Approach*, London: Routledge, 57–69.

Katz, H. and Anheier, H. (2006) 'Global connectedness: the structure of transnational NGO networks', in M. Glasius, M. Kaldor and H. Anheier (eds), *Global Civil Society 2005–6*. London: Sage, 240–65.

Keane, J. (2003) *Global Civil Society?* Cambridge: Cambridge University Press.

Keating, M. (2001) *Nations against the State: The New Politics of Nationalism in Quebec, Catalonia, and Scotland*. Basingstoke: Palgrave Macmillan.

Kellner, D. (1998) 'Globalization and the postmodern turn', in R. Axtmann (ed.), *Globalization and Europe: Theoretical and Empirical Investigations*. London: Pinter, 25–43.

Kellner, D. (2007) 'Globalization, terrorism and democracy: 9/11 and its aftermath', in I. Rossi (ed.), *Frontiers of Globalization Research*. New York: Springer, 243–68.

Keohane, R. O. (1984) *After Hegemony*. Princeton, NJ: Princeton University Press.

Keohane, R. O. (1995) 'Hobbes' dilemma and institutional change in world politics: sovereignty in international society', in H.-H. Holm and G. Sorensen (eds), *Whose World Order? Uneven Globalization and the End of the Cold War*. Boulder, CO: Westview Press, 165–86.

Kern, S. (1983) *The Culture of Time and Space 1880–1918*. Cambridge, MA: Harvard University Press.

Killick, T. (2004) 'Politics, evidence, and the new aid agenda', *Development Policy Review*, 22(1): 5–29.

King, A. D. (ed.) (1991) *Culture, Globalization, and the World System: Contemporary Conditions for the Reproduction of Identity*. Basingstoke: Macmillan.

Kleingeld, P. (1999) 'Six varieties of cosmopolitanism in late 18th century Germany', *Journal of the History of Ideas*, 60(3): 505–24.

Kline, S. (1995) 'The play of the market: on the internationalization of children's culture', *Theory, Culture and Society*, 12: 103–29.

Koenig-Archibugi, M. (2002) 'Mapping global governance', in D. Held and A. G. McGrew, *Governing Globalization*. Cambridge: Polity, 46–69.

Kopal, Z. (1973) 'Forward', in B. Bienkowska (ed.), *The Scientific World of Copernicus*. Dordrecht: Reidel, vii–xii.

Kotkin, J. (1993), *Tribes: How Race, Religion, and Identity Determine Success in the New Global Economy*, New York: Random House.

Krasner, S. (1985) *Structural Conflict: The Third World Against Liberalism.* Berkeley, CA: University of California Press.

Kymlicka, W. (1995) *Multicultural Citizenship.* Oxford: Oxford University Press.

Kymlicka, W. and He, B. (eds) (2005) *Multiculturalism in Asia.* Oxford: Oxford University Press.

Labonté, R. and Schrecker, T. (2009) 'Introduction: Global Challenges to People's Health', in R. Labonté, T. Schrecker, T. C. Packer, and V. Runnels (2009), *Globalization and Health: Pathways, Evidence and Policy.* London: Routledge, 1–33.

Labonté, R. Schrecker, T. Packer, C. and Runnels, V. (2009) *Globalization and Health: Pathways, Evidence and Policy.* London: Routledge.

Lash, S. and Urry, J. (1987) *The End of Organised Capitalism.* Oxford: Polity Press.

Lechner, F. (2005) 'Religious rejections of globalization', in M. Juergensmeyer (ed.), *Religion in Global Civil Society.* Oxford: Oxford University Press, 115–34.

Lechner, F. (2009) *Globalization: The Making of World Society.* Oxford: Wiley-Blackwell.

Lee, R. W. (1989) 'The cocaine dilemma in South America', in D. J. Mabry (ed.), *The Latin American Narcotics Trade and US National Security.* New York: Greenwood Press, 59–74.

Lever-Tracy, C., Ip, D. and Tracy, N. (1996) *The Chinese Business Diaspora and Mainland China.* Basingstoke: Macmillan.

Levi-Faur, D. (2005) 'The global diffusion of regulatory capitalism', *Annals of the American Academy of Political and Social Science,* 598(1): 12–32.

Lévi-Strauss, C. (1955) *Tristes Tropiques.* Paris: Plon.

Levitt, T. (1983) 'The globalization of markets', *Harvard Business Review,* May/June: 92–102.

Levy, M. A., Keohane, R. O. and Haas, P. M. (1993) 'Improving the effectiveness of international environmental institutions', in P. M. Haas, R. O. Keohane and M. A. Levy (eds), *Institutions for the Earth: Sources of Effective International Environmental Protection.* Cambridge, MA: MIT Press, 397–426.

Lewis, I. (1973) *Anthropologist's Muse,* London: London School of Economics.

Lillrank, P. (1995) 'The transfer of management innovations from Japan', *Organization Studies,* 16(6): 971–89.

Lockwood, B. and Redoano, M. (2005) 'The CSGR Globalisation Index', *CSGR Working Paper.* University of Warwick, 155/04.

Loh, C. (1995) 'The Vienna process and the importance of universal standards in Asia', in M. C. Davis (ed.), *Human Rights and Chinese Values.* Oxford: Oxford University Press, 145–67.

McChesney, R. (1999) *Rich Media, Poor Democracy.* Urbana, Ill: University of Illinois Press.

McDonald, S. (1988) *Dancing on a Volcano: The Latin American Drug Trade.* New York: Praeger.

McGrew, A. (1992) 'Conceptualising global politics', in A. McGrew and P. G. Lewis (eds), *Global Politics.* Oxford: Polity Press, 1–28.

McNeely, I, and Wolverton, L. (2008) *Reinventing Knowledge: From Alexandria to the Internet*, New York: Norton.

McNeill, W. H. (1964) *The Rise of The West: A History of the Human Community.* Chicago: Chicago University Press.

McNeill, W. H. (1986) *Polyethnicity and National Unity in World History.* Toronto: University of Toronto Press.

McNeill, W. H. (1990) 'The *Rise of the West* after twenty-five years', *Journal of World History*, 1: 1–21.

Maimbo, S. and Ratha, D. (eds) (2005) *Remittances: Development Impact and Future Prospects.* Washington, DC: World Bank.

Malachuk, D. (2007) 'Nationalist cosmopolitics in the nineteenth century', in D. Morgan and G. Banham (eds), *Cosmopolitics and the Emergence of a Future.* Basingstoke: Palgrave Macmillan, 139–62.

Mandle, J. (2003) *Globalization and the Poor.* Cambridge: Cambridge University Press.

Mann, M. (1986) *The Sources of Social Power*, vol. 1. Cambridge: Cambridge University Press.

Mann, M. (1993) 'Nation states in Europe and other continents: diversifying, developing not dying', *Daedalus*, Summer: 115–40.

Mann, M. (1997) 'Has Globalization Ended the Rise and Rise of the Nation state?' *Review of International Political Economy*, 4(3): 472–96.

Mann, M. (2005) *The Dark Side of Democracy: Explaining Ethnic Cleansing.* Cambridge: Cambridge University Press.

Marcuse, P. and van Kempen, R. (eds) (1999) *Globalizing Cities.* Oxford: Blackwell.

Martell, L. (2010) *The Sociology of Globalization.* Cambridge: Polity Press.

Martinelli, A. (1982) 'The political and social impact of transnational corporations', in H. Makler, A. Martinelli and N. Smelser (eds), *The New International Economy.* London: Sage, 79–116.

Marx, K. and Engels, F. (1962) 'Manifesto of the Communist Party', in K. Marx and F. Engels, *Selected Works*, vol. 1. Moscow: Foreign Languages Publishing House, 34–65.

Matthews, D. (2004) 'WTO decision on the implementation of paragraph 6 of the Doha Declaration on the TRIPS Agreement and Public Health', *Journal of Economic Law*, 7(1): 73–107.

Mayer, A. E. (1990) 'The Shari'a: a methodology or a body of substantive rules?', in N. Heer (ed.), *Islamic Law and Jurisprudence.* Seattle: University of Washington Press, 177–98.

Mazlish, B. and Buultjens, R. (eds) (1993) *Conceptualising Global History.* Boulder, CO: Westview Press.

Mazrui, Ali A. (1990) *Cultural Images in World Politics.* London: Currey.

Mennell, S. (1990) 'The globalization of human society as a very long term process', in M. Featherstone (ed.), *Global Culture.* London: Sage, 359–72.

Mernissi, F. (1993) *Islam and Democracy.* London: Virago.

Meyer, J. (2009) *World Society: The Writings of John Meyer*, ed. G. Krücken and G. Drori. Oxford: Oxford University Press.

Meyer, J., Boli, J., Thomas, G. and Ramirez, F. (1997) 'World Society and the Nation State', *American Journal of Sociology*, 103(1): 144–81.

Mignolo, W. (2000) 'The many faces of cosmo-polis: border thinking and critical cosmopolitanism', *Public Culture*, 12(3): 721–48.

Milanovic, B. (2005) *Worlds Apart: Measuring International and Global Inequality*. Princeton, NJ: Princeton University Press.

Mills, J. (1986) *Where Crime and Governments Embrace*. Garden City, NY: Doubleday.

Mitchell, J. (1992) 'The nature and government of the global economy', in A. G. McGrew *et al.* (eds), *Global Politics*. Cambridge: Cambridge University Press, 174–96.

Miyoshi, M. and Harootunian, H. A. (eds) (1989) *Postmodernism in Japan*. Durham: Duke University Press.

Modelski, G. (1978) 'The long cycle of global politics and the nation state', *Comparative Studies in Society and History*, 20: 214–35.

Moore, W. E. (1966) 'Global sociology: the world as a singular system', *American Journal of Sociology*, LXXI(5): 475–82.

Mosley, P., Harrigan, J. and Toye, J. (1991) *Aid and Power: The World Bank and Policy-Based Lending*, 2 vols. London: Routledge.

Mosse, G. (1985) *Nationalism and Sexuality*. Madison, WI: University of Wisconsin Press.

Nagel, J. (1986) 'The political construction of ethnicity', in S. Olzak and J. Nagel (eds), *Competitive Ethnic Relations*. New York: Academic Press, 93–112.

Negroponte, N. (1995) *Being Digital*. New York: Knopf.

Nisbet, R. (1980) *History of the Idea of Progress*. New York: Basic.

Norris, P. (2000) 'Global governance and cosmopolitan citizens', in J. S. Nye, and J. D. Donoghue (eds), *Governance in a Globalizing World*. Washington, DC: Brookings Institute, 155–77.

Norris, P. (2006) 'Confidence and the United Nations: cosmopolitan and nationalist attitudes', paper presented to the World Values Survey Conference, Politics and Values, 1981–2006, Istanbul, November, at http://ksghome. harvard.edu.au/'~pnorris/Acrobat/Cosmopolitan%20and%20nationalistic %20attitudes%20towards%20the%20UnitedNations.pdf.

Nye, J. S. (2004) *Soft Power*. New York: Public Affairs.

Office of Multicultural Affairs (1989) *National Agenda for a Multicultural Australia*. Canberra: AGPS.

Ohmae, K. (1990) *The Borderless World: Power and Strategy in the International Economy*. London: Fontana.

Ohmae, K. (1996) *The End of the Nation State*. London: HarperCollins.

Olessen, T. (2004), 'The Transnational Zapatista Solidarity Network: an infrastructural Analysis', *Global Networks*, 4(1): 89–107.

O'Neill, J. (2009), *Netherlands*. New York: Knopf Doubleday.

Oppenheim, L. (1905) *International Law*, vol. 1. London: Longmans.

Opsahl, T. (1992) 'The Human Rights Committee', in P. Alston (ed.), *The United Nations and Human Rights*. Oxford: Oxford University Press, 369–443.

O'Rourke, K. (2001) 'Globalization and Inequality: Historical Trends', Centre for Economic Policy Research, *CEPR Discussion Paper* no. 2865, at http://ssrn.com/abstract=277292.

Osiander, A. (2001) 'Sovereignty, International Relations, and the Westphalian Myth', *International Organization*, 55(2): 251–87.

Ozouf, M. (1988) '"Public Opinion" at the end of the Old Regime', *Journal of Modern History*, 60: S1–S21.

Papacharissi, Z. (2002) 'The Virtual Sphere: The Internet as a Public Sphere', *New Media and Society*, 4(1): 9–27.

Papastergiadis, N. (2000) *The Turbulence of Migration: Globalization: Deterritorialization, and Identity*. Cambridge: Polity Press.

Parry, G. (1993) 'The interweaving of foreign and domestic policy', *Government and Opposition*, 28(2): 143–51.

Pateman, C. (1988) *The Sexual Contract*. Cambridge: Polity Press.

Peters, J. D. (1995) 'Historical tensions in the concept of public opinion', in T. L. Glasser and C. T. Salmon (eds) *Public Opinion and the Communication of Consent*. New York: Guilford Press, 3–32.

Petras, J. and Veltmayer, H. (2007) *Multinationals on Trial: Foreign Investment Matters*. Aldershot: Ashgate.

Phillips, K. (2006) *American Theocracy: The Peril and Politics of Radical Religion, Oil, and Borrowed Money in the 21st Century*. London: Penguin.

Pierson, C. (1991) *Beyond the Welfare State?* Cambridge: Polity Press.

Pieterse, J. N. (1995) 'Globalization as hybridization', in M. Featherstone, S. Lash and R. Robertson (eds), *Global Modernities*. London: Sage, 69–90.

Pieterse, J. N. (2007) *Ethnicity and Global Monoculture*. Lanham, MD: Rowman and Littlefield.

Piore, M. and Sabel, C. (1984) *The Second Industrial Divide*. New York: Basic.

Polanyi, K. (1957) *The Great Transformation*. Boston: Beacon Press.

Polegato, R. and Bjerke, B. (2006) 'The link between cross-cultural value associations: the case of Benetton and its advertising', *Journal of Advertising Research*, 46(3): 263–73.

Pollard, S. (1965) *The Origins of Modern Management*. London: Edward Arnold.

Porat, M. U. (1977) *The Information Society*. Washington, DC: US Department of Commerce.

Pratt, M. L. (1992), *Imperial Eyes*, London: Routledge.

Price, V. (2008) 'Democracy, global publics and world opinion', in M. Albrow, H. Anheier, M. Glasius and M. Price (eds), *Global Civil Society 2007/8*. London: Sage, 20–33.

Pryke, S. (2009) *Nationalism in a Global World*. Basingstoke: Palgrave Macmillan.

Ravitch, D. (1990) 'Multiculturalism. E Pluribus Plures', *American Scholar*, 59: 337–54.

Ravitch, D. (1991) 'Multiculturalism: an exchange', *The American Scholar*, 60: 272–6.

Raychauduri, T. (1988), *Europe Reconsidered: Perceptions of the West in Nineteenth Century Bengal*, New Delhi: Oxford University Press.

Raychauduri, T. (1994), 'Dominance, Hegemony, and the Colonial State: the Indian and African experiences', in D. Engels, and S. Marks (eds) *Contesting Colonial Hegemony: State and Society in Africa and India*, London: Britsh Academy Press, 267–81.

Reich, S. (1989) 'Roads to follow: regulating direct foreign investment', *International Organisation*, 43(4): 543–84.

Renault-Nissan (2010) Renault-Nissan Strategic Alliance Model, http://www.slideshare.net/nevenaz/renault-nissan-strategic-alliance (accessed 15 October 2010).

Reynolds, R. (2002) 'American globalism: mass, motion, and the multiplier effect', in A. G. Hopkins (ed.), *Globalization in World History*. London: Pimlico, 243–60.

Rex, J. (1995) 'Multiculturalism in Europe and America', *Nations and Nationalism*, July: 243–59.

Rex, J. and Singh, G. (2003) 'Multiculturalism and political integration in modern nation states: thematic introduction', *International Journal on Multicultural Societies*, 5(1): 3–19.

Richmond, A. (1991) 'Immigration and multiculturalism in Canada and Australia', *International Journal of Canadian Studies*, 3: 87–110.

Richmond, A. (1993) 'Open and closed borders: is the New World Order creating a system of global apartheid?', *Refuge*, 13(1): 10–14.

Rieger, E. and Leibfried, S. (2003) *Limits to Globalization*. Cambridge: Polity Press.

Righter, R. (1995) *Utopia Lost: The United Nations and the World*. New York: Twentieth Century Fund Press.

Ritzer, G. (1993) *The McDonaldization of Society*. Thousand Oaks, CA: Pine Forge Press.

Ritzer, G. (2004) *The Globalization of Nothing*. Thousand Oaks, CA: Pine Forge Press.

Robbins, B. (1999), *Feeling Global: Internationalism in Distress*, New York: New York University Press.

Roberts, M. (1992) '"World music" and the global cultural economy', *Diaspora*, 2(2): 229–42.

Robertson, R. (1992) *Globalization: Social Theory and Global Culture*. London: Sage.

Robertson, R. (1995) 'Glocalization: time-space and homogeneity-heterogeneity', in M. Featherstone, S. Lash and R. Robertson (eds), *Global Modernities*. London: Sage, 25–44.

Robertson, R. (2003), 'Antiglobal religion', in M. Juergensmeyer (ed.), *Global Religions: An Introduction*. Oxford: Oxford University Press, 110–23

Robinson, F. (1979) 'Islam and Muslim separatism', in D. Taylor and M. Yapp (eds), *Political Identity in South Asia*. London: Curzon Press.

Rodrik, D. (1997) *Has Globalization Gone Too Far?* Washington, DC: Institute on International Economics.

Rodrik, D. (2006) 'Goodbye Washington consensus, hello Washington confusion', *Journal of Economic Literature*, XLIV, December: 973–87.

Rodrik, D. (2007) *One Economics, Many Recipes: Globalization, Institutions and Economic Growth*. Princeton, NJ: Princeton University Press.

Rosenau, J. N. (1980) *The Study of Global Interdependence*. London: Francis Pinter.

Rosenau, J. N. (1990) *Turbulence in World Politics: A Theory of Change and Continuity*. Princeton, NJ: Princeton University Press.

Rosenau, J. N. (1996) 'The adaptation of the United Nations to a turbulent world', in R. Thukur (ed.), *The United Nations at Fifty: Retrospect and Prospect*. Dunedin: University of Otago Press, 229–40.

Rowlands, I. (1995) *The Politics of Global Atmospheric Change*. Manchester: Manchester University Press.

Rowthorn, R. (2008) 'The renaissance of China and India: implications for the advanced economies', in P. Arestis and J. Eatwell (eds), *Issues in Economic Development and Globalization*. Basingstoke: Palgrave Macmillan, 49–72.

Rudolph, S. H. (2005) 'Religious transnationalism', in M. Juegensmeyer (ed.), *Religion in Global Civil Society*. Oxford: Oxford University Press, 189–200.

Runblom, H. (1994) 'Swedish multiculturalism in comparative perspective', *Sociological Forum*, 9(4): 623–40.

Russell, R. B. and Muther, J. (1958) *A History of the United Nations Charter*. Washington, DC: Brookings Institution.

Said, E. W. (1978) *Orientalism*. New York: Penguin.

Said, E. W. (1993) *Cultural Imperialism*. London: Chatto & Windus.

Sartori, G. (1989) 'Undercomprehension', *Government and Opposition*, 24(4): 391–400.

Sassen, S. (1991) *The Global City, New York, London, Tokyo*. Princeton, NJ: Princeton University Press.

Sassen, S. (1994) *Cities in a World Economy*. Thousand Oaks, CA: Pine Forge Press.

Sassen, S. (1996) *Losing Control? Sovereignty in an Age of Globalization*. New York: Columbia University Press.

Sassen, S. (1998) *Globalization and its Discontents*. New York: New Press.

Sassen, S. (2006) *Territory, Authority, Rights: From Medieval to Global Assemblages*. Princeton, NJ: Princeton University Press.

Sassen, S. (2007) *A Sociology of Globalization*. New York: Norton.

Sassen, S. (2008) 'The good and the bad: multiple meanings of globalization', in T. Morris-Suzuki (ed.), *Contradictions of Globalization*. Tokyo: International House of Japan, 17–50.

Sassen, S. (2009) 'The global city perspective: theoretical implications for Shanghai', in X. Chen and Z. Zhou (eds), *Shanghai Rising: State Power and Local Transformation in a Global Megacity* [*Globalization and Community* series no 15]. Minnesota: University of Minnesota Press, 3–29.

Savun, B. (2009) 'Mediator types and the effectiveness of information provision strategies in the resolution of international conflict', in J. Bercovitch and S. Gartner (eds.), *International Conflict Mediation: New Approaches and Findings*. London: Routledge, 96–114.

Schama, S. (1991) 'Homelands', *Social Research*, 58(1): 11–30.

Schapiro, M. J. (1994) 'Images of planetary danger: Luciano Benetton's ecumenical fantasy', *Alternatives*, 19: 433–54.

Scharpf, F. W. (2000) 'Globalization, and the welfare state: constraints, challenges, and vulnerabilities', paper delivered to International Research Conference on Social Security, Helsinki, 20at http://www.issa.int/pdf/topico/2scharpf'.pdf

Schiller, H. (1976) *Communication and Cultural Domination*. New York: International Arts and Sciences.

Schlesinger, A. (1992) *The Disuniting of America*. New York: W. W. Norton.

Schmitter, P. C. (1996) 'Imagining the future of the euro-polity with the help of new concepts', in G. Marks, F. W. Scharpf, P. C. Schmitter *et al.* (eds), *Governance in the European Union*. London: Sage, 121–50.

Schneider, C. and Wallis, B. (eds) (1988) *Global Television*. Cambridge, MA: MIT Press.

Schneider, J. (1977) 'The world-system and its dangers', *Journal of Peasant Studies*, 6: 29–32.

Scholte, J. A. (2005) *Globalization: Critical Perspectives*. Basingstoke: Palgrave Macmillan.

Schreiner, M. (2003) 'A cost-effectiveness analysis of the Grameen Bank of Bangla Desh', *Development Policy Review*, 21(3): 357–82.

Scott, A. (ed.) (1997) *The Limits of Globalization: Cases and Arguments*. London: Routledge.

Seade, J. (1995) 'The World Trade Organisation', *Global Economic Institutions Newsletter* 1: 3–4.

Sell, S. K. (2004) 'The quest for global governance in intellectual property and public health: structural, discursive and institutional dimensions', *Temple Law Review*, 77: 363–400.

Sen, A. (2005) *The Argumentative Indian*. London: Penguin.

Shah, A. (2004) 'Nigeria and oil', *Global Issues*, 3 July, at http://www.globalissues.org/article/86/nigeria-and-oil.

Shibata, T. (1993) 'Sony's successful strategy for compact discs', *Long Range Planning (Journal of Strategic Management)*, 26(4): 16–21.

Sklair, L. (1989) *Assembly for Development: The Maquila Industry in Mexico and the US*. Boston: Unwin Hyman.

Sklair, L. (1991) *The Sociology of the Global System*, London: Harvester Wheatsheaf.

Sklair, L. (2001) *The Transnational Capitalist Class*. Oxford: Blackwell.

Skrbis, Z. (1999) *Long-distance Nationalism*. Aldershot: Ashgate.

Smart, N. (2003) 'The global future of religion', in M. Juergensmeyer (ed.), *Global Religions: An Introduction*. Oxford: Oxford University Press, 124–32.

Smith, A. D. (1971) *Theories of Nationalism*. London: Duckworth.

Smith, A. D. (1986) *The Ethnic Origins of Nations*. Oxford: Blackwell.

Smith, A. D. (1990) 'Towards a global culture?', *Theory, Culture, and Society*, 7: 171–91.

Smith, A. D. (1995) *Nations and Nationalism in a Global Era*. Cambridge: Polity Press.

Smith, J. (ed.) (1988) *Racism, Sexism, and the World-System*. Westport: Greenwood.

Soros, G. (2010) *The Soros Lectures*. New York: Public Affairs.

Soysal, Y. N. (1994) *Limits of Citizenship*. Chicago: Chicago University Press.

Stam, R. (1992) 'Mobilising fictions; the Gulf War, the media, and the recruitment of the spectator', *Public Culture*, 4(2): 101–26.

Steger, M. (2003) *Globalization: A Very Brief Short Introduction*. Oxford: Oxford University Press.

Stephenson, C. (1989) 'Going to McDonald's in Leiden: reflections on the concept of self and society in the Netherlands', *ETHOS, Journal of the Society of Psychological Anthropology*, 17(2): 241–62.

Stiglitz, J. (2002) *Globalization and its Discontents*. London: Penguin.

Strange, S. (1996) *The Retreat of the State. Diffusion of Power in the World Economy*. Cambridge: Cambridge University Press.

Sturmer, C. (1993) 'MTV's Europe', in T. Dowmunt (ed.), *Channels of Resistance: Global Television and Local Empowerment*. London: BFI, 50–66.

Suter, K. (1996) 'Reforming the United Nations', in R. Thukur (ed.), *The United Nations at Fifty: Retrospect and Prospect*. Dunedin: University of Otago Press, 241–62.

Swidler, A. (1986) 'Culture in action: symbols and strategies', *American Sociological Review*, 51: 273–86.

Swyngedouw, E. (1992) 'The Mammon Quest: 'glocalization', interspatial competition and the monetary order: the construction of new scales', in M. Dunford and G. Kafkalis (eds), *Cities and Regions in the New Europe: The Global–Local Interplay and Spatial Development Strategies*. London: Belhaven Press, 39–67.

Swyngedouw, E. (1997) 'Neither global or local: "glocalization" and the politics of scale', in K. Cox (ed.), *Spaces of Globalization*. New York: Guilford Press, 137–66.

Sylvan, L. (1995) 'Global trade, influence and power', in P. Alston and M. Chiam (eds), *Treaty-Making in Australia: Globalization versus Sovereignty?*. Sydney: Federation Press, 107–14.

Szerszynski, B. and Urry, J. (2002) 'Cultures of cosmopolitanism', *Sociological Review*, 50(4): 461–81.

Szerszynski, B. and Urry, J. (2006) 'Visuality, mobility, and the cosmopolitan inhabiting the world from afar', *British Journal of Sociology*, 57(1): 113–31.

Tai, S. H. C. (1997) 'Advertising in Asia: localize or regionalize?', *International Journal of Advertising*, 16: 48–61.

Taylor, P. (2004) 'Local consumption cultures in a globalizing world', *Transactions of the Institute of British Geographers*, 29(2): 165–78.

Telò, M. (ed.) (2009) *The European Union and Global Governance*. London: Routledge.

Templeton, M. (1996) 'The achievements and shortcomings of the United Nations', in R. Thukur (ed.), *The United Nations at Fifty: Retrospect and Prospect*. Dunedin: University of Otago Press, 41–58.

Thernstrom, S. (ed.) (1980) *Harvard Encyclopaedia of American Ethnic Groups*. Cambridge, MA: Belknap Press.

Thompson, G. (2003) *Between Markets and Hierarchies: The Logic and Limits of Network Forms of Organization*, Oxford: Oxford University Press.

Thomson, J. E. and Krasner, S. (1989) 'Global transactions and the consolidation of sovereignty', in E. O. Czempiel and J. N. Rosenau (eds), *Global Changes and Theoretical Challenges*. Lexington, MA: Lexington, 195–219.

Thomson, J. E. (1995) 'State sovereignty in international relations: bridging the gap between theory and empirical research', *International Studies Quarterly*, 39, 213–33.

Tibi, B. (1988) *The Crisis of Modern Islam*. Salt Lake City: University of Utah Press.

Tibi, B. (1994) 'Islamic law/*Shari'a*, human rights, universal morality and international relations', *Human Rights Quarterly*, 16(2): 277–99.

Tilly, C. (1984) *Big Structures, Large Processes, Huge Comparisons*. New York: Russell Sage Foundation.

Todeva, E. and Knoke, D. (2005) 'Strategic alliances and models of collaboration', *Management Decision*, 43(1): 123–48

Toennies, F. (1955) [1887] *Community and Association*. London: Routledge.

Toynbee, A. (1934–61) *A Study of History*, 12 vols. Oxford: Oxford University Press.

Tuckey, B. (1997) 'Discordant variations on a world car theme', *Business Review Weekly*, 21 July.

Turner, B. (2007) 'Globalization, empire, and religion in Asia', in P. Beyer and L. Beaman (eds), *Religion, Culture, and Globalization*. Leiden: Brill, 145–66.

UNCTAD, Programme on transnational corporations (1993) *World Investment Report: Trans-National Corporations and Integrated International Production*. New York: United Nations.

UNESCO (1999) 'The globalization of the drug trade', *Sources*, April, at http://www.unesco.org/most/sourdren.pdf, (accessed 17 May 2010).

UNODC (2009) *World Drug Report 2009*. New York: United Nations.

United Nations (2008) Department of Economic and Social Affairs, *International Migrant Stock: The 2008 Revision*, http://esa.un.org/migration/p2k0data.asp

Urry, J. (2000) *Sociology Beyond Societies*. London: Routledge.

Usenier, J.-C and Lee, J. (2009, 5th edn) *Marketing Across Cultures*. Pearson: Harlow.

Van der Ven, H. (2002) 'The onrush of modern globalization in China', in A. G. Hopkins (ed.), *Globalization in World History*. London: Pimlico, 167–93.

Vans, T. (1988) 'Trends in international television flow', in C. Schneider and B. Wallis (eds), *Global Television*. New York: Wedge Press.

Vargas, V. (2003) 'Feminism, globalization, and the global justice and solidarity movement', *Cultural Studies*, 17(6): 905–20.

Verne, J. (1873) *Le Tour du Monde en Quatre-vingts Jours*. Paris: Hetzel.

Vertovec, S. and Cohen, R., (2002) 'Introduction', in S. Vertovec and R. Cohen (eds), *Conceiving Cosmopolitanism*, Oxford: Oxford University Press, 1–22.

Vines, D. (1995) 'Reforming the international monetary system: lessons from the Mexican experience', *Global Economic Institutions Newsletter*, 1: 7–12.

Vines, D. (1996) 'Global economic institutions: a historical overview and a modest reform agenda', unpublished paper, Australian National University, April.

Vogelstein, F. (2008) 'The untold story: how the iPhone blew up the wireless industry', *Wired Magazine*, 16(02), accessed at www.wired.com/gadgets/wireless/magazine/16-02/ff_iphone?currentPage=4.

Wallerstein, I. (1976) 'A world system perspective on the social sciences', *British Journal of Sociology*, **27**(2), 343–52.

Wallerstein, I. (1974) *The Modern World System: Capitalist Agriculture and the Origins of the European World-Economy in the Sixteenth Century.* New York: Academic Press.

Wallerstein, I. (1979) *The Capitalist World Economy.* Cambridge: Cambridge University Press.

Wallerstein, I. (1984) *The Politics of the World-Economy.* Cambridge: Cambridge University Press.

Wallerstein, I. (1990) 'Culture as the ideological battleground of the modern world system', in M. Featherstone (ed.), *Global Culture.* London: Sage, 31–56.

Wallerstein, I. (1991) *Geopolitics and Geoculture.* Cambridge: Cambridge University Press.

Wang Fanqing (2010) 'Food makers catering to local tastes in China', *Just Food*, 11 March, at http://www.justfood.com/analysis/food-makers-catering-to-local-tastes-in-china_id110151.aspx (accessed 18 October 2010).

Warner, M. (1994) 'Japanese culture, western management: Taylorism and human resources in Japan', *Organization Studies*, 15(4): 509–33.

Waxer, L. (2001) 'Llegó la Salsa: the rise of salsa in Columbia and Venezuela', in L. Waxer (ed.), *Situating Salsa: Global Markets and Local Meanings in Latin Popular Music.* New York: Routledge, 219–46.

Weber, E. (1976) *Peasants into Frenchmen: The Modernisation of Rural France 1870–1914.* Stanford, CA: Stanford University Press.

Weiss, L. (1998) *State Capacity: Governing the Economy in a Global Era.* Cambridge: Polity.

Weissbrodt, D. (1988) 'Human rights: an historical perspective', in P. Davies (ed.), *Human Rights.* London: Routledge, 1–20.

Wells, H. G. (1933) *The Shape of Things to Come: The Ultimate Revolution.* London: Hutchinson.

Werbner, P. (1999) 'Global pathways and working class cosmopolitans: the creation of transnational worlds', *Social Anthropology*, 7(1): 17–35.

Werbner, P. (ed.) (2008) *Anthropology and the New Cosmopolitanism: Rooted, Feminist, and Vernacular Perspectives.* Oxford: Berg.

Wete, F. N. (1988) 'The new world information order and the US press', in C. Schneider and B. Wallis (eds), *Global Television.* Cambridge, MA: MIT Press, 137–46.

Wickham, C. R. (2005) 'The Islamist alternative to globalization', in M. Juergensmeyer (ed.), *Religion in Global Civil Society.* Oxford: Oxford University Press, 149–70.

Wight, M. (1992) *International Theory: The Three Traditions.* New York: Holmes & Meier.

Wilkinson, D. (1987) 'Central civilization', *Comparative Civilizations Review*, Autumn, 31–59.

Wilkinson, D. (1993) 'Civilizations, cores, world economies, and Oikumenes', in A. G. Frank and B. K. Gills (eds), *The World System: Five Hundred Years or Five Thousand?* London: Routledge, 221–46.

Williams, G. A. (1994) *The Search for Arthur.* London: BBC.

Williams, R. (1993) 'Technical change: political options and imperatives', *Government and Opposition*, 28(2): 152–69.

Williamson, J. (1990) 'What should the World Bank think about the Washington consensus', *World Bank Research Observer*, 15(2): August, 251–64.

Wimmer, A. and Glick Schiller, N. (2002) 'Methodological nationalism and beyond: nation state building, migration, and the social sciences', *Global Networks*, 24, 301–34.

Wolf, E. (1982) *Europe and the People Without History.* Berkeley, CA: University of California Press.

Wolf, M. (2010) *Fixing Global Finance: How to Curb Financial Crises in the 21st Century.* New Haven: Yale University Press.

Wood, F. (2002) *The Silk Road.* London: Folio Society.

World Bank (2005) *Economic Growth in the 1990s: Learning from a Decade of Reform.* Washington. DC: World Bank.

World Bank (2009) *Poverty Net: Information Disclosure: The Case of Nike in Vietnam*, http://go.worldbank.org/8RO75XZZX0.

Worsley, P. (1980) 'One world or three? A critique of the world system theory of Immanuel Wallerstein', *Socialist Register*, 298–338.

Worsley, P. (1990) 'Models of the modern world-system', in M. Featherstone (ed.), *Global Culture: Nationalism, Globalization and Modernity.* London: Sage, 83–96.

Yapp, M. (1979) 'Language, religion and political identity', in D. Taylor and M. Yapp (eds), *Political Identity in South Asia.* Atlantic Highlands: Curzon Press, 1–34.

Yapp, M. (1992) 'Europe in the Turkish mirror', *Past and Present*, 37: 134–55.

Young, I. M. (1989) 'Polity and cultural difference: a critique of the ideal of universal citizenship', *Ethics*, 99: 250–74.

Zheng, C., Hyland, P. and Soosay, C. (2007) 'Training practises of multinational corporations in Asia', *Journal of European Industrial Training*, 31(6): 472–94.

Index